What Your Colleagues Are Saying . . .

Rebecca G. Harper combines play and purpose throughout *Writing Workouts, Grades 6–12: Strategies to Build Students' Writing Skills, Stamina, and Success*. Using the analogy of fitness training throughout the book, she brilliantly explains the importance of each component. The accompanying lessons and ideas follow a format that is not only easy to follow but also relevant and meaningful. Full of current and relatable resources, teachers will find inspirational and turnkey ideas in Harper's latest book—ideas that will bring laughter, engagement, joy, and learning to the students in their classrooms.

—**Melanie Meehan, author**
Answers to Your Biggest Questions About Teaching Elementary Writing

Rebecca G. Harper has created the hyper-practical guide I wish I had had as an early-career writer's coach. I love the emphasis on writing as a discipline and growth as the fruit of practice. There is a lot to play with and try in this volume.

—**Dave Stuart Jr., author**
Answers to Your Biggest Questions About Teaching Middle and High School ELA

Rebecca G. Harper cleverly leads us to rethink how we teach writing. She reminds us of the recursive nature of writing and demonstrates how writers move through their process not in a regimented lockstep but in a focused and deliberate manner with attention to various aspects at different times. Harper has created an impressive collection of strategies that students can use to build their writing muscles wherever they are in their process. *Writing Workouts, Grades 6–12* is a book you'll return to over and over as you plan instruction and confer with individual writers.

—**Lester Laminack, author**
Critical Comprehension: Lessons for Guiding Students to Deeper Meaning

Developing as a writer is a hard lift for many students. Luckily, we now have Rebecca G. Harper's *Writing Workouts, Grades 6–12*—an all-in-one guide for helping students develop the writing fitness needed to engage in such a difficult journey. Offering both an innovative framework and hundreds of practical resources and writing lessons, this is that rare writing-instruction book that offers clever and effective lessons and tips that will improve one's lessons today and thought-provoking larger suggestions to improve one's overall approach to writing instruction.

—**Matthew Johnson, author**
Flash Feedback and *Answers to Your Biggest Questions About Teaching Middle and High School ELA*

Writing Workouts, Grades 6–12

Writing Workouts, Grades 6–12

Strategies to Build Students' Writing Skills, Stamina, and Success

Rebecca G. Harper

CORWIN Literacy

FOR INFORMATION:

Corwin
A SAGE Company
2455 Teller Road
Thousand Oaks, California 91320
(800) 233-9936
www.corwin.com

SAGE Publications Ltd.
1 Oliver's Yard
55 City Road
London EC1Y 1SP
United Kingdom

SAGE Publications India Pvt. Ltd.
Unit No 323-333, Third Floor, F-Block
International Trade Tower Nehru Place
New Delhi 110 019
India

SAGE Publications Asia-Pacific Pte. Ltd.
18 Cross Street #10-10/11/12
China Square Central
Singapore 048423

President: Mike Soules
Vice President and Editorial Director: Monica Eckman
Executive Editor: Tori Mello Bachman
Content Development Editor: Sharon Wu
Editorial Assistant: Nancy Chung
Project Editor: Amy Schroller
Copy Editor: Deanna Noga
Typesetter: C&M Digitals (P) Ltd.
Proofreader: Lawrence W. Baker
Indexer: Integra
Cover Designer: Scott Van Atta
Marketing Manager: Margaret O'Connor

Printed in the United Kingdom

ISBN 978-1-0718-6704-4

This book is printed on acid-free paper.

23 24 25 26 27 10 9 8 7 6 5 4 3 2 1

CONTENTS

For downloadable resources related to *Writing Workouts, Grades 6–12,*
visit the companion website at

resources.corwin.com/WritingWorkouts.

NCTE/ILA STANDARDS FOR ENGLISH LANGUAGE ARTS

Standard	Lessons
Students read a wide range of print and nonprint texts to build an understanding of texts, of themselves, and of the cultures of the United States and the world; to acquire new information; to respond to the needs and demands of society and the workplace; and for personal fulfillment.	• Music Infographics • Sounds Like • Stretch to See • Resource Roundup • Character Props • Character Evolution • Whose Line Is It? • Most Valuable Character • Cast the Character • Songs for Voice • Pictures for Mood • Claims and Evidence Matchup • Stop/Go Sources • Wordless Picture Books • Social Media Profile Slide • Pop-Up Poems • Descriptive Writing Calendars • Paint Strip Arguments • Source Synthesis • Mix and Match Remix • Paint Strip Paraphrase • Top Ten Plays • Writing Wordle • Soap Opera Stories • Blackout Poems

(Continued)

(Continued)

Standard	Lessons
Students apply a wide range of strategies to comprehend, interpret, evaluate, and appreciate texts. They draw on their prior experience, their interactions with other readers and writers, their knowledge of word meaning and of other texts, their word identification strategies, and their understanding of textual features (e.g., sound-letter correspondence, sentence structure, context, graphics).	• Music Infographics • Sounds Like • That's What They Said • Memory Maps • Expert/Know Nothing List • Stretch to See • Picture Point of View • Resource Roundup • Character Props • Character Evolution • NVA² • Whose Line Is It? • Most Valuable Character • Cast the Character • Songs for Voice • Pictures for Mood • Claims and Evidence Matchup • Stop/Go Sources • Wordless Picture Books • Descriptive Writing Calendars • Paint Strip Arguments • Mix and Match Remix • PK/NK • Exit-Slip Variations • Top Ten Plays • Writing Wordle • Soap Opera Stories • Walk-Out Songs • Social Square Challenge
Students employ a wide range of strategies as they write and use different writing process elements appropriately to communicate with different audiences for a variety of purposes.	• Music Infographics • Say, Say, Say • Sounds Like • Memory Maps • Stretch to See • Picture Point of View • Resource Roundup • Character Props

Standard	Lessons
	• Text Translations • Character Evolution • Most Valuable Character • Greeting Cards • Cast the Character • Claims and Evidence Matchup • Musical Transitions • Wordless Picture Books • Social Media Profile Slide • Pop-Up Poems • Descriptive Writing Calendars • Paint Strip Arguments • Sticky Note Paragraphs • Source Synthesis • Mix and Match Remix • Paint Strip Paraphrase • Fun Way/Test Way • Out of the Gate Annotate • APW (Annotate, Plan, Write) • ACDC (Assess/Craft/Determine/Conclude) • First Word • Bless, Press, Address • I.N.K. • P.E.N. • Candy Revisions • Walk-Out Songs • Social Square Challenge • Post Promise or Story Worthy? • Do I Need to Repeat Myself? • Blackout Poems • Block Poems • Prepositional Phrase Poems • Partner Poems
Students adjust their use of spoken, written, and visual language (e.g., conventions, style, vocabulary) to communicate effectively with a variety of audiences and for different purposes.	• Say, Say, Say • Sounds Like • Memory Maps • Picture Point of View • Character Props

(Continued)

(Continued)

Standard	Lessons
	• Text Translations • Greeting Cards • Pictures for Mood • Claims and Evidence Matchup • Musical Transitions • Wordless Picture Books • Social Media Profile Slide • Pop-Up Poems • Descriptive Writing Calendars • Paint Strip Arguments • Mix and Match Remix • Paint Strip Paraphrase • Slinky Paragraphs • Level Up • Soap Opera Stories • Social Square Challenge • Post Promise or Story Worthy? • Do I Need to Repeat Myself?
Students use spoken, written, and visual language to accomplish their own purposes (e.g., for learning, enjoyment, persuasion, and the exchange of information).	• Say, Say, Say • Sounds Like • Memory Maps • Stretch to See • Picture Point of View • NVA^2 • Most Valuable Character • Cast the Character • Pictures for Mood • Claims and Evidence Matchup • Social Media Profile Slide • Pop-Up Poems • Descriptive Writing Calendars • Paint Strip Arguments • Sticky Note Paragraphs • Mix and Match Remix • Walk-Out Songs • Do I Need to Repeat Myself?

Standard	Lessons
Students apply knowledge of language structure, language conventions (e.g., spelling and punctuation), media techniques, figurative language, and genre to create, critique, and discuss print and nonprint texts.	• Picture Point of View • NVA² • Songs for Voice • Pictures for Mood • Claims and Evidence Matchup • Musical Transitions • Descriptive Writing Calendars • Paint Strip Arguments • Source Synthesis • Paint Strip Paraphrase • Do I Need to Repeat Myself? • Prepositional Phrase Poems
Students participate as knowledgeable, reflective, creative, and critical members of a variety of literacy communities.	• Memory Maps • Resource Roundup • Wordless Picture Books • Pop-Up Poems • Descriptive Writing Calendars • Source Synthesis • Paint Strip Paraphrase • Bless, Press, Address • Writing Surgery • Living Paragraph • Partner Poems
Students conduct research on issues and interests by generating ideas and questions and by posing problems.	• Resource Roundup • Claims and Evidence Matchup • Stop/Go Sources • Social Media Profile Slide • Paint Strip Arguments • Sticky Note Paragraphs • Source Synthesis • Mix and Match Remix • PK/NK • Paint Strip Paraphrase • Social Square Challenge

ACKNOWLEDGMENTS

Writing a book—any book—can't be done without a community of people who support, encourage, cheer, and critique a writer's work. I am certainly not an easy person to love or work with, yet there are some who show their support, despite my faults.

Much of my appreciation is owed to my family who put up with and love me, though I remain unorganized and chaotic, and who accept, for the most part, my idiosyncrasies and odd behaviors, especially when I am on deadline. To my husband, Will, thanks for listening, or at least pretending to, when I have ideas for books, classes, and suggestions for changing the world. To my children, Amelia, Macy Belle, and Vin, who allow me to ask their friends about their literacy practices, provide student work samples, and keep their eye-rolling contempt at bay while I set out to if not completely change, at least disrupt the traditional teaching world.

I continue to be grateful to my parents, Mom, Dad, and Kathy, who instilled the hustle and the "What the hell? Let's try it" attitude that continues to be the compass that guides my work today.

On a professional note, I would not be here without my students, all of whom I love and adore, and who push me to be better, stronger, and smarter because they deserve such. Thanks to my OG university colleagues for supporting me from way back. Y'all know who you are.

I would be remiss if I did not give a shout-out to the National Writing Project network. I was fortunate enough to take part in an NWP Summer Institute at the University of South Carolina (Go Gamecocks!) in the summer of 2005. I can trace every professional accomplishment back to that summer and often refer to it as my professional pivot. NWP changed my life, not only that summer, but also through the multitudes of committed, compassionate, and daring educators who I am honored to call my colleagues and friends. A special thanks to all my NWP writing friends, but especially my friend and fellow Dolly Parton fan, Tanya Baker; my NWP site cheerleader from the very beginning, Tom Fox; and my soul sister, Mary Jade Haney.

A huge thanks goes to every single one of my Augusta University Writing Project peeps. The best part of my job is the Summer Institute and getting to meet a new group of world-changing educators every single summer. A special thanks to those who came through with samples that are included in this book.

Those are:

Brittney Byrd
Nicole Cain
Kirsten Douglas
Ashley Elvis
Kelly Evans
Olga Malin
Alison Mason
Afinju McDowell
Alysha Mooney
Carley Robertson
Shelly Tanner
Candi Washington

Thanks to the awesome teachers and young people who contributed to this book.

Tre' Cain
Mark Epps
John David Groves
Paul Hankins
Amelia Harper
Macy Belle Harper
Vin Harper
Lauren Hofstetter
SJ Ingram
Jocelyn Johnson
Henry Johnston
Kay Lilly
Bekah List
Brandon McCormick

People in this world who I just love:

Lachonna Avery
Donnella DeBerry-Bull (Ms. DB)
Dr. Carletha Doyle (Dr. D)
Kourtney McCormick

As I wrap up this manuscript, I can't leave without saying a huge thank-you to my editor, Tori Bachman. Thank you for taking a chance on this lady.

And y'all, keep on asking me if I do hair, because if this teaching gig doesn't work out, I've got a solid second career plan. Seriously.

With a full and grateful heart,

Rebecca

Publisher's Acknowledgments

Corwin gratefully acknowledges the contributions of the following reviewers:

Jarred Amato
English Teacher
Nashville, TN

MarLynda Holley
High School Teacher
Beaufort, SC

Lynn Angus Ramos
Curriculum and Instruction Coordinator
Decatur, GA

Alicia Stephenson
K–12 Educator and Instructional Coach
Valdosta, GA

ABOUT THE AUTHOR

Rebecca G. Harper, PhD, is an associate professor of literacy at Augusta University. She has served as an invited speaker and keynote for a variety of literacy conferences and has delivered literacy professional development sessions across the country. Her research interests include sociocultural theory and critical literacy and content and disciplinary literacy. She is the author of *Write Now & Write On: 37 Strategies for Authentic Daily Writing in Every Content Area*. She lives in Aiken, South Carolina, with her husband, Will, and children, Amelia, Macy Belle, and Vin.

For the teachers who changed my life:

Marilynn C. Powers

Larry Turney

Amelia P. Ellison

Ruthie McManus

Dr. Val Lumans

Dr. Diane Stephens

Dr. Gayle S. Lee (Mom)

Thank you for making a difference and for instilling a love of learning in me.

Chapter 1

WRITING FITNESS

January marks the beginning of a new calendar year and, for many, serves as the month of new commitments. This is the month when millions of individuals commit to a new year with better habits and behaviors. According to Forbes (Murphy, 2020) and *U.S. News and World Report* (Luciani, 2015), over half of Americans make New Year's resolutions. While resolutions involve several topics and ideas, some of the most popular New Year's resolutions involve some aspect of health and fitness. In fact, YouGov reports that at least half of all New Year's resolutions involve some type of health and fitness aspect including losing weight, changing eating habits, and exercising (Ballard, 2020).

For many, even those resolutions that are not fitness related are short lived, because over 80% of all New Year's resolutions get abandoned by mid-February (Luciani, 2015). This happens because often resolutions are unclear or are unrealistic due to the high expectations of the goal itself. In other cases, excitement and commitment to a new habit, especially a new fitness routine, are short lived. If a new fitness habit requires rearrangement of daily life and doesn't have clear, attainable goals, we abandon it because of time constraints, lack of enjoyment, or sheer difficulty.

Imagine setting "training for and running in a marathon" as a New Year's resolution. That takes training and discipline, but it looks different for someone who is already a runner versus someone who is a novice runner. An established runner is already training, but maybe for shorter distances like a 5K or 10K run. Training for a marathon, though more intense than their current training, is manageable because they are already conditioned for running. They already have the right shoes, they have been running on a regular basis, and they have completed some type of running task (5K, 10K, etc.). While this new training may be more intense, for someone who already has experience as a runner, even for shorter distances, this goal is more likely to be met.

Imagine that same task, training for and running a marathon, for someone who is not a runner. This person doesn't know anything about the art of running. They aren't sure how to train for the race or even what shoes they should wear. They may not know how often they should run, for how long, or how long their marathon training should last. They do not own a treadmill, they aren't sure what types of food runners eat, and they know little about any pre- or postrace rituals that should be in place. How easy will it be for that person to complete the goal of running over twenty-six miles? Do you think they will be successful? Probably not. Certainly, it would be more difficult than it would be for the person who has running experience. Because of this lack of experience and the nature of the goal itself, it is likely that the new runner's goal won't be met, simply because it is just too difficult.

For many students, writing feels like running a marathon without prior running experience. Many students fail to perform well for some of the same reasons that individuals struggle with lifestyle and fitness changes. They haven't been trained properly, and their goals are not clearly articulated. In some instructional cases, students are expected to run a marathon and they haven't had experience or success with a 5K or even a jog around the classroom. As a result, writing may seem like a difficult task to master and complete, let alone excel in performance. Why? Think about the writing tasks that many students take part in. Many of the write-on-demand tasks require students to write extended pieces with little time for warmup and brainstorming. Others require students to write about topics they have little experience with. Some are extended responses that require endurance and stamina, while others demand students quickly compile written evidence in a sprint task. Yet other written engagements warrant discipline-specific language and structure and a solid understanding of the foundational aspects of multigenre compositions. When students find that they are unsuccessful at the writing that is thrown at them, many of them do what runners do when they realize that training for a marathon every day without a plan or with the wrong shoes is too hard: They quit.

This is why the teaching of writing is a lot like a workout regimen. It takes discipline, practice, and a specific schedule with goals that are directly linked to results and products. Before a training program commences, the end goal should be clear as well as the steps needed to achieve that goal. Plus, time must be allocated to complete the training—you have to schedule the time for regular training.

When you think about a workout regimen, what tenets and components stand out to you? Do you find yourself comparing multiple aspects of fitness or lifestyle changes and find that there are some similarities? Regardless of the type of training or purpose, most workout regimes have some common components. These might include:

- A schedule
- Targeted results
- Goals
- Expected time commitment
- Varying level of difficulty
- A trainer or expert guide
- A fitness log or tracker
- A plan of activity
- Communities of support from peers
- Supplements and nutritional information that can increase performance

All these items assist individuals as they begin this new task. Because of the multifaceted nature of these characteristics, success is more likely simply because there are multiple components working in tandem to help an individual achieve this goal. In addition, many fitness programs include a preview of the plan, so users know exactly what to expect from the program.

When training students as writers, consider how the above characteristics transfer into instructional practices. Ask yourself some of these questions:

- Is writing a fixed component on the instructional schedule?
- Do the students have writing goals for their progress?
- As the instructor, are there class goals in place for writing?
- Do you know how much time you have for writing in the day?
- Do they see writing modeled by their teachers?
- Who is assisting with the training of the students? (Not just the teacher, but peers as experts and authors through the integration of author's craft.)
- What kind of writing community are students part of?
- How often is literature used as a supplement in writing class?

Taking an inventory of the items above can assist teachers as they begin to plan purposeful writing instruction and training. When planning for writing instruction, it helps to have a solid grasp not only of the *how* we plan to teach but also the *why*. Breaking an instructional goal down into specific chunks, as in the following table, can help teachers plan purposeful lessons that can lead to more effective instruction. (You can find a printable copy of this on the online companion website, resources.corwin.com/WritingWorkouts.)

Writing Instructional Goal	Why Is This Goal Relevant?	How Can This Goal be Achieved?
What do I want students to do?	Why do students need to know this?	What will I as the instructional leader do to facilitate the goal? What will the students do to achieve the goal?

Even though many students have the potential to become skilled writers, a significant portion of our writers are out of writing shape. Why?

- They haven't been trained properly.
- They don't have a steady diet of authentic writing.
- They suffer from writing injuries or conditions (fragmentitis, bad cases of the run-ons, FOWM—Fear of Writing More).
- They lack writing endurance and stamina.
- They have limited opportunities to practice their writing skills.
- Their literature diets lack variety.

Yet all these deficiencies can be remedied by implementing writing into the daily lives of students and their instructional experiences. By offering students multiple opportunities to practice and train, teachers can help their writing fitness to improve over time, which can lead to stronger writers who can lift heavier topics, write for longer amounts of time, and improve their overall writing health. Not only that, but writers who are in good writing shape can also write on demand, complete sprint writing tasks, and stretch their writing muscles by playing around with words and phrases. Good writing shape involves a solid baseline of multiple writing proficiencies, not just one area.

Getting Into Writing Shape

So what does getting into writing shape look like? First of all, just like real fitness plans, the writing workouts that have lasting results are not quick fixes and don't work overnight. In other words, this is not a five-paragraph juice cleanse that will make you produce a product that passes an assessment on Friday, only to have you struggle with the same skills the following week.

There is no one quick formula, no RACE to the constructed response finish line or RAFT for that multigenre writing task. While some formulas might work for some types of writings, when students only know that one approach, many attempt to utilize it for every single type of writing. Consider the RACE strategy, for example. RACE, simply put, stands for Restate, Answer, Cite, and Explain. While this strategy may work for a constructed response that demands textual evidence as a component of the composition, it simply won't work in a persuasive or narrative setting. Similarly, all constructed responses that require textual evidence won't work with this approach either. Several years ago, I was in a fourth-grade math classroom in a district that exclusively utilized the RACE writing strategy. I watched a fourth grader as she struggled with placing the right information into the appropriate letters of the acronym. When she asked her teacher how she should restate the problem, the teacher told her to simply rewrite the math problem for the R letter. The student did as she was instructed, then moved on to answer the problem, only to find herself confused again with the Cite section of the strategy. Her teacher told her skip that part and move on to the Explain portion. As a result, this strategy was not an effective one for this lesson and for this purpose. Why?

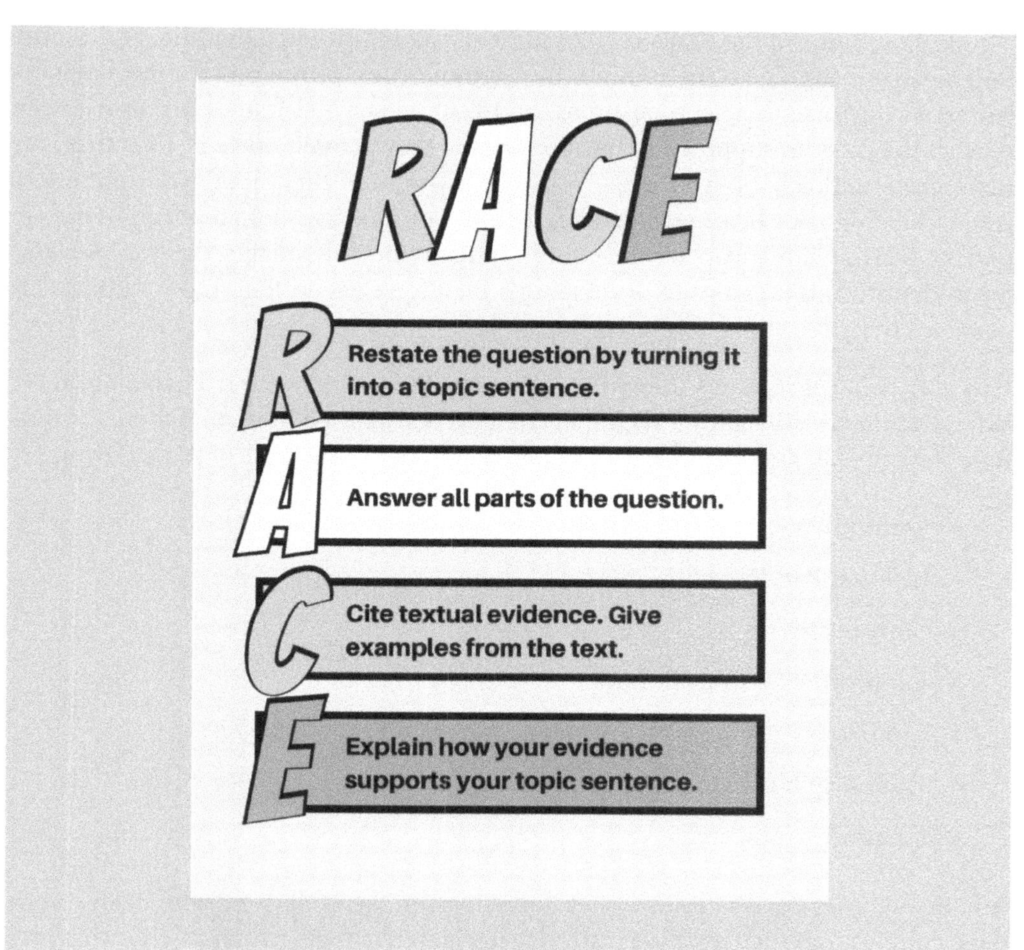

- It included components that were not necessary or possible due to the nature of the question.
- Due to its one-size-fits-all nature, specific goals and purposes of the lesson were not taken into account.

- Because this district was *only* utilizing this strategy for *all* their writing tasks, both the student and teacher did not have another strategy in their writer's toolbox that could be implemented.

In this case, this student was *overtrained* in the use of one specific strategy that was only useful for certain types of writing. Think of it like a weightlifting routine. If someone wants to enter the World's Strongest Man competition, would training focus on just the biceps? No. Instead, it would focus on all or most muscle groups since the end goal is to build overall strength. Similarly, in the classroom, getting into good solid writing shape involves training across genres and formats. A solid writing workout regimen acknowledges that the craft of writing cannot be exclusively restricted to a formulaic method of construction. Rather, it is a unique set of skills and competencies that work in tandem with subtle nuances and the craft of language, which create a story, an explanation, an account, an argument. Students who are in good writing shape have teachers and facilitators who recognize that they teach *writers* not writing.

Think about some of the strategies that students might use when drafting, brainstorming, or organizing. Take the outline, for example. The purpose of an outline is for writers to organize their compositions, and build a skeletal framework or overview of what the paper is supposed to be about *before* they actually write it. I bet there are many reading this book who wrote your paper *first*, and then wrote your outline. If you're nodding your head reading this, then the outline was not an effective strategy for you. (Hey, it didn't work for me either!) If that is the only strategy that was provided for students when it comes to developing a plan for a paper, then some students are going to struggle.

However, what if teachers offered students multiple methods for organizing ideas? What if students took part in writing instruction that showed them that there are multiple ways to plan and organize your paper? How about using any of the following?

- Outlines
- Colored Post-it maps
- Story boards
- Jamboard or Dabble online
- Timelines
- Paint strip blocks for multiple sources
- Graphic organizers

And the list goes on. A writer who has more tools in the toolbox is more likely to produce compositions that are more fully developed and effective than a writer who only has one or two tools at his/her disposal.

Now, let's think back to that runner who has training experience but is now preparing for a marathon. Of course, this new training is still going to be difficult. The runner may still struggle, but certainly not to the degree of the one who has never run anywhere before. The same goes for student writers. While new genres and writing tasks demand different subsets of skills, a student who writes often and for a variety of purposes is better prepared to take up a new writing task than one who writes on rare occasions. That's why a student who has a lot of experience writing in the persuasive genre will find that training in that genre can assist when they begin writing an argument. One who has experience with informational writing can use this experience when completing longer research writing tasks. This related training helps build stronger overall writers. Some of the related writings that students complete are listed in Figure 1.1.

Figure 1.1

Related Writings/Tandem Training		
Persuasive essays	Personal narratives	Informational writing
Argumentative papers	Historical fiction	Research papers
Position papers	Story scripts	Outlines
Movie/book reviews	Story boards	Summaries
	Autobiographies	Lab reports
	Memoirs	Biographies

Components of Effective Writing Training

What should an effective writing fitness program look like? What yields real writing results? What makes a healthy writer? Effective writing training includes several crucial components:

1. Daily opportunities for writing

When writing becomes a part of the daily routine, the expectation is set. When will we write? Today, tomorrow, and the next day. We write daily. Students who write daily become better writers (https://www.literacyworldwide.org/; https://ncte.org/; https://www.nwp.org/).

2. Inclusion of relevant and authentic writing tasks

Writing engagements that are relevant and authentic allow students to write for real purposes and real audiences. Plus, when students can write about what they know first, they are able to leverage background knowledge and create more developed writing pieces. In addition, because many students are already writing outside of the academic setting, but don't necessarily recognize the connection between home and academic writing (Lenhart, 2008), these authentic writing opportunities are imperative. Giving students opportunities to write for authentic purposes and establishing a link between personal and academic writing can help students become more aware of this crossover.

3. Goals-oriented, process-based instruction

Not only should instruction involve specific short-term and long-range performance goals, but writers also need support when developing goals for individual writing pieces. Because part of the writing process involves planning and thinking about the overarching purpose of the piece, setting goals and making plans for their writing helps writers think through their writing tasks, resulting in better final products. To effectively achieve this, students should have an intimate working knowledge of the writing process itself.

In a nutshell, the writing process involves planning, drafting, revising, and editing, but it is important to note that these processes are recursive and can occur at any given point in the construction of a piece. Recognizing that writing is not a linear process helps students view writing as fluid and dynamic rather than in a formulaic, scripted nature. Don't like how that sentence sounds now? Don't wait till your entire draft is complete; go ahead and revise it now. Make it halfway through your piece only to realize you need to include another section or component? Go back to your original plan and modify it. Showing students examples like these can help them realize that they can make shifts and changes throughout the process, not just at certain check points. Plus, when students understand the actual process of writing, their compositions become longer, more developed, and qualitatively better (Graham et al., 2012).

4. Training variety

To improve overall writing fitness, students should take part in training engagements that utilize a variety of formats and offer opportunities to practice writing across a wide variety of genres and purposes and for a number of audiences. Providing opportunities for students to take part in a variety of writing activities and tasks increases the likelihood that they will be stronger writers overall. Plus, students should take part in writing engagements that vary in complexity, overall length, and topic. For example, proficiency in a specific genre—take the persuasive one, for example—should involve training that utilizes multiple topics, formats, and audiences to prepare a writer who is in good persuasive shape.

5. Expert input

When training, students need the opportunities to engage and learn from and with a variety of experts. These experts should come from a number of areas and aren't exclusive to the teacher charged with teaching the class. Instead, utilizing peers, mentor texts and authors, as well as other writers from additional areas offers unique perspectives and breadth for young writers. Plus, when young writers see writers represented from a variety of backgrounds, it asserts and reaffirms the notion that anyone can be a writer. In addition, allowing students to see and hear how experts struggle is key when building confidence. Let students see how writers sometimes can't come up with a solid sentence, forget how to spell in front of the class, or have days where they can't come up with any ideas that seem *writable*. This can help students build confidence in their own writing and assist in building classroom community as well.

Stop & Think

While I enjoy a variety of fitness programs, I recently began one that was beyond intense. Although I have a lot of experience working out, this particular one was very hard for me. One of the main reasons I did not quit had to do with the "experts" who were leading this training. They ALL were in better shape than me, and most (truthfully, probably all) of them were younger than me, yet every single one of them struggled, too. As a result, I didn't feel defeated. In fact, I felt encouraged. If these experts were having a hard time, then it's ok for me to struggle, too!

6. Communities of support and feedback

Writers can grow and thrive within a supportive community of feedback. For writers to learn and improve their writing, opportunities for feedback are necessary. Because feedback drives revision, nurturing a supportive community and fostering relationships that capitalize on safe spaces can aid students in their writing endeavors. Building a community with this in mind puts the teacher and students as cooperative partners who learn from each other (NCTE, 2018).

Share with students select author interviews from YouTube or authors' websites that talk about the writing process, specifically the struggle involved. This past year our Writing Project Site has hosted over forty authors for book clubs. These virtual conversations revealed that every single one of these experts has their own writing struggles. Whether it was manuscript rejections, facing writer's block, or simply lacking the motivation to write, all our visiting authors agreed that writing can be a struggle sometimes!

7. Balanced diet of reading and writing

Not only do students need to train appropriately and often, but they also need a balanced reading and writing diet. To grow as healthy writers, students must digest a variety of literature types. Merging contemporary titles with canonical texts; utilizing digital texts, graphic novels, and poetry; and presenting students with choices that represent diverse authors, characters, and perspectives helps develop healthy readers and writers.

Using the components outlined previously when working with writers helps develop strong writers. When students are in good writing shape, they can accomplish a number of goals. Here's what a student in good writing shape can do:

- Write for a variety of purposes and audiences
- Write for extended amounts of time
- Complete short bursts of targeted writing
- Revisit and revise writing pieces
- Give and receive feedback used to guide and shape future revisions
- Plan, execute, and amend long- and short-term writing goals
- Implement different writing strategies and approaches for different writing engagements

Now, all these benefits for getting into writing shape don't mean that writers sometimes don't want to write, can't think of ideas, or get frustrated with the task. Even professional athletes and trainers have days where they don't want to go to the gym. Writers are no different. Just as a swimmer needs a day off after a three-day intense meet, sometimes writers need a day of recovery or rest. Yet don't be fooled by rest days; even on those days, students are still getting trained. Instead of high intensity training, it might simply include a quick one-sentence response to a reading or a paint strip collection of words they like, or it might be through a read-aloud where we ask them to think about a portion of the story and map it out in their heads. Regardless, all these can translate later into something they are doing in their writing.

How This Book Can Help

Chapters in this book outline and address specific types of writing training and explore what types of writing engagements fit within those areas. Sample schedules and goal documents follow on the companion website, along with recommended approaches for students at varying writing abilities.

Further are some highlights from each chapter that may help you determine just where you want to start reading first. However, you'll find that the layout of the book in some ways follows the natural progression and framework of a workout. Looking at the brief synopsis of the chapters provides information on what types of engagements are included in each section. Doing this first can help ensure that the time spent is not wasted on strategies or engagements that don't fit your purpose or time availability. You may find that you dip in and out of this book as you locate strategies that best fit the goals of your instruction. If you haven't been including as much writing in your instruction or are a little apprehensive with going full tilt right off, start with the Writing Warmups chapter, the Cold Starts and Cooldowns chapter, or the Rest, Recover, Revise chapter. Regardless, each chapter offers unique and novel approaches for developing and nurturing young writers.

Chapter 2—Writing Warmups

This chapter includes writing engagements that allow students to warm up and stretch their writing muscles. These tasks are quick and easy to implement because they require minimal planning and preparation. In addition, they transcend a variety of genres and delivery methods so they are natural winners in today's diverse classrooms. Plus, writing warmups serve as the precursor for larger, fully involved writing engagements to come. Although they require little planning and preparation, their strategic, purposeful placement can enhance and improve student performance in a longer writing task.

Chapter 3—Targeted Training

To strengthen specific types of writing or skills, targeted training is necessary. In this chapter you'll find specific ideas for the teaching of voice, grammar, comparing and contrasting, point of view, and textual evidence, which are just some of the specific training lessons included. If you are searching for ways to teach specific skills using contemporary and engaging material, this chapter offers excellent approaches with easy implementation ideas.

Chapter 4—High Intensity Training

Some of the academic writing engagements that students are charged with executing are intense. Not only are students required to write lengthy compositions, but many academic writing engagements also require them to analyze and synthesize multiple sources, apply sophisticated placement of textual evidence, and craft a solid position statement. In this chapter, high intensity writing tasks are offered, including argumentative compositions, multisource research, thesis statements, and more.

Chapter 5—Cold Starts and Cooldowns

Just like warmups, students need opportunities to cooldown from a writing task. Typically used at the end of a class period, at the culmination of a writing task, or following a unit of study, cooldowns offer students the chance to reflect, process, and respond to material they have completed. Some of these include new exit slip ideas, reflection formats, and other informal out-the-door assessments.

Chapter 6—Rest, Recover, Revise

Writers who are in good writing shape know that revising is an integral part of the writing process. In reality, there is no real final draft; we could keep revising and rewriting forever. In this chapter, ideas for revising and revisiting pieces are used including Bless, Press, Address; First Off; Stretch a Sentence; and more.

Chapter 7—Stretch Day

There are days when writers can stretch their muscles with writing tasks and ideas that allow them to play around with words and language. With these opportunities, students get to take part in playing with writing. Students will stretch by creating Blackout Poetry, Movie Soundtracks, Prepositional Phrase Poems, and more.

Chapter 8—A Balanced Diet of Reading and Writing: The Literature and Writing Students Need to Thrive

Part of developing healthy writers includes feeding them the right material along with their writing tasks. Learn why and how to integrate new and engaging literature in writing instruction that captures diverse perspectives and views, along with offering students opportunities for reading and research, publishing and sharing, and serving as literacy advocates.

Online Companion Website

On the companion website, you'll find all the handouts or templates needed to accomplish some of the strategies listed in the book: http://resources.corwin.com/WritingWorkouts.

Companion website to *Writing Workouts*

Chapter 2

WRITING WARMUPS

In a workout, warming up before strenuous activity has several benefits. It stretches muscles and loosens up your joints, gets your heart rate up before the real workout, and helps prepare the body for the activity that will follow. In other words, warming up helps get the body ready for what's to come. Plus, not only does a proper warmup provide a preview of the upcoming workout, but it can also help prevent injuries, alleviate early fatigue, and help the athlete perform better.

Much like a warmup before a physical workout, writers need opportunities to loosen up and warm up with words before they begin a longer writing task. When students warm up before they begin a strenuous writing engagement, they often produce better final products and can write longer, more extended pieces. While warming up is beneficial for longer, more involved writing compositions, even abbreviated writing tasks can benefit from a warmup to activate prior knowledge and experiences. Allowing students time to warm up before they start writing has a number of benefits:

- Gets ideas flowing
- Activates prior knowledge
- Allows time to stretch their writing muscles, through thinking and processing material
- Gives students time to prepare for an extended response
- Serves as a preview of the engagement to come
- Helps develop connections between the warmup and the task to follow

Warming up BEFORE an extended response can increase the likelihood for success since it allows students some preview and practice space over a short period of time. Plus, these warmups allow teachers the unique ability to integrate multiple writing practice opportunities on a regular and consistent basis, some with limited preparation and planning.

While writing warmups are typically short periods of writing that are low intensity, they can always be extended into longer engagements. For example, the Warmup With Music activity can easily become a fully involved piece, as you will see in a later chapter where we critically interpret a music video. Likewise, Quick Writes, which I have used for over a decade, can serve as warmups and also can be extended into longer responses, depending on the purpose of the overall lesson.

A writing warmup is most beneficial if it clearly relates to the larger task at hand. For example, in a physical workout, you would not typically see an intense cardio warmup before a yoga class. Instead, you might see a warmup that focuses on breathing, stretching, or balance. Why? Because those are the types of activities and moves that will be the focus for the yoga class that follows. With this principle in mind, writing warmups work best when they feed into the day's writing or help students practice a skill that might be used in a larger genre. Plus, you can use different types of warmups that address the same larger, overarching skill, which can help students by offering multiple opportunities for additional practice of a targeted skill.

For example, in my teaching, I noticed that the construction of dialogue was a difficult skill for some students to master, yet it was one that was required in ELA standard sets and included in the county-mandated writing rubric. However, when students implemented dialogue in their writing, their dialogue sounded canned, mimicking narration and less like the actual words that might come from a character. Thus, a variety of dialogue warmups would be beneficial for students to use when practicing this skill. If I wanted students to warm up with some dialogue activities, I might have them complete the Say, Say, Say warmup, the Sounds Like warmup, or the That's What They Said warmup. Each of those strategies addresses the subtle nuances of dialogue in a low- stakes, relaxed setting for a brief time, yet they all are meant as strategies that can assist students in the effective construction of dialogue. However, these could also be used as a drop-in, kind of like the Parachute Writing included in my book *Write Now & Write On* (2022).

While writing warmups that are centered around the same theme can be used to effectively address a skill over the course of multiple days, they can also be used as a way to review a type of writing that students are already familiar with. For example, the persuasive genre appears in almost all grade-level standards sets, starting as early as kindergarten. A writing warmup that addresses some sort of persuasive component can offer students the opportunity to limber up with something they are familiar with because their past experience can assist them in the task completion. Plus, because this genre is seen across content areas, in multiple formats, and is crafted for myriad audiences, completing warmups that are focused on this genre can be used for a number of purposes. And the persuasive genre is one that is especially prevalent in the real world, including social media. This offers another authentic example of writing in today's world.

The writing warmups in this chapter have been organized into different sections based on the nature and type of warmup. Each includes anchor National Council of Teachers of English and International Literacy Association ELA Standards included on the companion website as well as suggestions for modifications, extensions, and connections to overarching lesson goals. As you plan your instruction, think through the big ideas and concepts you will be teaching along with the skills and competencies that students need additional practice to master. Choosing appropriate warmups that can reinforce these skills can make for successful instruction.

MUSIC INFOGRAPHICS

One of my favorite types of texts to use with students is music. Warmups that incorporate music offer unique opportunities for students to interact with a variety of musical styles and capitalize on student interest and ideas in the classroom. Plus, because there are so many possibilities for variation with different genres and artists, they are an easy implementation tool that keeps students engaged. Music is also an easy win for students because they can make connections between their academic and nonacademic lives and can prolong the learning intentions of the lesson by adding their own suggestions from their personal music choices later.

While using music in lessons offers students the opportunity to connect their personal interests to academic learning, incorporating infographics in teaching can offer students opportunities to look at data and information in a new way. This allows students to take advantage of their creativity and artistic notions to effectively present information. Plus, an infographic makes data appear much more meaningful and adds a cool factor to what can sometimes be viewed as a boring and dull task.

Fitness Beat graphic designed by Alva Rovalino for National Geographic, 2011

One way to incorporate music and infographics is through this activity using one of Alva Rovalino's infographics called "Fitness Beat" (scan the QR code in the margin to see this graphic and share with students). It is a great warmup for presenting textual evidence and gives students an auditory textual example. And it capitalizes on student interest by allowing students to connect their personal interests with an academic task. It also allows students to see data presented in a different way, with a combination of figures and images in tandem with numbers and statistics.

Putting It to Work

1. Display the "Fitness Beat" infographic for the class. Hover over the QR code in the margin to show the infographic to students (you can find it online here: https://www.alvarovalino.com/Fitness-Beat).
2. Discuss the physical activities that are listed on the infographic.
3. Play a portion of one song from each physical activity listed. (This means you should play a portion of one of the songs from all categories including resting, walking, training, and high intensity training.)
4. Have students discuss as a class the characteristics of the samples played.
5. Discuss the appropriateness of each sample for the physical activity that corresponds with the song. Have students orally justify the song choices on the infographic with their classmates.
6. After all the samples have been played and discussed, instruct students to locate a new song that fits into each of the categories.

7. Students can record their new choices on sticky notes or on a piece of paper divided into sections.

8. Have students draft a one- to two-sentence explanation for their choice.

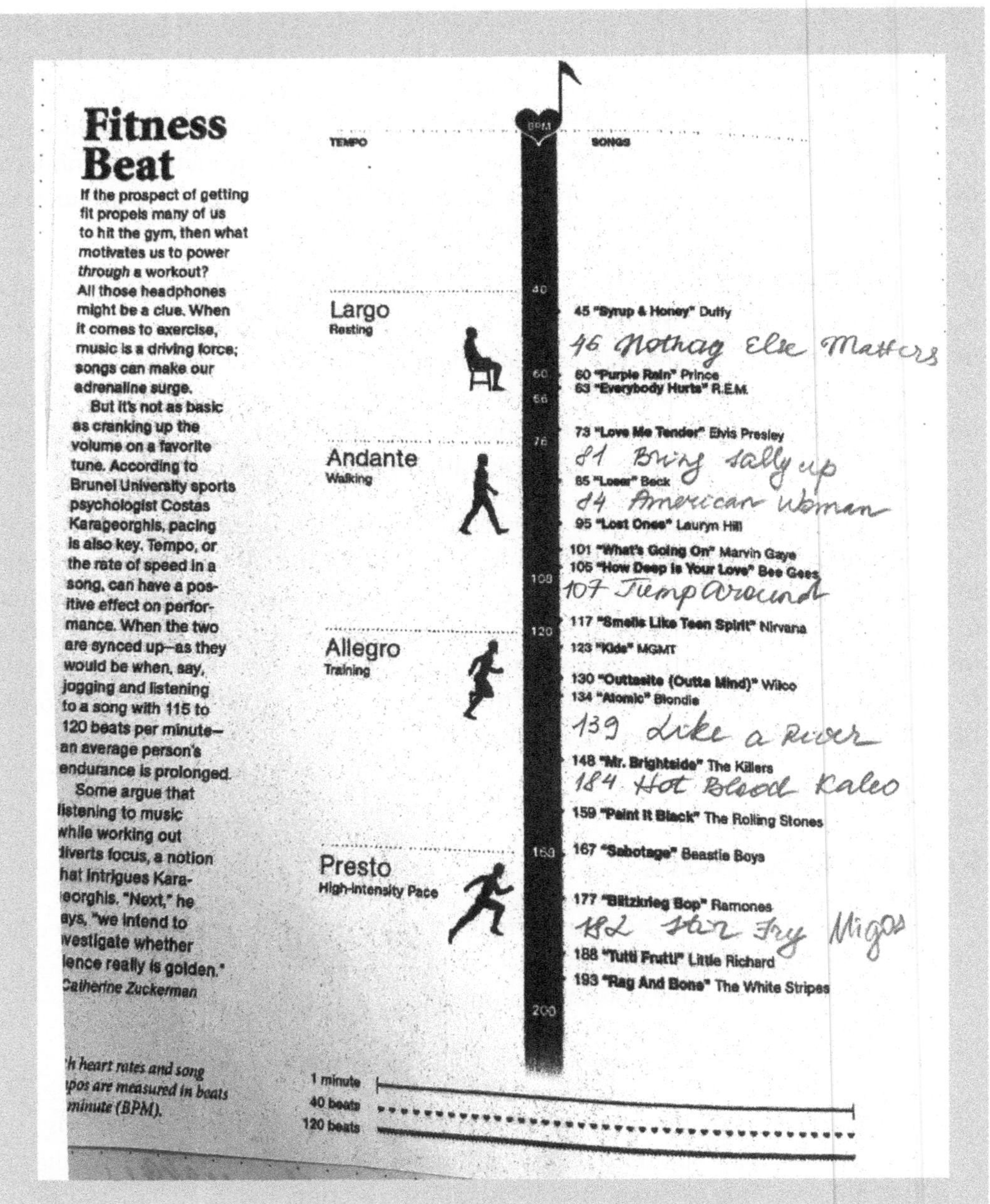

Fitness Beat

If the prospect of getting fit propels many of us to hit the gym, then what motivates us to power *through* a workout? All those headphones might be a clue. When it comes to exercise, music is a driving force; songs can make our adrenaline surge.

But it's not as basic as cranking up the volume on a favorite tune. According to Brunel University sports psychologist Costas Karageorghis, pacing is also key. Tempo, or the rate of speed in a song, can have a positive effect on performance. When the two are synced up—as they would be when, say, jogging and listening to a song with 115 to 120 beats per minute—an average person's endurance is prolonged.

Some argue that listening to music while working out liverts focus, a notion hat intrigues Karaeorghis. "Next," he ays, "we intend to vestigate whether lence really is golden." *Catherine Zuckerman*

h heart rates and song pos are measured in beats minute (BPM).

TEMPO | BPM | SONGS

Largo Resting
- 45 "Syrup & Honey" Duffy
- 46 Nothing Else Matters
- 60 "Purple Rain" Prince
- 63 "Everybody Hurts" R.E.M.
- 73 "Love Me Tender" Elvis Presley

Andante Walking
- 81 Bring Sally up
- 85 "Loser" Beck
- 84 American Woman
- 95 "Lost Ones" Lauryn Hill
- 101 "What's Going On" Marvin Gaye
- 105 "How Deep Is Your Love" Bee Gees
- 107 Jump Around
- 117 "Smells Like Teen Spirit" Nirvana

Allegro Training
- 123 "Kids" MGMT
- 130 "Outtasite (Outta Mind)" Wilco
- 134 "Atomic" Blondie
- 139 Like a River
- 148 "Mr. Brightside" The Killers
- 184 Hot Blood Kaleo
- 159 "Paint It Black" The Rolling Stones

Presto High-Intensity Pace
- 167 "Sabotage" Beastie Boys
- 177 "Blitzkrieg Bop" Ramones
- 182 Stir Fry Migos
- 188 "Tutti Frutti" Little Richard
- 193 "Rag And Bone" The White Stripes

When to Use It

- When introducing or reinforcing textual evidence.
- To integrate disciplines (health/fitness, the arts, and literacy).
- For lessons that involve data presentation and delivery.

- When you want students to practice utilizing textual evidence in a brief writing task.

Quick Tip!

Guess where I originally found this resource? In the *National Geographic* magazine. You never know where you'll find ideas for writing!

Why It Works

- It provides a second sensory experience with a literary element/competency.
- Choice is key here; there are multiple answer options for students.
- It capitalizes on student choice and background knowledge.
- It offers multiple connections between kinesthetic, verbal, and auditory means.

Modifications

- Instead of using music, try different scenes from movies that follow the same intensity levels.
- Have students complete this engagement with a partner.
- Instead of having students come up with their own new songs for each section, have a ready-made list of sample options that students can search and listen to from a song bank.
- Use artwork or photos instead of music.
- Play the music samples first and have students guess which physical activity might go with the music.

Extensions

- Have students create a pictorial image that corresponds with the song chosen.
- Have students create a word bank of adjectives that can be used to describe the chosen song.
- Get students to attack or defend a classmate's song choice using textual evidence from the infographic and song lyrics (for ideas using this strategy, see my book *Write Now & Write On* [2022]).
- Create a playlist using a compilation of student songs for each level of activity. Provide the playlists to PE teachers to use in their teaching based on the level of training the students are completing in class.

Digital Direction

- Post the infographic in a virtual classroom platform such as Google classroom.

- Use an add-on recording application like Mote for Google documents so students can record their comments with the infographic.
- Use a web application such as Diigo for digital annotation and comments.
- Have students video themselves completing the training listed in the infographic while listening to their chosen song. For example, for the resting phase, they may video themselves sitting on a couch listening to one of their songs associated with that activity. Students would create a trailer that includes video clips of all the physical training activities and songs associated with each.

Quick Tip!

Here's a super cool web tool for presenting text in a more visual manner: www.voyant-tools.org. Voyant is a web-based reading and analysis environment for digital text. Users can paste text into the search box to see their text represented in multiple ways.

Lesson Lead-Ins

- Use this as an introduction or warmup for research writing that includes a visual data representation component.
- Position this as an opening for a lesson on mood or tone in writing.
- Warm up with this activity prior to beginning an extended piece that requires the integration of textual evidence.
- Use this as a warmup for the Songs for Voice (see page 86).

SAY, SAY, SAY

My stepmother often used the expression “There’s more than one way to skin a cat” whenever she wanted us to acknowledge that there were multiple ways to approach a situation or solve a problem. Much like this old saying, there are multiple ways to say the same things. Yet in many cases, students resort to the same phrases or words, especially when constructing dialogue.

When constructing dialogue, students experience challenges with creating authentic and believable words that actually sound like real dialogue. Part of this difficulty can be attributed to the lack of experience many students have with writing dialogue. Because this is a sophisticated skill to master, multiple opportunities to practice are beneficial. Plus, students can benefit from practicing multiple ways to say the same thing. Take the phrase “I’ve got a lot of work to do.” Think of all the ways that you could say this. Some examples include

“I’ve got so much to do with this new project I’m working on.”

“I’m covered up with work.”

“I’m in the weeds.” (This is my own personal mantra.)

“I’ve got a full plate right now.”

“I’m slammed.”

“I’m swamped.”

I bet you could add a few examples that would work here as well. The point is, there are multiple ways to say the same thing. Students can practice this skill by warming up with Say, Say, Say.

Putting It to Work

1. Put a common statement on display for students to see.
2. Discuss the different ways that the phrase can be stated.
3. Make sure that items such as word tiers/levels (the formal or informal tone or use), audience, and person speaking are discussed. For example, a formal example might be “This new project has added a lot of extra tasks to my daily work.” An informal example might be “I’m up to my eyeballs in work!”
4. Divide the class into pairs or groups. Have each group draft a new way to say the statement.
5. Have students share with the class.

6. As a class, determine the three best ways to revise the target statement.

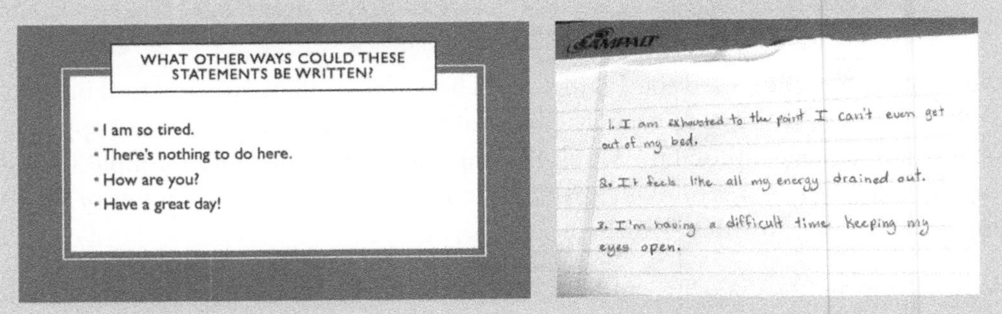

When to Use It

- When introducing or reinforcing dialogue.
- To practice constructing dialogue.
- To practice revising dialogue to make it sound more authentic.

Why It Works

- It allows students the opportunity to practice writing and rewriting a common phrase.
- Because students are all working on revising the same statement, collaborative partnerships are easy since the overarching focus is the same.
- Revising on the small scale makes this phase of writing more attainable.

Modifications

- Instead of using a printed statement, use a video clip of dialogue instead.
- Use clips from a movie that has been remade and compare the differences between the actor's dialogue.
- Take lines from famous speeches and have students complete the same activity.
- Provide students with the modified statements ahead of time and have students choose which statement is best.
- Provide students with a character sketch of the person who might be saying the dialogue. Have them use this information to help them determine what would sound like their assigned character.

Extensions

- Have students take their dialogue options and draft character descriptions for the character who might say them.

- Continue the engagement by formally punctuating and inserting the dialogue into a written composition.
- Match a character from a literary work to the dialogue that sounds like that character.

Digital Direction

- Use an application like Make Belief Comix (https://www.makebeliefscomix.com/Comix/) to develop a multipane comic with the options for dialogue.

- Use the PuppetMaster app to create an animated drawing of the character with the recorded dialogue.
- Adobe Character Animator can be used to design a digital character that can be animated with motion and sound.

Lesson Lead-Ins

- Use this warmup as a lead-in when students are incorporating dialogue into their writings.
- Position this warmup when working on character analyses or character development in writing.
- When beginning a unit on research writing and academic language, use this warmup as a way to illustrate formal and informal tone.

SOUNDS LIKE

Sometimes, when we really get to know a person or character, we hear certain words or phrases and say, "That sounds like . . . !" This happens because we know enough about that person that we can assign certain attributes and characteristics to them, which we then connect to the words they say or might say. Because of our past experiences with a person or character, we are often able to use this knowledge to make assertions and assumptions about a figure. Students can warm up and practice the skills that help them build dynamic characters with the Sounds Like activity. This can also be related to students' social media savvy by calling it Tweets Like, Posts Like, Snaps Like, Toks Like, etc.

Putting It to Work

1. Determine which characters or figures are the focus of the lesson. These could be characters from a novel, pop culture icons, or historical figures.
2. Locate multiple quotes that come from each of the figures. If using a fictional character from a novel or movie, use the character's quotes from the novel or from the video clip. See some examples in the image below.

Who said it? Which character from The Odds of Getting Even said these?
"We should put gossip on the menu."
"Ride with me, Soldier."
"A smart leader knows when to step aside, and let others lead."
"Church at 11 hours."

3. Post the quotes on notecards or sticky notes, but don't reveal the source of the quote.
4. Make a chart with each character's name on it or write the character's name on a sentence strip and put it on the floor in a designated area.
5. At the beginning of the class period, provide students with sticky notes. Have them record character traits or characteristics on their sticky notes for each of the focus characters. Place these in the designated location in the classroom.

6. Discuss the traits with the class.

7. Next, provide each student with a quote.

8. Have the students place the quote with the name of the character who they think said it. (If they are unsure, they can use the character descriptors/traits that they compiled at the beginning of the activity.)

This is an important prior knowledge activator. It gets students thinking about the focus figures/characters and aids them in determining which quotes sound like the character.

9. After students have placed their quotes where they believe they belong, discuss as a class.

10. Reveal the true origin of any of the misplaced quotes.

When to Use It

- When you want students to match dialogue to a particular type of character.
- As another way to address dialogue.
- As a way for students to address quotes out of context.
- When you want students to begin a character analysis composition.

Why It Works

- It offers students a different way to examine character and character traits.
- Because the figures/characters used are ones that students are familiar with and have experience with, this activity leverages background knowledge and aids the student in making connections.
- The task is more attainable for readers and writers who are below grade level, students who are neurodiverse, or students learning English as a new language because students are focusing on small bursts of reading and writing (sticky notes with character traits and one- to three-line quotes from characters).

Modifications

- Instead of using direct quotes from characters, use social media tweets or posts.
- Play audio recordings of the quotes and have students determine who said them.
- Use mock Instagram posts complete with images and have students determine who posted them.

Extensions

- Instead of identifying specific figures as a focus, choose random quotes, tweets, or posts and have students group them in categories based on which ones sound alike. Once students have a large group of quotes that they think sound like a certain person/character, have them draft a list of character traits that that person might have.

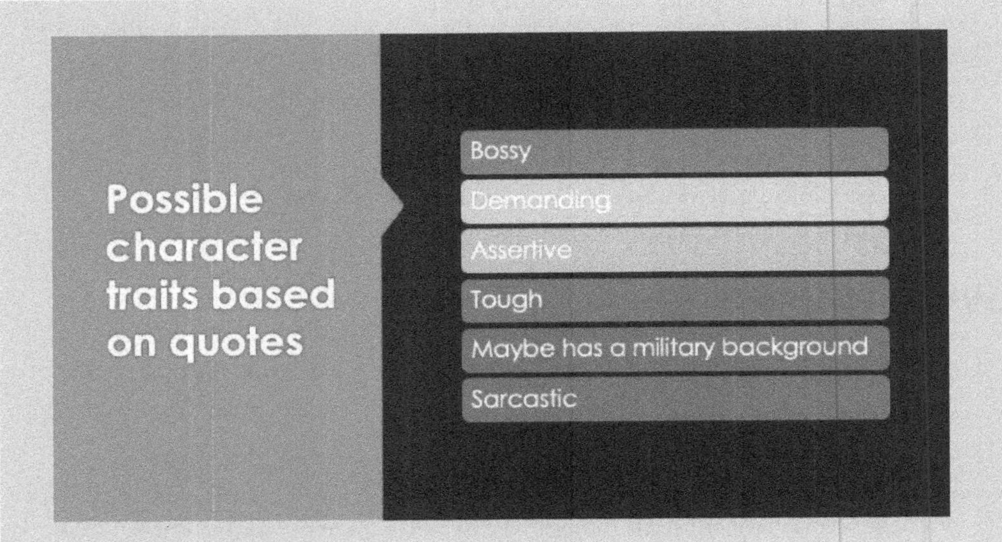

- Start the lesson with quotes on Day 1, then extend it to include social media posts such as tweets and Instagram stories. In this extension, the warmup progresses daily. Day 1 warmup would be Sounds Like (using direct quotes), Day 2 warmup would be Tweets Like (using tweets for classification), and Day 3 would be Posts Like (using Instagram stories for classification).
- Have students create a mock social media handle for the characters and create sample tweets or posts for the character.
- Have students create their own quotes similar to the ones classified on the charts.

Digital Direction

- Use an application like PicStitch, PicCollage, or Canva to collect the quotes along with images of the focus figure.
- Use the breakout room feature in Zoom to engage students in collaborative discussions in the virtual environment.
- Have students animate the quotes of their characters using a digital application like Toon Boom or Pow Toon.

Lesson Lead-Ins

- Begin lessons that capitalize on the importance of prior knowledge with this warmup.
- Incorporate this warmup in lessons that require students to make connections between multiple texts, figures, or concepts.
- Use this warmup as a lead-in to tasks that center around character analyses and/or character development.
- When working on writing pieces that involve the integration of dialogue, have students complete this warmup to practice different ways for their character to speak.

THAT'S WHAT THEY SAID

When incorporating dialogue effectively into a composition, there's much more to consider than just *who* is saying it. In fact, good writers pay close attention not just to the *who* but also the *how*, *where*, and *why*. Certain words or phrases might be employed in specific settings, conversations might occur about a specific subject based on the characters doing the talking, and so on. For example, the dialogue that occurs in a funeral setting is completely different than what might transpire between the same characters at an amusement park. Plus, think about how we modify what we say based on who is our audience. I bet there are words you don't use when your grandmother is around! Crafting quality dialogue is not just finding the right words that sound natural; it's about juxtaposing those words so that they fit with the conflict in the story, the other characters, and the setting. Getting students to pay attention to those qualities can help them write better dialogue. Warming up with That's What They Said is one way to practice this skill.

> *Quick Tip!*
>
> Several years ago State Farm ran a series of commercials where they used the same dialogue dropped into two totally different scenarios. The overall meaning could not have been more different! Check them out at https://www.ispot.tv/ad/ASxV/state-farm-jacked-up.

Putting It to Work

1. Locate an image that has multiple individuals in the picture.
2. Pass out blank dialogue bubbles to the students.
3. Instruct students to look at the different characters in the photo. Ask them to make a list of who might be speaking in this photo.
4. Record this list for students to see.
5. Have students use their dialogue bubble cut outs to write possible dialogue that the different characters in the photo might say. Remind them to consider the setting, event portrayed, and other individuals pictured.
6. Have them brainstorm possible dialogue options for 5 to 7 minutes.
7. Share with the class.

> *Quick Tip!*
>
> Individuals do not have to be people. They can be animals as well. That would be a fun dialogue lesson—imagining what a room full of dogs would say!

When to Use It

- When you want students to practice writing dialogue but want to draw attention to the factors that influence and impact the words a character might say.
- As a warmup for additional dialogue writing.
- As a low-stakes brainstorming session.

Why It Works

- Because this strategy focuses mainly on a picture as a starter, students are not tasked with reading a lengthy passage.
- It gives students a specific focus: the crafting of dialogue that is specifically connected to the image shown.
- It provides students an opportunity to consider the other factors in a scene that influence dialogue.

A great place to find free images online is www.pixabay.com. Search based on a topic or concept and find free photos to download.

Modifications

- Instead of having students write possible dialogue options for all the individuals/characters depicted in the image, assign students a specific character to focus on.
- Have ready-made quotes that students can match to the characters in the image and justify their selections.
- To draw more attention to the other elements in the photo, have students write down observations they have of what is presented in the image. Then have them start composing the dialogue.
- Place images on the floor of the classroom. Have students drop their written dialogue bubbles around the images that correspond with the appropriate pictures.

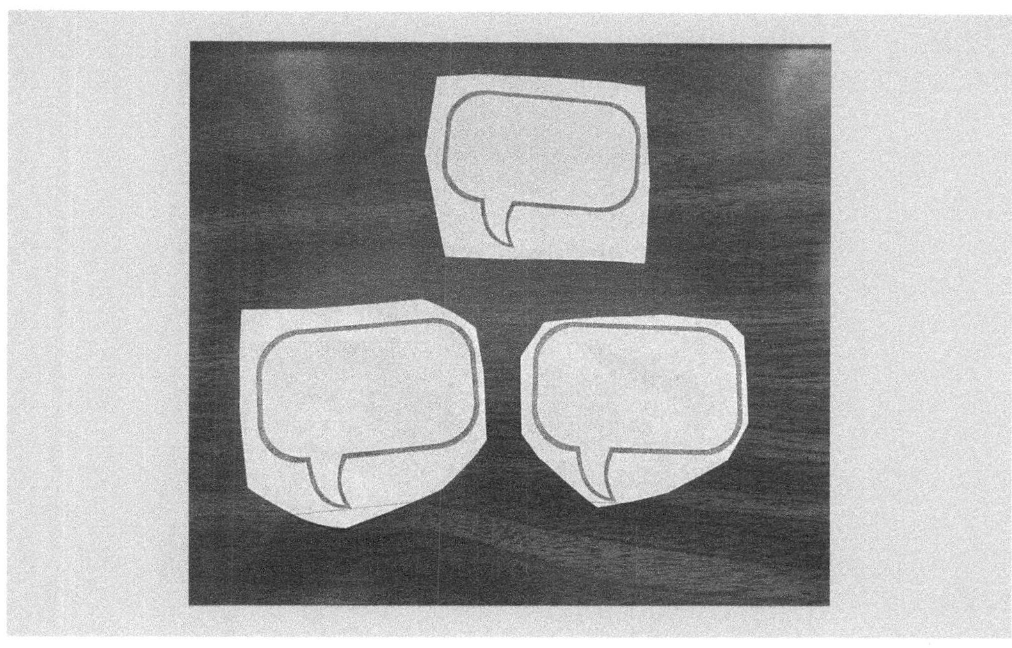

Extensions

- Have students continue this activity by completing a collaborative extension with new photos. Provide each group of students a new photo and have them repeat the engagement.
- Use the dialogue that the students generated to begin drafting an extended composition that incorporates the material they used in their dialogue brainstorming session.
- Use scripts from plays to generate new dialogue.
- Have students use their dialogue to write a scene based on the image.

Digital Direction

- Use an application like PicStitch, PicCollage, or Canva to collect the quotes along with images.
- Have students discuss dialogue options on Padlet using the wall option.
- Transfer the image and the dialogue into the web application Storyboard That and add speech bubbles and characters right on the screen.

Lesson Lead-Ins

- Use this as a lead-in for writings that incorporate dialogue.
- Provide this as a warmup for the Soap Opera activity on page 226.
- Connect this to the Memory Maps strategy on page 29 by encouraging students to add dialogue to their maps.

MEMORY MAPS

Memoir was one of my favorite genres to teach in middle school writing classes. Memoir writing can offer opportunities for students to realize that even simple moments in their lives can be blown up into full-fledged stories simply by paying attention to that time period in their lives. When teaching memoirs, I often read sections from Gary Paulsen's book *How Angel Peterson Got His Name* (2003) because it is a perfect example of how a writer can expound on a certain period in their life. Plus, the story is hilarious and makes for an awesome read-aloud.

Memory Maps are like the Neighborhood Map I wrote about in *Write Now & Write On* (2022) yet differ because they discuss a specific memory in preparation for drafting of a memoir. It might be helpful if your students have some experience with the Neighborhood Maps before they move into Memory Maps, but it's not necessary.

While I used Neighborhood Maps as an icebreaker activity to get to know my students or to illustrate a particular character in a literary work or historical event, Memory Maps are useful to help students think through specific events in their lives and generate ideas and memories of the event. As a result, they are natural warmups when students are working on memoirs.

Putting It to Work

1. Begin by brainstorming a list of memories students have about specific events. For example, you might ask students to think about memorable celebrations, events at school, family vacations, sporting events, and so on.
2. Record this list for the class to see.
3. Show students some examples of maps. Ask students questions about them. For example, you might ask what the map is for, what information is typically included on maps, where might you see maps, and so on.
4. Model how to complete a Memory Map. Begin by choosing a memory of your own to draw about.

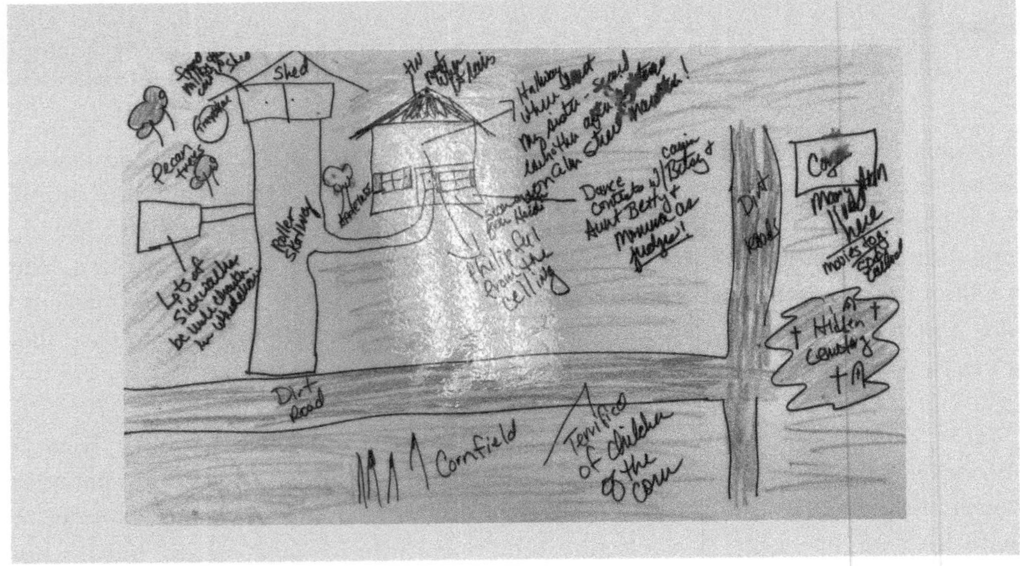

5. When drawing the Memory Map, make sure to include items such as the characters/people involved, setting, problem or theme, and possibly the resolution.
6. While modeling, make sure you talk through the pieces of the event that you are remembering. Include who was there, what was going on, where the memory occurred, and so on. This can serve as a reminder or nudge about items students can include in their own maps.
7. Encourage students to ask questions about your Memory Map.
8. Provide students with paper and have them first choose their memory that they are going to map out.
9. Have students draw their Memory Maps and then share with a partner.

When to Use It

- When you want students to focus on a specific moment or event for writing.
- As a warmup for memoir writing.
- As a low-stakes brainstorming session.

When working on the genre of memoir, it is helpful to begin priming the pump earlier with read alouds and other texts that might help students brainstorm ideas. Some of my favorites are:

- Jacqueline Woodson's *We Had a Picnic This Sunday Past*
- Eve Bunting's *The Memory String*
- Maribeth Boelts's *Those Shoes*
- Yangsook Choi's *The Name Jar*
- Jamilah Thompkins-Bigelow's *Your Name Is a Song*

Why It Works

- Because this strategy focuses mainly on pictorial images and representations, students are not bound by spelling, grammar, or sentence structure.
- It offers layers of communication and meaning: pictorial representation, oral retelling, and written words.
- There is no definitive final product; students can continue adding to their Memory Map indefinitely.
- It never has to move beyond this brainstorming/drafting stage if needed.

Modifications

- Have students work collaboratively with a partner to map out a classroom memory that they both shared.
- Instead of having students draw Memory Maps about themselves, have them map out a character's memory from a novel or a memory of historical figure.
- Working with a partner, have one student orally retell their memory while their partner draws the Memory Map. Switch roles.

Extensions

- Have students connect their Memory Maps to the Stretch to See on page 37.
- Encourage students to add sensory details to their Memory Maps.
- Use this strategy in tandem with the Neighborhood Map Activity (Harper, 2022).

Digital Direction

- Have students design a digital Memory Map using an application like Canva, PicCollage, or Pixpa.
- Use a digital drawing application like Sketchbook, Procreate, or iArtbook.

Lesson Lead-Ins

- Use this as a lead-in for memoir writing.
- Provide this as a warmup for descriptive writing.
- Connect this to culminating writings at the completion of a literary work. Use Memory Maps to recall different events in an extended work.

EXPERT/KNOW NOTHING LIST

One of the hardest parts of writing is simply starting and getting the words on the page—much like going to the gym when the most difficult part is getting in the car and heading that way. Writing, for some, is no different. Facing an empty page and trying to craft words into sentences is daunting, when in fact, many of us have a wealth of knowledge about several concepts as well as unique ideas that can manifest themselves into solid written pieces.

Having students generate an Expert/Know Nothing list provides students with a working list of possible options for writing and research. While this strategy is a little more simplistic than others in this chapter, don't let the simplicity fool you. By incorporating this easy-to-drop-in strategy, you'll find that it addresses several of the main roadblocks of writing: topic generation, research subjects, and background knowledge. Plus, lists are low-stakes writing engagements that are short and simple, but purposeful—just the right combination for today's busy classroom.

Try this strategy yourself by making your own chart. Now ask yourself, "Which of these topics would I want to write about?" My guess is that you would pick the Expert side, right? Yet every day we ask students to write about topics from the Know Nothing side and wonder why the writing is a struggle. Let that sink in for a minute.

Putting It to Work

1. Begin by having students make a T Chart on their papers.
2. Instruct them to label one side Expert and one side Know Nothing.
3. Have them brainstorm a list of items that they know a lot about. These could be school related, but more than likely, they will come from personal experiences and interests. Ask students to consider items/skills/tasks they enjoy, such as music, sports, crafts, trivia, and so on.
4. Have them share this list with the class.
5. Next, have students complete the part of the chart that includes information they don't know much about. These can serve as research ideas.
6. Share with the class.

Keep this running list in student folders for future additions and lesson ideas. Students can add to it throughout the year, too.

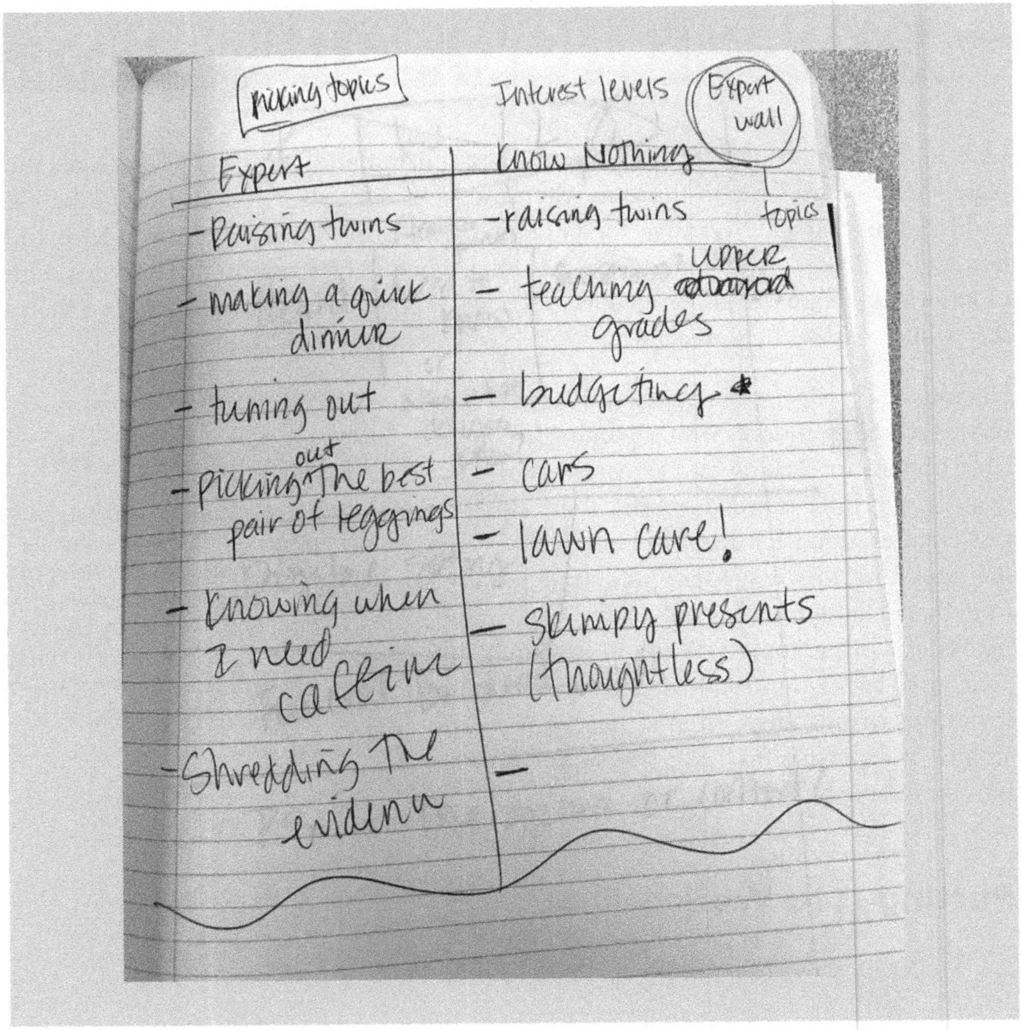

When to Use It

- When you want to have a running list of topics your students know about and ones they have limited knowledge with.
- As an alternative to an interest inventory, this Expert/Know Nothing list can provide teachers with suggestions for writing ideas that capitalize on student background knowledge.
- When you want to generate *researchable* topics without saying the word *research*. The Know Nothing section becomes a starting point for research.

Quick Tip!

Don't skip the share-outs! They are important because they can offer additional ideas for classmates to add to their own papers.

Why It Works

- It is a low-stakes type of writing a list, which can be completed in a short amount of time.
- It never has to move beyond this brainstorming/drafting stage if needed.
- Making a list of what they know about and what they don't can help students start to generate ideas for writing and research.

> **Quick Tip!**
>
> In addition, this list can help teachers pick appropriate texts and read-alouds that take student interest into account.

Modifications

- Have students interview their classmates and record the information learned from their classmates on the template found on the companion website.
- Use pictures instead of words to complete the template.
- Complete one part of the chart at a time. Start with the Expert side and then later return to the Know Nothing side.

Extensions

- For self-selected writing days, have students refer to their lists for writing ideas.
- When discussing research topics, have students check their Know Nothing lists for possible paper ideas.
- Post your experts about certain subjects on a chart in your classroom. Need an expert reader on a specific topic? Refer to the chart to find a peer who can help.
- Match up students with other experts in the same content area or topic for collaborative projects. Do the same for research possibilities.
- You can take this a step further by having a trivia session in class the next day. For example, you might take the information you collected from the expert list and start class off by saying, "Jake is an expert in archery. What questions might we ask him about archery?" Or you could have students choose one item from their expert list and record it on a notecard. Have each student in class draft questions (they can only be yes or no questions) that they would ask their classmates to try to figure out their expertise that is recorded on the notecard.

Digital Direction

- Have students create a pictorial list of their information using a program like PicCollage or Canva.

- Use Flipgrid to have students respond and collaborate with other experts or researchers of specific topics.
- Use the wall feature on Padlet for students to pose questions for the experts or share topic ideas.

Lesson Lead-Ins

- Use this as a lead-in for research writing as the Know Nothing list offers multiple topic ideas for research.
- Provide this as a warmup for topic generation.
- Use this as a different type of icebreaker when getting to know your students.

STRETCH TO SEE

One of the best resources for writing ideas and topics comes from images and photos. Because the number of images available are infinite, the possibilities for a writing class are endless. Plus, images offer another awesome added benefit: You can drop in any number of photos into a lesson with very little planning (Forgot your bell ringer for the day? Google a unique image and start writing about it.), or they can be strategically placed and purposely connected to a bigger idea or lesson. In this activity, you're asking students to describe an image or a portion of the image, which helps build observation and descriptive detail skills in a fun, low-stakes way, both of which aid them when writing. Images can also be helpful in setting up a reading, either fiction or nonfiction. For example, when reading a novel like Bryan Bliss's *Thoughts and Prayers* (2020), you might include an image of a teenager on a skateboard heading down a sidewalk next to a snow-covered field. This image is strategic and purposeful because it could represent a specific character in Bliss's novel. Pictures really can be worth a thousand words, especially in an ELA class!

If your students have not done this activity before, do one together as a class. Don't be tempted to skip this part, especially if you are asking them to make connections to abstract concepts. Working on the first one together will make independent work much easier.

Putting It to Work

1. Post an image for the entire class to see. Discuss the image and talk about what you notice about the photo.

2. Give them a specific item/concept to find in the photo. For example, you might ask students to find the math in the picture. Have them record their noticings on their paper. (By the way, you'd be amazed at how many math concepts are hidden in photos: angles, lines, shapes, volume, reflections, and more.)

3. Have students share their observations.
4. Choose another item for students to find. For example, you might ask them to find the figurative language in the photo.
5. Share with the class.

When to Use It

> **Quick Tip!**
>
> You can have students find as many concepts as you'd like for a number of subjects. However, it is important to have them focus on abstract concepts and not literal ones. For example, don't ask them to find all the animals in the picture—too easy—this isn't a seek and find, but rather a stretch to see.

- When you want students to focus on abstract concepts that might be overlooked or unseen.
- As a way to have students pay close attention to different aspects of images.
- When you want students to examine a photo through a critical lens. This could be done with a number of photos, but the questions would shift. You might ask questions like these:
  - What systems of power are present in this photo?
  - Where are the biases in this photo?
  - Make a list of the inequities in this image.

Penguin Photo → find all math items
- # of penguins
- depth of water
- temperature of air
- height/weight of penguins
- elevation
- time of day

↳ find science items
- habitat
- animal
- coral
- water

↳ find SS items
- population
- emigration
- leadership
- nat. resources
- environment

Why It Works

- Because this strategy focuses mainly on pictorial images and representations, it gives students a visual starting point. While they are still reading, instead of reading words, they are reading an image.
- Students are tasked with generating a list of words, not sentences, which can make the task more accessible for some.

Modifications

- Have students locate their own images and develop potential writing prompts and quick writes that can be used with their images.
- Instead of having students come up with all the words on their own, post a word bank or provide words listed on notecards that students can use as starters for their own collection.
- Show students several images (3–5) and a group of words. Have them determine which photo best represents the descriptor words based on the prompt/question.

Extensions

- Extend this into a grammar lesson with the NVA^2 activity on page 66.
- Have students connect this warmup to the Pop-Up Poems on page 114, the NVA^2 strategy on page 66, or the Wordless Picture Books strategy on page 107.
- Instead of having students find abstract concepts, ask students to develop questions that might be either generated by viewing the image or answered by looking at the details in the image.
- Connect this to the Pictures for Mood lesson on page 90.

Digital Direction

- Use PicCollage to collect images and words for this strategy.
- Have students collaboratively discuss their ideas using a digital application like Parlay or dotstorming.

Lesson Lead-Ins

- Use this as a lead-in for extended pieces focusing on description.
- Focus your questions and prompts with the pictures on specific lessons that address concepts such as figurative language, prepositional phrases, point of view, and more.
- Connect this to lessons that focus on adding more details including Descriptive Writing With Calendars (page 125) and Pictures for Mood (page 90).

PICTURE POINT OF VIEW

One ELA focus that is constant across grade levels is point of view (POV). While early literacy classes tend to focus on who is telling the story, as students progress in their schooling, POV becomes more specific and detailed, with students reading and writing stories told from multiple points of view. Now students must recognize, identify, and navigate multiple options for POV including first person, second person, third person limited, and third person omniscient. For some, the lines between the different types of third-person points of view becomes a little blurry, and yet for others, sometimes when they see the pronoun "I," they make the leap that the text they are reading must be written in first person.

Most ELA engagements that address this skill tend to approach it from an identifiable stance, meaning students are asked questions like "Identify the point of view in passage A." "From what point of view is passage B told?" Those types of questions or tasks require students to read and label: Passage A is first person; Passage B is third person limited. The problem with these types of tasks is that they do not allow for the *experience* of POV. One way that teachers can attempt to create a more thorough understanding of POV is through a strategy called Picture Point of View.

Putting It to Work

1. Begin by discussing each form of narrative POV as a reminder and review. This is especially important when you are utilizing first person, second person, and third person limited and omniscient.
2. Divide the class into four groups of students.
3. Pass out different colored sticky notes to the students. Use four different colors, one for each POV.
4. Explain what color represents which POV. Explain to students that the color sticky note they received indicates which POV they will focus on for this activity.
5. Show students an image. This image might include a photograph of a group of people, an image with one character, a piece of artwork with multiple individuals present, or a drawing with multiple characters.

Quick Tip!

A lot of students confuse perspective with POV. Perspective addresses the attitudes and stance, if you will, that the narrator assumes when telling a story. POV focuses on the type of narrator telling the story. Some great books that help drive this point home are:

- *Counting by 7s* by Holly Goldberg Sloan (This novel alternates between first person narration and third person.)
- *Zoom* by Istvan Banyai (This book is a great visual example of perspective.)
- *Because of Mr. Terrupt* series by Rob Buyea (These books utilize the same type of narration but tell the story from multiple perspectives.)
- *The Pain and the Great One* by Judy Blume (This book tells a story from the differing perspectives of a brother and sister.)
- *Flipped* by Wendelin Van Draanen (This novel is told from two different narrator perspectives.)

6. Have students work with their group to brainstorm narration that would fit the picture in the POV they were assigned.
7. Give students about 5 to 7 minutes to complete this task.
8. Have each group share their ideas.
9. Take up the blank sticky notes and redistribute to different students. (By doing this, you are modifying the group structure.)
10. Direct students to areas in the room where new pictures are posted.
11. Explain to students that they will be completing a gallery walk around the room and will be writing about each image from the new POV they have been assigned.

> **Quick Tip!**
>
> I suggest that you post images on large pieces of chart paper like shown in the example. This way, students can post their ideas all around the picture as they complete their gallery walk around the room.

12. Give students about 5 minutes at each station before moving on to the next station.
13. Once the class has rotated to all stations, have the last group at each station share all the collected information from each POV with the class.
14. Ask students to comment on how the POV affected the details that were provided in the writings.

When to Use It

- When you want students to practice writing with images as a starter.
- As a warmup for writing in different points of view.
- As a collaborative engagement.

Why It Works

- Because this strategy uses images as the central method for developing a story, students aren't spending significant amounts of time unpacking text.
- It allows students the ability to capitalize on their individual ideas and background knowledge when drafting their ideas.
- It never has to move beyond this brainstorming/drafting stage if needed.

Modifications

- Have students complete the task using different colored markers to designate the POV they are focusing on. Instead of requiring students to always write in a designated POV, students can choose to add to the chart in the POV of their choice. (Make sure students know what colors are for which POV so the information and ideas don't get mixed up.)

- Have sample narration examples already created for students to use. Based on the POV assigned, students have to locate which ready-made details fit that POV.

Extensions

- Have students practice modifying the perspective from which they write, but keep the POV constant. Discuss how perspective alters the story.
- Encourage students to take an existing piece of their writing and switch the POV. Compare how those POVs affect the story.

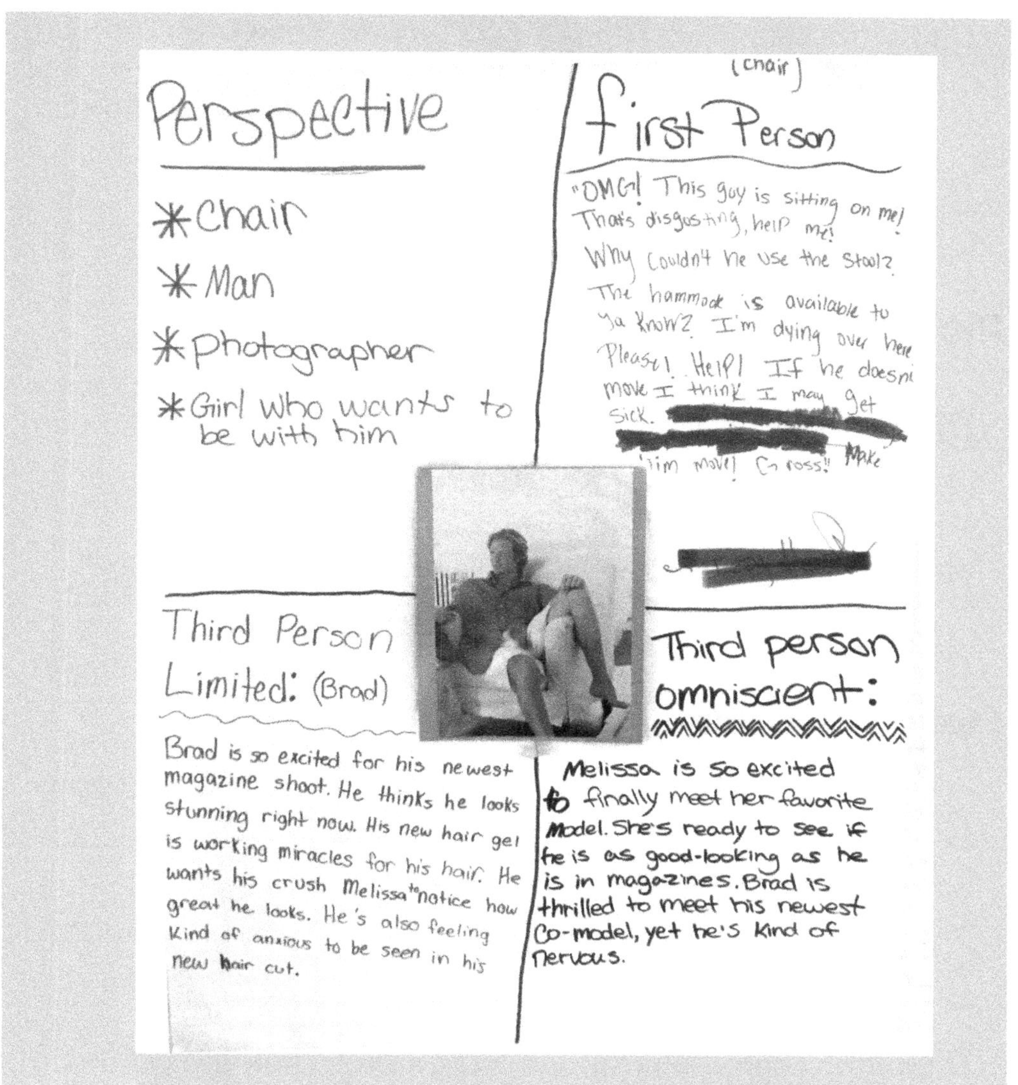

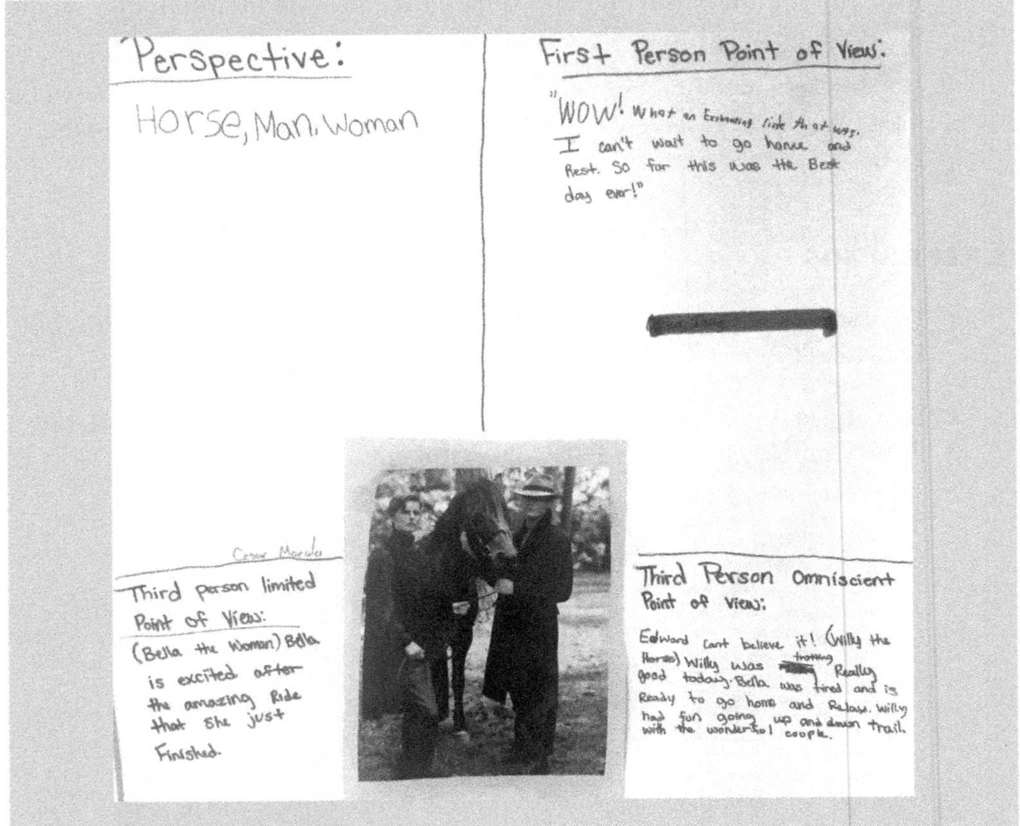

Digital Direction

- Map out different possible POV details using a digital program such as MindMeister.
- Use an online brainstorming application like dotstorming for a digital connection.
- Compare different POVs using an online application like PicCollage to collect the images and associated descriptions in a "Pinterest-like" board setup.

Lesson Lead-Ins

- Use this as a lead-in for writing in different POVs and in a variety of genres.
- Connect this lesson to ones on voice, mood, and perspective, because each adds a unique layer to a text's overall meaning.
- Use this as a lead-in for discussions of audience and purpose and how POV might be modified based on those.

RESOURCE ROUNDUP

So many extended writing engagements require students to read and write widely across multiple sources. This is especially true in high school classrooms where Document Based Questions (DBQs) are a frequent resident. Yet developing a response that is well-thought out, articulates a clear argument or position, and incorporates multiple pieces of evidence from several sources can be intimidating for some students. In many instances, the sheer volume of material they must read just to be able to write their response can be overwhelming.

One way to address this complex task is by breaking it down into more manageable pieces. Students are likely to be more successful at writing a fully involved DBQ composition if they have had time and experience with the process, one component at a time. An easy way to start breaking down a large task like this is to begin with the documents themselves. That's where Resource Roundup comes into play. With this strategy, students start with the documents and examine them first before they start constructing a specific response that requires them to complete a response that incorporates material from all the sources.

> **Quick Tip!**
>
> Before you start this lesson, students should have a solid understanding of *how* artifacts should be examined, especially if you are utilizing different types of documents such as infographics, charts, historical quotes, and more.
>
> Questions students should ask themselves when examining the documents might include
>
> - What is the intended audience? Who is this written for?
> - What is the purpose?
> - Are there titles, headings, or other text features that should be attended to?
> - Is there a graphic or figure incorporated in this document?
> - What about annotations? Footnotes?

Putting It to Work

1. Start by determining what theme you would like your documents or artifacts to focus on. You might include several works by the same author, multiple sources about a particular topic, or different writing samples that focus on a specific genre.
2. Develop a few questions, no more than three or four, that could be used as part of a constructed or extended response task associated with these documents.
3. Divide students into groups and give each group one of the questions.

> **Quick Tip!**
>
> Because many constructed response questions are often multipart and have several questions built into one task, I like to use those as my starting points. I simply break those multipart questions into individual questions and use those as my starters for this lesson. Then, I can piece those questions back together for the full constructed response task. For instructions on this extension, visit the companion website at **resources.corwin.com/WritingWorkouts.**

4. Provide students with the Resource Roundup template on the companion website.

Resource Roundup

Directions: Record the constructed response question in the table below. List the title of each document in the corresponding box in the table below. Include any information from the document that addresses the question posed.

Constructed Response Question	Document 1 Football and Brain Injuries: What You Need To Know.	Document Exactly How Dangerous is Football?	Document 3 NFL Rulebook Safety Rules + Reg.	Document 4 Infographic	Document 5 photo
What are the dangers of football?	-concussions -headaches -brain damage	TBI's	~~[illegible]~~ ~~[illegible]~~	Memory Neck loss injury Concussion back/Spine	
What are some safety measures in place?	Helmets mandatory sit-outs	helmet research long term studies			helmets pads
What is the NFL doing to address this?		helmet research studying former players	changing rules for hitting in head or neck area	testing former players for CTE	

5. Have students record their assigned question at the top of the template.

6. Show students where the resources are posted in the classroom and how many are displayed.

7. Before setting them loose, ensure that students have a solid understanding of how artifacts should be examined, especially if you are utilizing different types of documents such as infographics, charts, historical quotes, and more. Questions students should ask themselves when examining the documents might include

- What is the intended audience? Who is this written for?
- What is the purpose?

- Are there titles, headings, or other text features that should be attended to?
- Is there a graphic or figure incorporated in this document?
- What about annotations? Footnotes?

8. Have the students rotate around the room with their question and template. They should visit every document station and examine the document to determine if any information on that item would help them answer their question. Students should mark their templates accordingly. (For groups with experience with this strategy, you can include as many as eight sources. For those who haven't practiced this strategy yet, keep it to around four samples.)
9. Once the groups have circulated around the room to all the samples, have them share their questions and which artifacts they deemed would be helpful when answering their questions.

When to Use It

- When you want students to view multiple sources on the same topic, genre, or idea.
- As a way to expose students to multiple texts in a short period of time.
- When you need to utilize multiple sources on a variety of reading levels.

Why It Works

- This strategy breaks a complex task (DBQ) into a series of steps, with Resource Roundup being the first.
- It gets students up and moving as they walk through the multiple sources station.
- Collaboration and discussion are key in this strategy as students can discuss with their groups which sources best answer their assigned question.
- It offers students the opportunity to examine sources for their quality and relevance to their question. Students can not only choose which sources should be used to answer their question but also the ones that can be omitted.

Modifications

- Start with one article or document but utilize multiple questions. Have students determine which questions can be answered by the selected document.
- Mix the types of texts used for this strategy to include pictures and other graphic representations of the content. Not only can this help striving readers, but it also gives students another opportunity to engage with texts in multiple formats.

Extensions

- Have students return to class with their completed template on Day 2 and revisit only the documents/artifacts that they indicated would answer their question. Have them locate information from each document that answers their assigned question.
- Encourage students to find another document or artifact that could be used in conjunction with the activity.
- Use this strategy in tandem with the Annotate, Plan, Write strategy on page 168.

Digital Direction

- Instead of physical documents, use links to web resources like videos, virtual exhibits, or websites for students to examine.
- Collect responses using an application like Mural.
- Have students collaboratively examine documents using a Google document or have them digitally annotate using Diigo.

Lesson Lead-Ins

- Use this as a lead-in for extended constructed responses.
- Try this as a warmup for critically examining sources for credibility.
- Warm up to research writing with this strategy. With this approach, students are able to practice examining multiple sources for information, something that is required when completing research.

CHARACTER PROPS

One of the best parts about teaching ELA is the ability to read and utilize a wide range of literature in daily teaching. There are so many wonderful novels that introduce students to dynamic, rich characters who can make us love them, hate them, cry for them, and more. My favorite works of literature are often the ones that leave me feeling unsettled, changed, and bothered, but I also love books whose characters feel like people I know or wish I did know, like Miss Lana in *Three Times Lucky* by Sheila Turnage. As students interact with characters across multiple literary works, opportunities to write about characters in multiple settings can assist them as they are tasked with completing in-depth character analyses. One way to warm up with character writing is with Character Props.

Putting It to Work

1. Determine which characters or figures from reading will be the focus of the lesson.
2. Choose one character to use as a demonstration model for the class.
3. Display four or five physical objects in the front of the room for students to see.
4. Introduce each object. You might hold up each object so everyone can see and tell the class what it is.

5. Remind students about the novel or other literary work they have been reading.
6. Give students a notecard or sticky note to record which character they think owns the displayed items. Have them explain and justify their reasoning.
7. Share with the class.
8. Put students in collaborative groups or with a partner.
9. Provide them with a list of possible characters to choose from.
10. Instruct students to come up with five objects that their character would have based on what they know about them. Make sure they know to justify and explain their choices. Use sticky notes to record their thoughts or use the template on the companion website.
11. Share with the class.

Character Props

Character Chosen: Ms. Lana

Character Traits: caring, dedicated, loyal

Prop	Justification	Textual Evidence (if applicable)
wig	Ms. Lana is always changing her appearance by wearing wigs and different clothes.	"Miss Lana tucked a strand of her glossy Ava Gardner wig behind her ear. . ."
Eiffel Tower	The cafe had a Paris themed menu.	"Glancing around, I pegged today's theme as 1930's Paris— her favorite. Amiriature [sic] Eiffel Tower graced the counter."
menu	Ms. Lana runs the cafe.	She, "wrote the day's specials on the chalboard [sic]."
order pad	Ms. Lana takes orders at the cafe and she wrote a note to the colone [sic].	"She scrawled across her order pad + handed it to him."

When to Use It

- When you are reading a novel or other literary work that has multiple characters.
- If you want students to review and collectively discuss characters from multiple works of literature.
- To get students to think beyond using words to convey meaning and include objects and items.
- When you want students to take part in an oral presentation component in addition to writing.

Why It Works

- Because this strategy includes an oral sharing component, having objects to hold or refer to can help students remember the details of the character since the object serves as a reminder.
- It utilizes collaborative learning and discussion.
- There is an element of student choice involved because students are able to decide which character they want to explore.

Modifications

- Instead of focusing on characters from a specific novel, have students develop a character based on objects you provide. For example, I often use my prom dress as a character starter warmup. I bring the dress into class and show it to students. While I walk around and let them see and feel the sequins and beads on the dress, I ask questions like:
    - Who might wear this dress?
    - Where would you wear this?
    - If this dress could talk, what would it say?
- Choose one character from a novel and have the class focus on the same character for the activity.
- Set the class up initially like a museum exhibit and have students travel to each teacher-created exhibit and record their character choices on the template on the companion website.

Extensions

- Once students have collected all their objects, instead of having them share aloud, have them set up their objects on display like an exhibit. Then have the entire class rotate through each exhibit and examine the artifacts chosen. Students can then guess which exhibit is for which character.
- Have students use these objects as idea starters when they begin drafting a character analysis.

Digital Direction

- Have students create virtual exhibits using online programs such as Art.Spaces or Artsteps.
- Present this lesson using Nearpod, an online interactive lesson program.

Lesson Lead-Ins

- Use this as a lead-in for character analysis engagements.
- Provide this as a warmup for the Character Evolution strategy on page 62.
- Connect this to culminating writings at the completion of a literary work.
- Use this strategy in tandem with the Most Valuable Character on page 74.

TARGETED TRAINING

Good overall physical fitness involves a carefully mixed cocktail of exercises, fitness plans, lifestyle choices, and healthy eating habits. When thinking of physical fitness, it is important that individuals take part in training that focuses on a variety of components. While total body wellness and health is important, the way individuals get to that end goal is through specific and targeted training that addresses multiple body parts and aspects of physical fitness. Writing fitness is similar. For students to be competent writers overall, they have to take part in training that addresses different components of writing. Now, this doesn't just mean that students train on a variety of genres, though that is part of it; rather, it means that students have a variety of writing experiences that address genre, structure, voice, dialogue, grammar, and more. Instruction that targets specific writing skills is a hallmark of a writing classroom that focuses on building writers who are fit to write in many genres, for various purposes and audiences.

While there are many engagements that focus on the developing writing proficiency, certain lessons focus on specific skills, genres, and craft moves. Plus, when teaching certain genres, there are some mini-lessons that can be built in strategically that contribute to a student's overall writing wellness and also that can help them improve and address components of a genre. The following table shows some targeted training ideas that might be employed when teaching specific genres.

Genre Focus	Targeted Training
Argumentative Writing	Claims lessons Credible sources Academic language Citing sources Bias
Persuasive Writing	Effective hooks Citing evidence Voice
Personal Narrative	Dialogue construction Character development Voice Vivid vocabulary Point of view Describing a setting using sensory details
Research Writing	Credible sources Language formality Citing sources Thesis construction
Poetry	Figurative language Sensory details Vivid vocabulary

Now, the table is certainly not exhaustive, but you get the general idea. Knowing how a particular genre functions and is structured can help you and students determine what targeted training experiences should be planned. Sometimes, there are specific, main components that can be easily targeted, and you may find that there are examples of certain types of author's craft that might be more subtle and get dropped in as possibilities but are not necessities in a genre. For example, sometimes authors arrange the words on the page to simulate the meaning of a word. In Julie Danneburg's *First Day Jitters*, the author mimics the action of the word *stumbled* by writing it like this:

s

t

u

m

b

l

e

d.

Do you see how with that example the author shows the reader visually what the word means? Another example is in Jeron Ashford Frame's book *Yesterday I Had the Blues,* where the author writes this phrase:

The kind of blues
make you just wanna just
turn
down
the
volume.

A targeted training lesson about this example of author's craft might not be used with every poetry unit created, but it would be a great example to include for targeted training if students are writing poems about natural disasters, as shown in these poems about earthquakes, tornadoes, and wildfires in the following image.

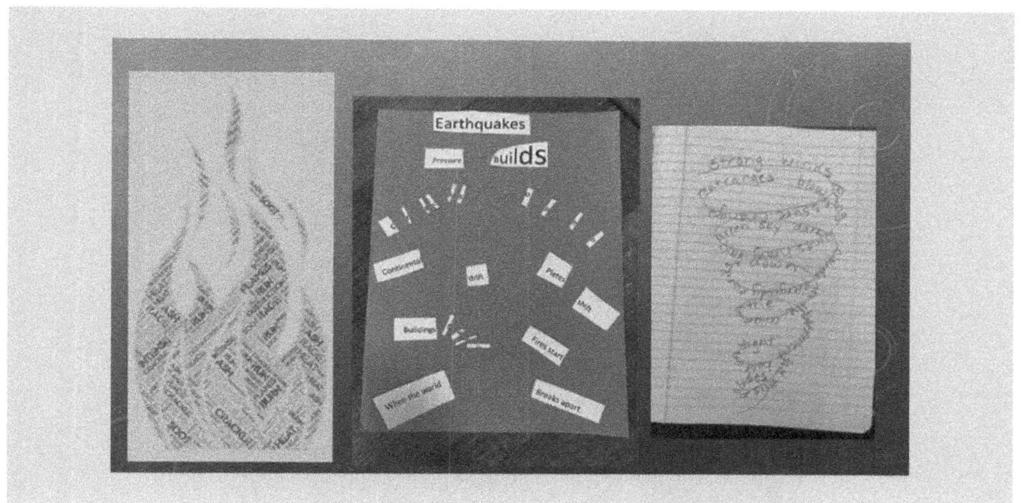

Targeted training lessons offer students another opportunity to engage with different components and characteristics of writing and provides them with the much-needed experience to be successful and competent writers. Plus, it helps ensure that students have better *overall* writing fitness, which can transfer into multiple writing genres and engagements.

Targeted writing training also helps both the teacher and students set a clear focus for a lesson or day. Having a specific focus for an instructional task can help ensure success across the board. In fact, one of my very favorite focus activities is a hands-on activity with peacock feathers. Yes, you read correctly: peacock feathers. Let me explain.

During writing presentations and at our National Writing Project Summer Institute, we use peacock feathers as a tangible example of how important having a focus can be on an individual's performance. I distribute peacock feathers to each teacher and give them very specific instructions:

- You must balance the peacock feather on the tip of your finger.
- You may not hold or assist the feather; it must be balanced.
- Walk around the room.
- Find five people you do not know.
- Tell each one of them one item about you and have them tell you one item about them.
- During this activity, you must do all the items listed above for success.

Can you imagine the results? These teachers always do horribly even though I gave them specific instructions AND I model the behavior.

For the next part of the task, I give them the following instructions:

- Look at the top of the peacock feather; each one has a place on the feather that is called the eye.
- You may balance the feather on the palm of your hand.
- Focus on the eye of the feather as you balance the feather on your palm.

What do you think happens when they are given this new task? They are much more successful than when they attempted the first task they were given. Why? Because in the second task, they had a specific focus. They were not required to do multiple tasks at once, but instead, were focusing on one specific task.

Here's the other important part to note. Prior to coming into class, almost no one had any experience balancing a peacock feather on their finger. As a result, their baseline of prior knowledge of this type of task was limited. Now, take into consideration that these participants had limited experience with the basics of the task I asked them to perform (balancing the feather), and yet I also asked them to do multiple tasks in *addition* to that one. It was only when they were given one specific direction that required them to perform one part of the task that the teachers were successful.

How in the world does this relate to writing? You see, on a frequent basis, our students are asked to demonstrate proficiency for a variety of writing skills on one specific writing composition. Students are often asked to craft compositions that are well organized, have effective hooks, use vivid or academic vocabulary, employ transitional phrases, incorporate textual evidence, and more. Do you see where I am going with this? Just like the students in my Summer Institute, many of our students in the P–12 setting haven't mastered the basics, not because they can't, but because they have not had the experience and opportunity.

Now let's go back to my Summer Institute students and that peacock feather task. What if instead of hitting them with the most sophisticated version of the task, I started with a clear focus? First, we practiced simply balancing the feather on our hands. Then we progressed to the tip of the finger, which is harder because there is less surface area. Now imagine, once students master this, we have students balance the feather and find one classmate to talk to. We would continue this progression through that entire list of demands posted above until students had added each component of the task to their repertoire. It is much more likely that students will be successful because they had a targeted focus *and* they built individual components of the culminating task on each other until the end result was achieved.

When teachers have a specific focus in their writing instruction, it can aid students in creating and crafting more successful pieces of writing. Just as setting a purpose for reading aids in understanding and comprehension, having a focus in writing can help students develop a deeper understanding for the craft and can aid them in drafting better final products.

Targeted training does just that. Because these strategies address different writing skills, craft, and components, students are aware of their focus for the task. Plus, they can see how that focused lesson connects back to the bigger idea or the writing composition they are constructing.

Strategies in this section have precise purposes and focus on the acquisition, practice, and refinement of specific writing skills that can be implemented in a variety of genres and subject areas. While there are several strategies in this book that focus on the writing skills that are more holistic in nature, the strategies in this chapter focus on writing skills that might be used in a specific setting or purpose.

TEXT TRANSLATIONS

For students, sometimes learning how to write for a variety of purposes and audiences can be daunting. In fact, in my work with teachers, one of the main complaints has to do with students' tendencies to write for one audience: the informal one. In fact, many lament that their students utilize text language and abbreviations in their writings that *should* be written using formal, academic language.

A fantastic book that illustrates this in the best, most humorous way is *Understand Rap: Explanations of Confusing Rap Lyrics You and Your Grandma Can Understand* by William Buckholz (2010). In this book, Buckholz takes rap lyrics from a variety of songs and then translates them into formal English. This hilarious book is a great example of how many of our students feel when we start using formal academic language in our instruction when many of them are well-versed in the informal version of language. (*Note*: Although this is a great resource to use in your classroom as a tangible example of informal and formal language in the real world, this is not a book I would recommend putting out in your classroom library simply due to the mature nature of some of the content. However, it is worthwhile to have in your personal library because specific sections can be used in teaching as examples of informal and formal written language.)

One way that students can practice bouncing in and out of formal and informal language is through text translations. With these strategies, students either translate portions of a text into more formal language or they translate it into informal language, based on the original sample. Either way, this is a great strategy for drawing attention to the levels of language that exist both in and outside of the classroom.

> **Quick Tip!**
>
> Here are some other text possibilities that can achieve the same goal:
>
> - *Pop Sonnets: Shakespearean Spins on Your Favorite Songs* by Erik Didriksen
> - *Darcy Swipes Left (OMG Classics)* by Jane Austen and Courtney Carbone
> - *William Shakespeare's The Phantom Menace: Star Wars Part the First* by Ian Doescher

Putting It to Work

1. Show students an example from the book, *Understand Rap: Explanations of Confusing Rap Lyrics You and Your Grandma Can Understand* by William Buckholz (2010), or a selection from another book of your choice. I like to use the examples in *Understand Rap* that fall under the headings of Cars and Money.
2. Read students the lyrics from the rap song and ask them to tell you what it means.
3. Show students the formal translation included in the book.

4. Discuss how these versions differ. You might ask them questions like this:
   - Is the overall message the same?
   - What types of words are used in each sample?
   - How does the language change in the different versions?
5. Provide students with a quote, excerpt from a text, or other sample that students will translate.

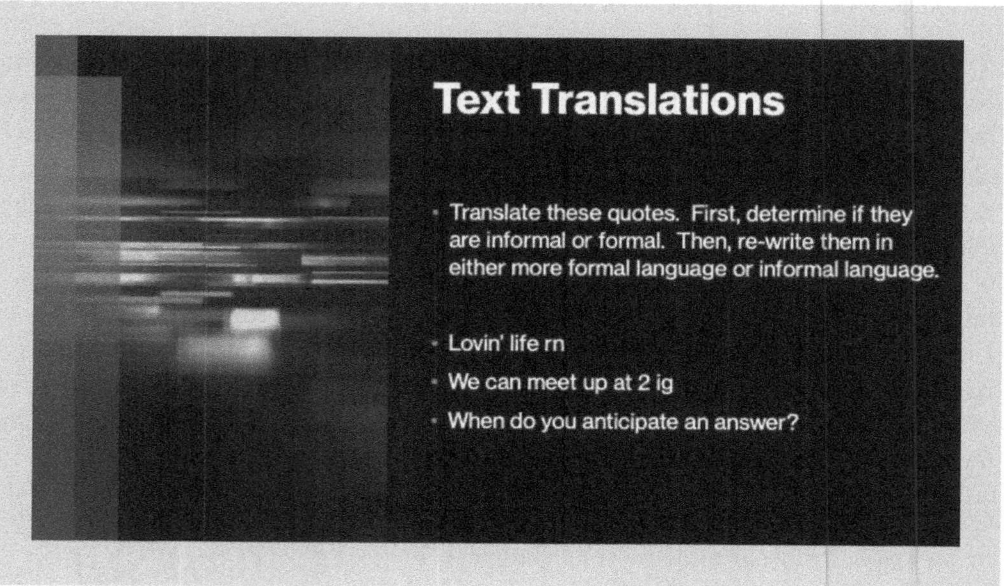

6. Have students first determine if the sample they are given is informal or formal. Once they have made this determination, they can proceed with translating the text.
7. Using the example discussed earlier as a guide, instruct students to either translate the sample into more formal text or translate it into informal text.
8. Share with the class.

When to Use It

- Use this as a way to make especially dense text more manageable and easier to understand.
- When you want students to practice writing for formal and informal audiences and you want them to explain the distinctions between the two.

> **Quick Tip!**
>
> A good resource for students to reference during this lesson are the leveled word charts in my book *Write Now & Write On* (2022). These can provide language options based on the formality of the text.

Why It Works

- It starts off with a real-world example of formal and informal language that many students are familiar with.
- It is a short, manageable task that students can complete in a short amount of time.
- Students are writing for a specific purpose—language formality—which can aid them in constructing effective writing responses.

Modifications

- Instead of using written examples of texts, use video clips of speeches or audio recordings.
- Provide the entire class with the same text to translate. Have half the class translate it into either formal or informal language. Have the other half of the class identify the language in the sample that classifies it as either formal or informal.
- Start with one quote that students translate instead of a longer piece of text.

Extensions

- Have students extend their translations by writing a justification sample that explains their changes.
- Get students to locate their own text samples for translation and have them lead the lesson.
- Connect this lesson to the Sounds Like strategy on page 22.
- Carry this over into research writing and channeling the academic voice.

Digital Direction

- Have students record their translations using VoiceThread or a movie maker program like iMovie to share.
- Use Padlet for students to record their translations and have their classmates respond digitally.
- Have students collaboratively draft their translations using an online program like Etherpad (https://etherpad.org/) or Draft (https://draftin.com/).

Lesson Lead-Ins

- Use this as a lead-in when students are focusing on writing engagements that are heavy on academic language and are highly formal.
- Connect this to lessons that focus on levels of words (Harper, 2022).

CHARACTER EVOLUTION

Standards that address character evolution are present across grade levels because this skill is one that is important for students to master. However, especially when students are reading an extended work like a novel, remembering exactly how a character has changed and evolved over multiple chapters can be overwhelming. In fact, many students focus on the event that happened most recently and can sometimes omit important events that occurred earlier in the novel.

An easy way to address this is by tracking these events over the course of the novel using paint strips (yes, the little paint samples you collect at the hardware store before painting a wall of your living room). Because of the way that paint strips are designed, they are excellent vehicles for recording details that occur in a sequential or linear fashion, much like what is required in a character evolution task. By keeping track of all the different events and occurrences in a character's life as they occur, it can make it easier for students to complete the task at hand. Plus, because the strategy utilizes a medium other than plain paper, it doesn't feel as intimidating as other written tasks.

Don't have paint strips or want to use those? Use the template on the companion website.

Putting It to Work

1. When beginning an extended work or novel, start by explaining to students how characters evolve over time based on events in the novels or other text.
2. Provide students with two paint strips. You will want to make sure you use ones that look like the configuration in the image on the facing page.
3. Have students tape the two paint strips together as shown in the photo.
4. As students are reading their novel, have them record any major events they think have an effect on the main character on the top paint strip. Students should do this throughout the course of reading the novel. The point is to record the information as they go so they can draft a higher quality culminating piece.

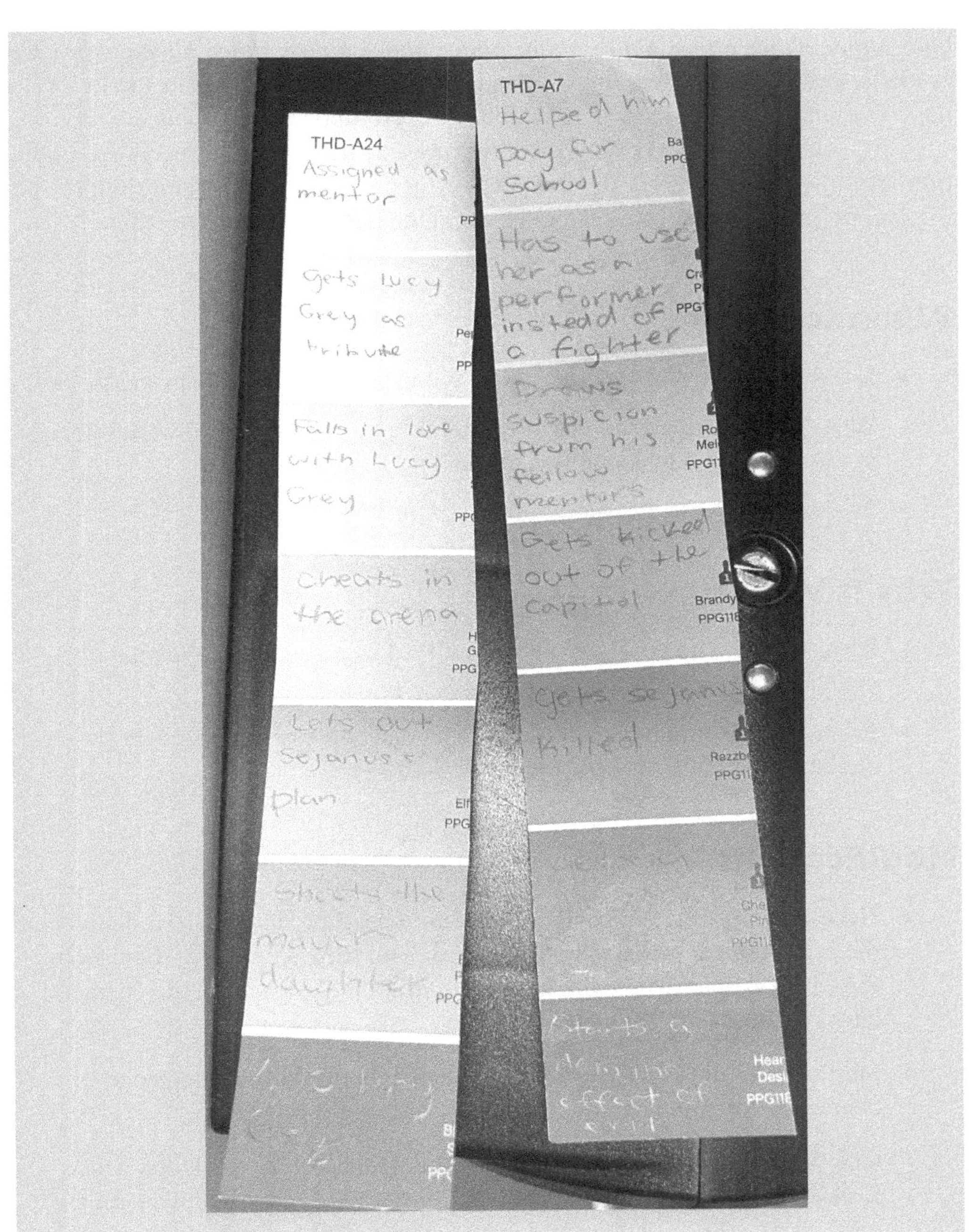

5. For the companion paint strip, have students write how they think the event affected their character.

6. Have students continue to record events and the impacts throughout the novel.

Once students have finished the entire novel and have recorded all the impactful events as well as the results of the events, use the paint strips as a starting point for students to draft an extended essay on the following prompt: "Explain how the character ________ changed/evolved throughout the course of the story. Use specific examples from the novel for evidence." You can modify this prompt to best fit your students, but the overarching idea/task is the same: How did the character evolve over time?

When to Use It

- Use this as a way to break up a large writing task into more manageable tasks.
- When reading an extended work with multiple characters you want students to examine individually and relative to one another.
- As a way to integrate purposeful note-taking and responses.

Why It Works

- It breaks the writing task down by front-loading most of the evidence collection throughout the reading.
- Because students have a specific focus, it makes it easier for them to be deliberate with the material they include.

Modifications

- Have students work with a partner to complete this. Have each student record the events for each character on the first paint strip. Then have them swap their strip with a partner and have them fill in the impacts on the character based on the events their classmate included.
- Start off with simply taking notes on significant events that affected a character. Later, have students add the companion paint strip.
- Color code characters using specific color paint strips for each character. Instead of having students always focus on the same character, take up the paint strips at the end of each class period and then redistribute the next day so students can record information on a different character.
- Use a shortened version of the paint strip configuration like the one in the picture. This way, students don't have as much to write initially.

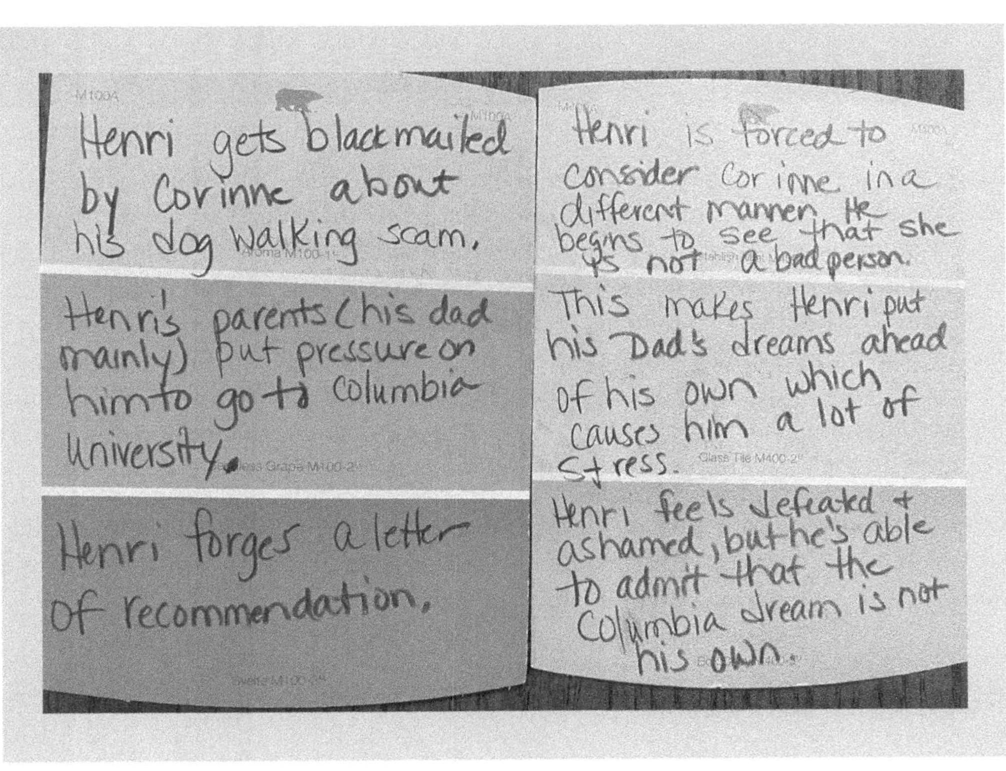

Henri gets blackmailed by Corinne about his dog walking scam.
Henri is forced to consider Corinne in a different manner. He begins to see that she is not a bad person.
Henri's parents (his dad mainly) put pressure on him to go to Columbia University.
This makes Henri put his Dad's dreams ahead of his own which causes him a lot of Stress.
Henri forges a letter of recommendation.
Henri feels defeated + ashamed, but he's able to admit that the Columbia dream is not his own.

Extensions

- Extend this to a comparison essay where students compare multiple characters from the same work or compare characters from different literary works.
- Have students extend this strategy to other character strategies like the Cast the Character on page 82, Most Valuable Character (MVC) on page 74, or the Whose Line Is It? on page 70.

Digital Direction

- Use VoiceThread for students to record their material, and then have their classmates respond.
- Have students use a digital assessment tool or quiz-making software to load their evidence, and have the class choose from a list of multiple-choice options how that event impacted the character.

Lesson Lead-Ins

- Use this as a lead-in for any lessons that focus on character analyses.
- When thinking about a culminating writing piece for an extended literary work, use this strategy to help students collect evidence and plan for the culminating writing task.

NVA^2

Traditional methods of grammar instruction rely on skills-based worksheets or grammar exercises in isolation. As a former writing teacher, I remember that finding ways to make grammar instruction effective and engaging was a struggle. Instead of traditional methods of grammar instruction that rely on skills-based worksheets or grammar exercises in isolation, I learned that grammar instruction worked best when I found ways to incorporate grammar into the writing the students were already doing. Experiencing grammar in context helps students not only also identify grammatical elements in writing but also experience grammar as they are writing. This offers kids more authentic opportunities to engage with the ways in which language and words work and function.

One of my favorite strategies to integrate grammar into the teaching of descriptive writing is NVA^2. For this strategy, students focus on parts of speech (nouns, verbs, and adjectives) to help them write more descriptive compositions.

Putting It to Work

1. Post an image on the SmartBoard or projector for the entire class to see. A great image repository is www.pics4learning.com or images found on www.nationalgeographic.com.
2. Explain to students the importance of descriptive language in writing because it helps readers create a visual image in their heads. This is especially important in compositions that do not include visual images and rely on words to paint the pictures.
3. Have students use the NVA^2 template on the companion website or create their own on a piece of paper.
4. Instruct students to make a list of nouns that describe the image. These should be recorded in the N column.
5. Have students move on to the V column and make a list of verbs that go along with the image.
6. Move next to the A column and have students make a list of adjectives that describe the image.
7. Once students have filled up their template, write the term *NVA^2* for the students to see. Instruct them to take one noun, one verb, and two adjectives and write an NVA^2 sentence that describes the image posted for the class to see.
8. Share with the class.

Noun	Verb	Adjective
1. Palm tree	1. People walking	1. blue sky
2. sand		2. blue ocean
3. beach		3. green leaves
4. shells		4. brown would
5. ocean		5. brown pinestraw
6. Pine straw		6. white clouds
7. clouds		7. tan sand
8. leaves		8. orange poles
9. poles		9. white poles
		10. clean beach

The beach is where a lot of people walk when the sky is blue with no clouds because they think it is gonna rain and ruin there walk and they are gonna be soaked wet so that is why I pick that sentence.

When to Use It

- As a way to incorporate grammar into writing engagements.
- When you want students to practice crafting descriptive sentences that include specific parts of speech.
- As a low-stakes way to have students practice descriptive writing.

Why It Works

- It starts with a list that becomes a word bank for students to use, which makes sentence construction much easier.
- Students are tasked with drafting one sentence at a time, which makes the task manageable.
- Starting with a visual image can help students focus as they begin brainstorming.

Modifications

- Start with one or two parts of speech first and have students practice with those before you move on to the next.
- Provide students with a ready-made word bank that they use to select the words they think compliment the image.
- Divide the students into groups and assign a specific letter for each group. Have one group focus on the nouns, another on verbs, and another on adjectives. Then put students back into groups and have them collaboratively write their NVA^2 sentences.

Extensions

- Add a fourth A category for adverbs. Have students write a new NVA^2 sentence that incorporates a noun, verb, adjective, and adverb.
- Have students repeat the sentence-construction process and construct a descriptive paragraph.
- Extend this strategy into a fully involved descriptive writing composition as shown in the Descriptive Writing With Calendars activity, page 125.
- Have students collect their own images and complete their lists and sample sentence. Display the images in the class for everyone to see. Then pass out the sentences and have the students see if they can match the sentence to the correct image.
- When students orally share their sentences, have their classmates identify which words were used for the different parts of speech in their sentences.

Digital Direction

- Upload the images into PicCollage and have students draft the sentences in text boxes on the image.
- Use www.text2photo.com to add text to the image. This can be used when making a list of the different parts of speech.
- Upload the photo to www.picmonkey.com to add text to the chosen image.

Lesson Lead-Ins

- When starting a descriptive writing unit, use this as a lead-in lesson.
- Connect this to the Stretch to See lesson on page 37.
- Extend this to the fully involved Descriptive Writing With Calendars lesson (see page 125).
- Use this as a connection to the Wordless Picture Books lesson on page 107.

WHOSE LINE IS IT?

Many of these targeted training strategies address skills related to character analysis, development, and traits. For students to be able to develop dynamic characters, analyze and critique characters, and compare them as well, students need to have multiple chances to practice these skills and explore the subtle nuances of characters in literature using a variety of strategies. In fact, strategies that help students practice different strategies that address multiple aspects of character development, including dialogue construction, character traits, and character evolution, can aid students as they complete character analysis writing tasks. Whose Line is It? is a strategy that can be used when you want students to use what they know about different characters to determine who said what.

Putting It to Work

1. When finishing up a novel or other extended work, make a list of characters from the work. Display for the students to see.
2. Have students brainstorm character traits that can be associated with each of the characters.
3. Discuss with the class each of the characters and their list of character traits.
4. Display a quote or piece of dialogue from the novel or extended work that one of the characters said.

WHO SAID IT?

- "You're the one wearing the yellow tights! I told you this would happen. I didn't care as long as it was just you. But it's not just you anymore, now is it? This was taped to my locker." (From *The Wednesday Wars* by Gary Schmidt)

5. Using the list of characters and their associated character traits, students determine which character from the list is the speaker of the line.
6. Students use notecards or sticky notes to record their ideas. They must use evidence from the brainstorming session to support their inferences.
7. Share with the class.
8. Provide students with a list of five to ten quotes from the novel that can be attributed to different characters.
9. Have students refer to the brainstorming information to complete the activity independently.

When to Use It

- When you want students to interact and engage with character dialogue in a different way.
- To review the important characters in an extended work or novel.
- If you want students to consider a character's words and dialogue when they complete a character analysis.

Why It Works

- Because students are focusing on short snippets of text each time, task completion becomes easier.
- Students are reading a few sentences at a time and then connecting them to their list of known characters.
- It starts with a brainstorming review of the characters and their lists of traits and then progresses into the connection of quotes/dialogue with each character.

Modifications

- Post each character and their traits on large pieces of chart paper around the room to create character stations. Have students partner up and give them a few sample quotes. Instruct them to rotate around the room to each character station and determine where their quotes should be placed.

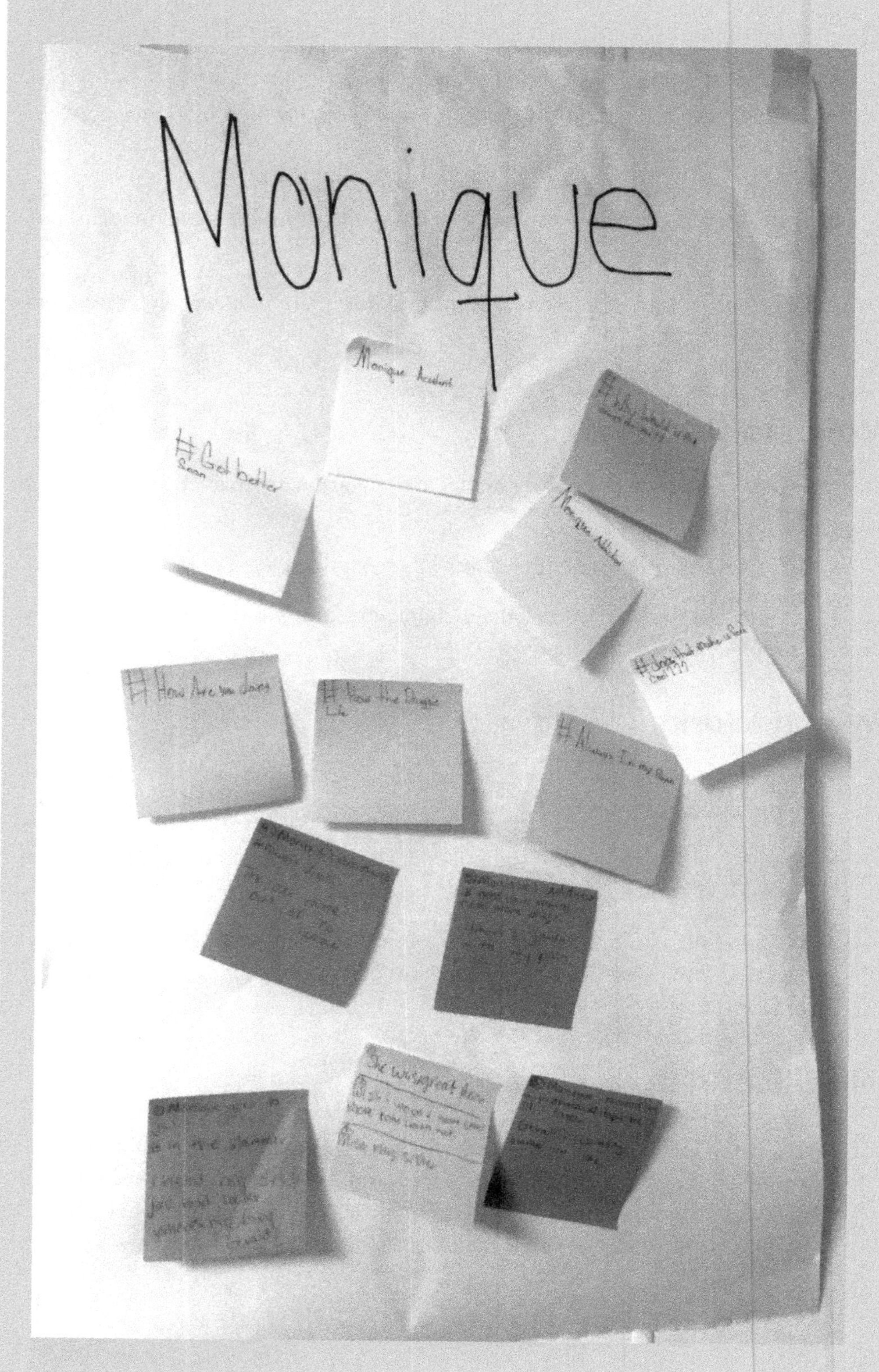
Monique

- Instead of focusing on characters in one novel, use characters from multiple novels as a more comprehensive review.
- For a cross curricular connection, have students focus on historical figures instead of fictional characters.
- Instead of focusing on characters, try a lesson that compares literary legends to music icons. Locate lyrics from musical artists and quotes from works of literature. Create a slideshow of each quote and have students guess whether or not the quote came from a music icon or a literary legend. The results will surprise you!

Extensions

- Connect this to the Sounds Like lesson on page 22.
- Have students use the direct quotes as a frame for them to write new dialogue that their selected character might say.
- Extend this into the Cast the Character strategy on page 82 or the Most Valuable Character (MVC) strategy on page 74.
- Connect this to the Attack or Defend strategy (Harper, 2022).

Digital Direction

- Use a digital animation program like Powtoon or Pixton to animate the characters digitally.
- Use a program like Google Slides to create a digital interactive character notebook that students can use to complete this strategy.
- A program like Voki can allow students to record the character quotes using their voices for a variety of avatars.

Lesson Lead-Ins

- When students have a culminating task that involves a character analysis or comparison, use this strategy as a lead-in for this formal assessment task.
- Use this as a review tool when finishing up an extended work of literature.
- When completing high intensity writing tasks that address character components, use this strategy as a lead-in. Character Evolution (page 62) is an example of a complimentary task that can be used in tandem for a high intensity writing.

MVC (MOST VALUABLE CHARACTER)

It is important for students to have multiple opportunities to think about characters in a variety of ways. For example, students should consider how characters interact with others in the story, what traits they have and how these impact their actions, and how they change over time. In addition, comparing characters in and across works can help students analyze and synthesize material from a wide variety of sources. The Most Valuable Character (MVC) engagement can offer students an authentic opportunity to evaluate a character's flaws and strengths and determine who is worthy of the MVC Award.

Putting It to Work

1. Determine if your lesson will focus on characters in one extended work or if you want students to focus on characters across several works.
2. Ask students what they know about a Most Valuable Player (MVP) award.
3. Have students brainstorm criteria for a sports figure to be chosen as an MVP.
4. Using this material as a frame, have students consider what criteria they should assign for an MVC award. For example, they might consider a character's heroic efforts, their commitment/friendship to other characters in the story, their role in the main events of the story, or other characteristics specific to the story.
5. As a class, draft a list of criteria for award selection.
6. Provide students with a list of character nominees. These can be from one literary work or from multiple works. Just make sure the students have read each of the works first!
7. Using the award selection criteria, have students determine who is the best candidate for the MVC award.
8. Have students use textual evidence from the work to justify their selection.
9. Share with the class.

Quick Tip!

This can be completed as a class, in a collaborative group/partner setting, or individually. The first time students use this strategy, I would suggest using a collaborative format.

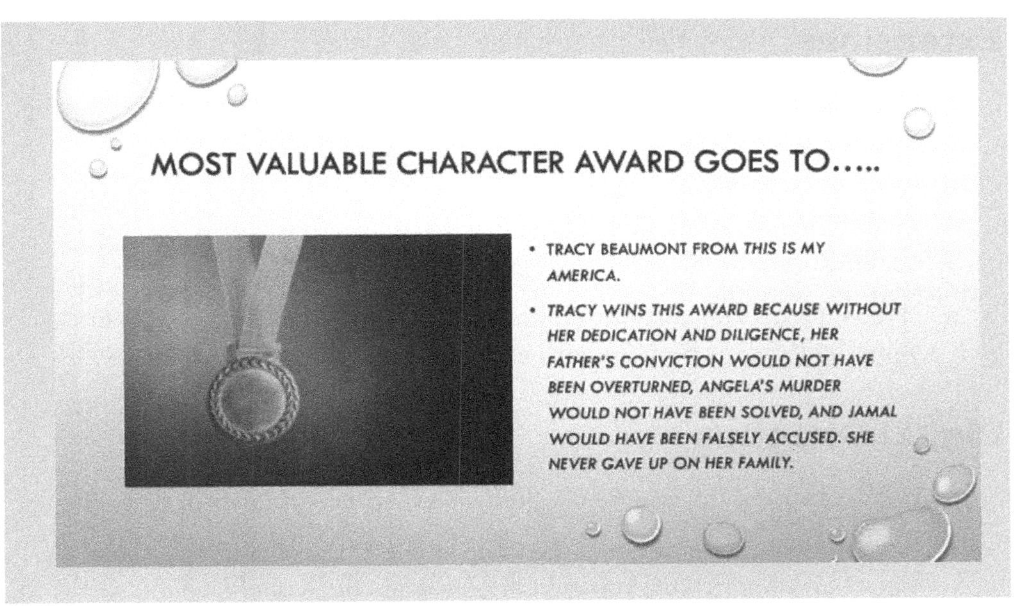

When to Use It

- When you want students to compare characters in a work or across multiple texts.
- To have students evaluate a character in a nontraditional format.
- Use this strategy around big award weeks like the Emmys, Oscars, or VMAs.

Why It Works

- It connects a real-world concept to the classroom. (MVP awards are used extensively in sports.)
- Looking at specific components of a text, in this case characters, can make the task more manageable for students.
- It can easily be modified or extended based on the focus of the lesson.
- This strategy can encourage creativity.

Modifications

- Have a word bank list of character traits that can help students as they brainstorm information about their character.
- Create one sample list of criteria for students to use first. Model the entire activity using the sample criteria list and then have students create their own.
- Break the task into chunks. Have students brainstorm traits one day, develop criteria for the award on the next day, and then select the recipient on the next.

Extensions

- Have students draft an acceptance speech for the character who is receiving the award.
- Get students to write a speech announcing the award. In this speech, they should include information about the character and why they meet the qualifications for the award.
- Have students draft additional awards such as Most Likely to . . . , Game-Winning Read, or Best Supporting Character.

Digital Direction

- Use a movie making program to film an awards ceremony with the students.
- Have students post a video in the voice of one of the characters on VoiceThread or Padlet explaining why they are the best choice for the award.
- Use Jamboard or Miro to collectively compile evidence for a character's nomination.

Lesson Lead-Ins

- Use this as a lead-in to the Cast the Character strategy on page 82.
- When completing reviews, use this strategy as a way to remind students about characters in a work.

GREETING CARDS

Navigating the realms of audience and purpose can take some practice and skill. In fact, lack of understanding about audience and purpose is one of the main reasons students make missteps in language, format, or genre. While identifying the purpose may be easier, understanding who the audience is and how that impacts the composition and construction of the writing piece sometimes is a little harder to see. One easy way to focus on purpose and audience is by using Greeting Cards.

Putting It to Work

1. Collect a variety of greeting cards that have the same purpose. (I have found that birthday cards work best, but "thinking of you" cards or ones focused on encouragement work well, too.)
2. Provide students with a stack of birthday cards that vary in form, function, and aesthetics, including images, written messages, and layout. Give students a copy of the Greeting Card template on the companion website.
3. Give students a list of various yet specific individuals to whom they must send cards. Some possible audiences include your best friend from elementary school, your Sunday School teacher who is turning 80, your soccer coach, your sibling, a neighbor who loves animals, and so on.
4. Instruct students to select the most appropriate card for each individual.

Stop & Think:

Here's a real-world example of knowing your audience. When my mother was diagnosed with brain cancer, she began a regimen of chemotherapy. Her doctors provided her with an information sheet of all the things she could and could not do while taking chemo. As she was reading the sheet, she told me, "Good news, Rebecca. It says I can still take birth control." To which I replied, "Better news, Mom. You are 60; you don't need it!"

When I wrote her eulogy, I included this as a funny moment in a crisis where we found laughter. However, when I stood in the pulpit of the Higher Ground Baptist Church and looked at my audience, which included my mother's fourth grade students, my grandmother, Mom's principal, and elders from the church, I knew there was NO WAY I could speak the words "birth control" in that moment and with that audience. As a result, I revised that eulogy right there and gave a different example story. Why? Because I understand how audience impacts both what and how I write or say something.

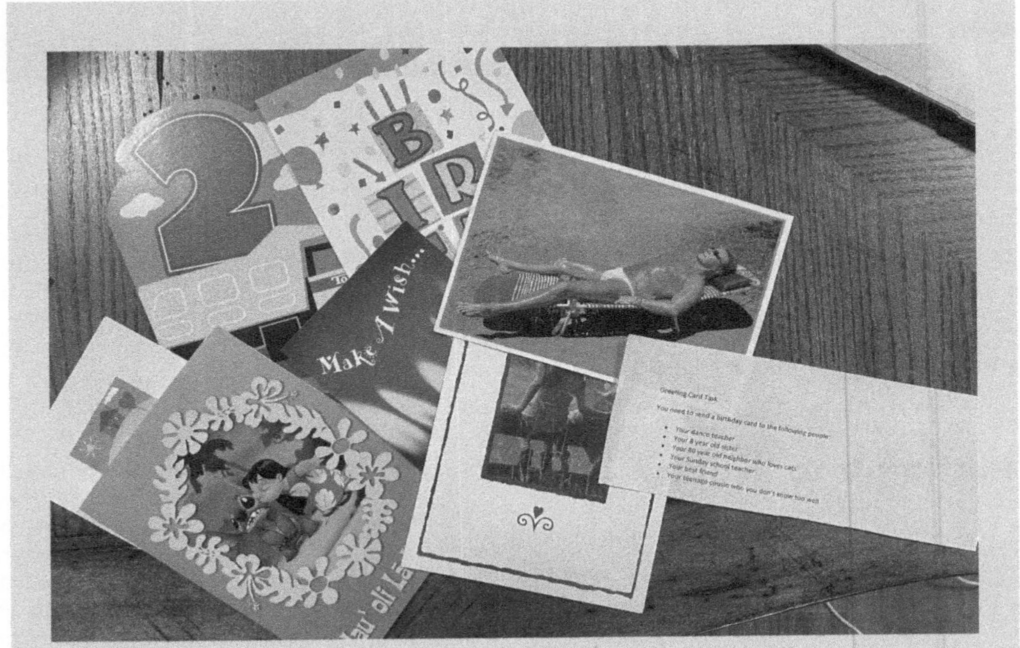

5. Record their choices on the template.
6. Have students justify their reasoning for their choices by providing supporting evidence from the cards and record them on the template.
7. Share with the class.

When to Use It

- When you want students to focus specifically on audience and purpose.
- As a way to connect a real-world example to an academic demand.
- When you want students to see the impact audience has on crafting a written response.

> **Quick Tip!**
>
> Another approach might be to have students determine how they might relay the same message to different audiences. How might they modify their delivery based on who they are speaking with? How might they deliver the same information to their teacher, friends, parents, and principal? Would they use different language? Different tactics?

Why It Works

- It's a low-stakes way to address audience and purpose.
- It combines a real-world example with an academic standard.
- Using greeting cards can be less intimidating than traditional audience and purpose lessons.
- Greeting cards with the same type of message can help students see that while their purpose is the same, the audience impacts what type of written message should be employed.

Modifications

- Instead of greeting cards as examples, have students use other forms of writing such as email and text messages.
- Use images of different types of audiences and have students use sticky notes or address labels to write words that might be used for a specific audience.
- Have students work with a partner to determine which cards should be used for which audience.
- Instead of having students focus on multiple audiences and cards, divide the task up. As students enter the classroom, pass out individual greeting cards and audiences (written on notecards) to each student. Then have students mingle to try to find the appropriate match for their audience or card.

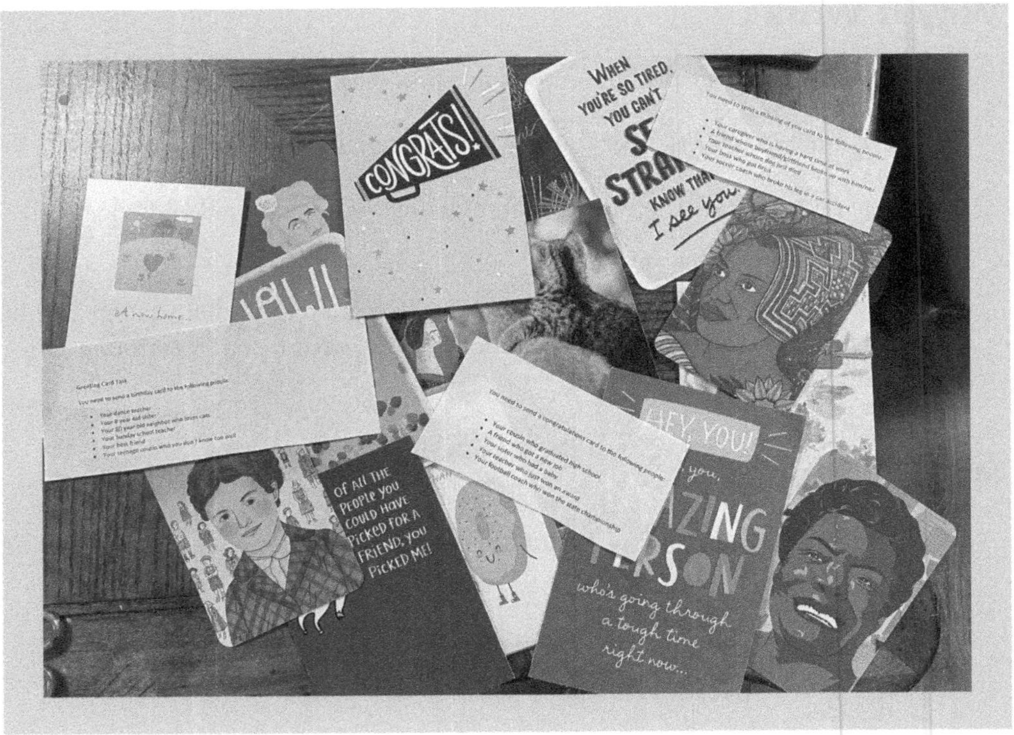

Extensions

- Have students extend this activity by writing an appropriate message in the card that best fits the audience.
- Ask students to brainstorm additional audiences they might consider for this activity.
- Transfer this activity into extended writing assignments that require students to write for the same purpose but for a different audience.

Digital Direction

- When teaching online, put students into breakout rooms and have them collaborate online to determine their selections.
- Use a program like PicCollage or Canva for students to upload images of their greeting cards along with text boxes that explain which audience they would use for each.
- Display this activity using a program like Lucidchart, Miro, or MindMeister, which creates digital thinking maps. Have students map out their choices using a tree map or other template.

Lesson Lead-Ins

- Use this activity to address writing tasks that require students to write for a variety of audiences.
- Connect this to the Text Translations lesson on page 59.
- Tie this into Levels of Words (Harper, 2022) or the AKA Charts (Harper, 2017).

CAST THE CHARACTER

I was shocked when my friend broke the news that Lenny Kravitz would play the character Cenna in the theatrical version of *The Hunger Games*. How could Lenny Kravtiz be Cenna? I had pictured someone more "Elton John-esque." So I started asking others who had read the series what their mind's version of Cenna looked like. The descriptions couldn't have varied more! People gave examples like:

- Slim, Italian, and well-dressed
- Dark-skinned, elegant, and sophisticated
- Mousy, pale, and nondescript.
- Flamboyant, flashy, and elaborately dressed

Every person I spoke with had a distinctively different idea of what this character looked like. How? After all, they had read the same words on the page. Yet each reader fills in the descriptive blanks with their own past experiences, mental images, and ideas. Thus, Cenna, looked different for everyone.

And although I was floored initially to hear of the casting choice, after watching the movie and rereading the books, Lenny Kravitz is now who I see when I read. (Sorry, Lenny, for my brief disappointment; you are my Cenna.)

When students read, drawing attention to mental images and visualization is key to comprehension. As students read extended texts, and especially those without pictorial images, visualizing the characters, setting, and events can help students better understand the overall message and theme of the text. In fact, when done well, students should visualize a running movie or image in their heads about what is happening in the material. One of the best ways to have students focus on visualization *and* using textual evidence is through the strategy Cast the Character. Plus, this lesson has multiple connections to the descriptive writing genre because the composition relies heavily on descriptive and visual language.

Putting It to Work

1. Choose a main character from an extended work, preferably a novel. Make sure the students have completed reading the entire work before you start this activity.
2. Based on the textual evidence provided in the novel, locate images of individuals online who might be possibilities of visual representations of the character. For example, if your novel includes a male character who is a teenager, you might locate multiple images of male teenagers who might look like your character. If there is additional textual evidence in the novel such as height, race, hair color, physical build, and so on, include those

considerations when you decide which images to include.

3. Display the images using a slide presentation with a program like PowerPoint, Google Slides, or Prezi, starting with a slide that includes the character's name.

4. Have students brainstorm/recall items about the listed character to activate prior knowledge. Record these on the board or have students record them on their papers.

5. Show students the first image. Have them locate textual evidence that supports the character's picture from the novel. Ask students to record these on sticky notes or you can type them on the slide.

6. Go through each slide and each image, repeating Step 5.

There are a plethora of choices for engaging, modern novels with rich characters. Some favorites of my students include

- *The Crossover* by Kwame Alexander
- *Black Brother, Black Brother* by Jewell Parker Rhodes
- *Bang* by Barry Lyga
- *We'll Fly Away* by Brian Bliss
- *Track* series by Jason Reynolds
- *How It All Blew Up* by Arvin Ahmadi

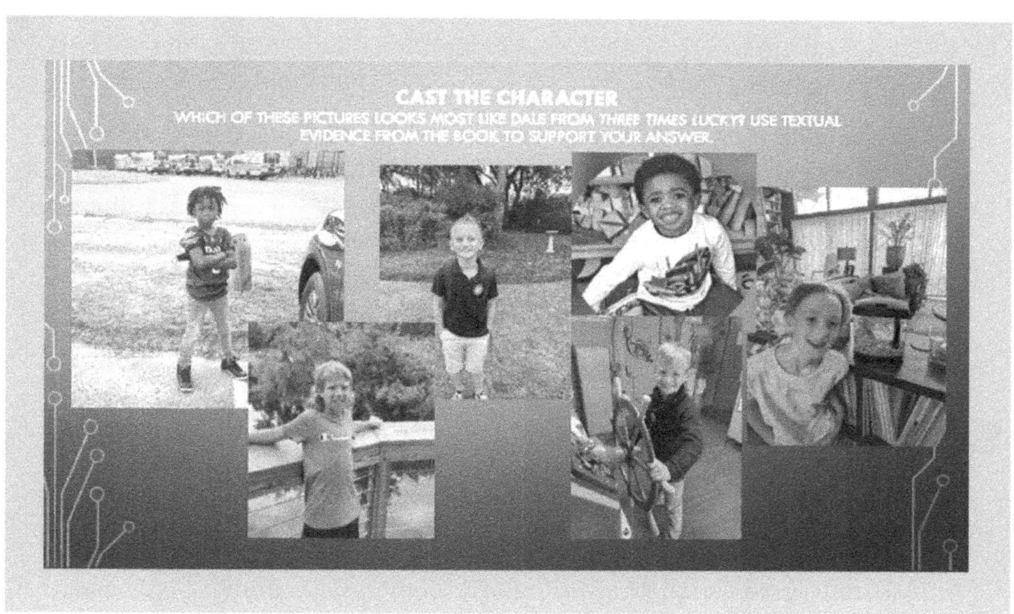

7. After students have viewed all possible images, have the class determine which one is the best visual representation of the character from the novel using the textual evidence as a guide. Using descriptive vocabulary along with textual evidence from the work, have students draft a justification for their choice on a notecard.

8. Discuss as a class the choices.

When to Use It

- To revisit characters at the end of a novel.
- When you want students to discuss how they visualize what characters look like.
- To merge textual evidence with character and visualization lessons.

Why It Works

- It includes a pictorial image as a reference point for the characters.
- There is a specific focus for the lesson as students are only concerned with what a character looks like based on details from the novel.
- Textual evidence is addressed in this strategy, but in small doses, which makes locating the supporting evidence much easier.

Modifications

- Instead of posting the images on a digital program, post each image on a large piece of chart paper and have students do a gallery walk with a partner and record supporting evidence on the poster.
- Have students locate possible images for the lesson instead of the teacher providing them.
- Do this with the setting of a novel or a specific event that occurred in the novel. For example, when I read *A Snicker of Magic* by Natalie Lloyd (2014) with a fifth-grade class, we did a similar activity, but we focused on the main character's car, which was referred to as the "Pickled Jalapeño" because of its green color. In another class, we focused on a character's pet dog, and when we read *Black Duck* (Lisle, 2006), we focused on a character's beach shack when we chose read images (Harper, 2022).

Extensions

- Have students visualize multiple parts of the novel including characters, the setting, and specific events.
- Ask students to complete a version of a Memory Map from page 29 where they draw what they remember from a specific part of the story.
- Have students to write an argument that supports their choice for who should be cast as the main characters.
- Connect this to the Character Evolution on page 62.

Digital Direction

- Have students assume the identity of one of the pictured characters and have them create an audition clip video that would be submitted to a casting company. In this video, they might give reasons why they should be cast and also perform some dialogue from the novel.
- Use a digital polling program like Centimeter or Poll Everywhere to capture student votes for a particular character choice live during the lesson.

Lesson Lead-Ins

- Use this as a lead-in for culminating engagements when students finish reading a novel.
- Connect this to lessons like Character Evolution on page 62, Most Valuable Character (see page 74), or Character Props (see page 49).

SONGS FOR VOICE

One of the most nebulous parts of writing to teach, in my opinion, is voice. Sometimes, it is hard to define exactly what voice is and how writers can use it in their written compositions. In fact, one of the best ways to teach voice due to this nebulous and ambiguous nature of the concept is through tangible examples, like mentor texts, and even music. Giving students examples of how voice *sounds* can help them develop their own voice when writing. Voice can be defined as the narrator or author's individual tone, emotion, and point of view through specific word choice and construction of phrases.

Putting It to Work

1. Find a song that has been covered by multiple music artists. Include a variety of covers, but no more than five. (My absolute favorite to use is Michael Jackson's song "Billie Jean." Cover versions of this iconic song completely change the overall tone and meaning. The versions I use are recorded by Honeywagon, David Cook, and of course, Michael Jackson.)
2. Make a copy of the lyrics (these will all be the same no matter who the artist is covering the song).
3. Provide students with the Songs for Voice template on the companion website and a copy of the lyrics.
4. Encourage students to follow along with the lyrics as they listen.
5. Play a portion of one of the songs. Have students make notations of their observations on the template. Encourage them to consider the following:
   - How does this song make you feel?
   - What is the overall mood?
   - What do you notice about the singer's performance?
6. Repeat Step 4 with each sample cover.
7. After students have listened to each cover song, have students discuss the differences in each version.

It's a good idea to make sure that the covers vary in musical genre. For example, the genres might include rock and roll, blues, country, ballad, and so on since each of those has a distinctively different style.

Make sure you play the most well-known cover last. For example, when I use "Billie Jean," I always play Michael Jackson's version last.

Songs for Voice

Song Title	Noticings *(mood, feeling, tempo, etc.)*
Billie Jean	
SONG 1	blues nostalgic sad soul melancholy missing guitar
SONG 2	rock ballad like Coldplay passion hard times blames himself bluesy
SONG 3	upbeat her fault irritated denying trifling don't know her fast beat

8. Have students discuss how each artist's individual performance affected the overall message of the song. Make sure to draw attention to how the lyrics were the same for all the versions; instead, the tempo, key, style, and artist changed.

9. Connect this concept back to writing by explaining that writers use certain words and phrases to create a distinct voice for the writing. Explain that how words are used and in what context affects voice along with perspective and point of view.

Quick Tip!

Several years ago, State Farm Insurance ran a series of commercials called "My Car." In these commercials, two separate scenes are played with different characters. However, the exact same dialogue is used in both scenes, yet two entirely different events with opposite meanings are played out. Check it out here: https://www.ispot.tv/ad/ASxV/state-farm-jacked-up

When to Use It

- When you want students to have a tangible example of what voice sounds like.
- To connect music to writing.
- For making real-world connections between writing in the world and writing in the classroom.
- To also address the skill of comparison and contrast indirectly.

Why It Works

- It offers students a tangible, auditory example of a writing concept.
- Connecting a real-life example can help students see the connection between the academic and personal world.
- It offers authentic evidence of a writing concept.

Modifications

- In addition to the song examples, layer this with the inclusion of a variety of excerpts from novels or picture books. Some favorites are:
  - *Voices in the Park* by Anthony Browne
  - *We Had a Picnic This Sunday Past* by Jacqueline Woodson
  - "My Name" from *The House on Mango Street* by Sandra Cisneros
  - *The Absolutely True Diary of a Part-Time Indian* by Sherman Alexie
- Provide students with a word bank that they may use when describing each song.

Extensions

- Provide students with one anchor song. Have them locate their own covers of the song and complete the template with a partner.
- Have students locate images that match the overall mood and voice of each version of the song.
- Encourage students to find another cover for the anchor song and evaluate it for voice as well.

Digital Direction

- Create a TikTok as a summary of the entire template. Have students include samples of each song and summarize it using recorded video or subtitles/text on TikTok.

- Use a collaborative brainstorming application like Jamboard for students to record their initial observations of each song.

Lesson Lead-Ins

- Use this as an opener for lessons on mood or tone.
- Connect this lesson to strategies that address different components of character.

PICTURES FOR MOOD

Several years ago, I was standing in the card aisle of CVS and noticed that each section of cards (sympathy, birthday, encouragement, etc.) all had certain similarities based on their purpose. For example, sympathy cards tended to use muted colors for their images or illustrations and often included script fonts and still-life images. Correspondingly, the birthday cards often included primary colors, bold fonts, and more animated images. This observation led me to think about how this is a real-world example of mood. The images, colors, and fonts all contribute to the overall mood of the card. Because mood is something that is a focus in ELA standards, greeting cards can serve as a real-world connection. (This engagement works well with images from magazines or print ads, too; just be sure to show only images, no words.)

> **Quick Tip!**
>
> To activate prior knowledge for this, complete a brainstorming session of mood words prior to starting the activity.

Putting It to Work

1. Collect a variety of greeting cards that are written for a variety of purposes. Make sure to choose cards that do not have written messages on the front. Instead, focus on ones that only have images or art on the front of the card. You don't want words to give away the purpose of the card.

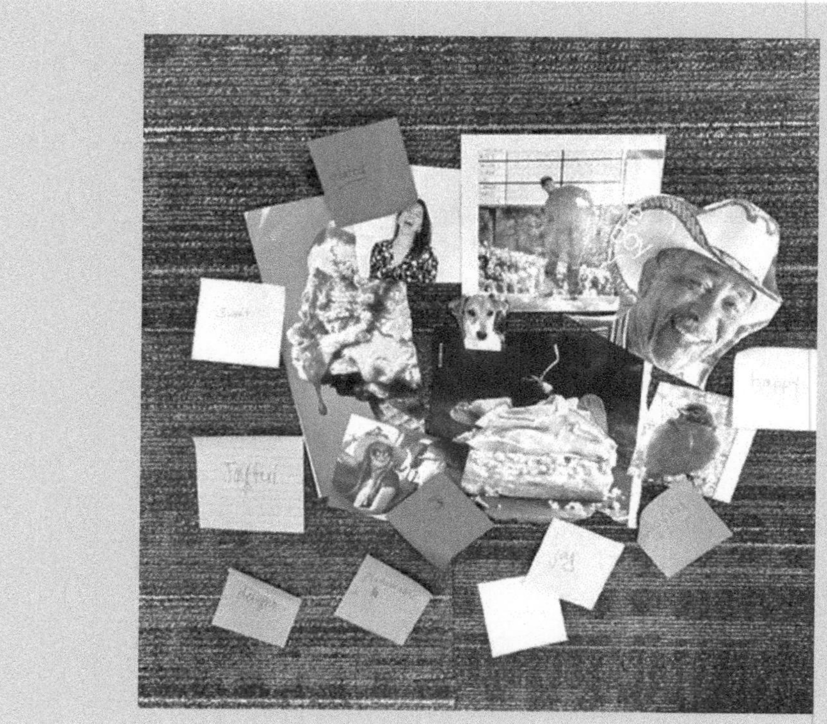

2. Cut the cards in two pieces so only the front image is visible.
3. As student walk into the room, hand them a greeting card cover.
4. Instruct them to group the cards in piles based on which images they think have similar moods.
5. Have students walk around and look at the piles to determine if any images need to be moved. If so, have students adjust them and place them in different piles. Remind them to keep in mind the reason for moving the image.
6. Give students a stack of sticky notes. Have students walk around and view the piles.
7. Ask students to write down words on their sticky notes that describe the mood evoked in the images.

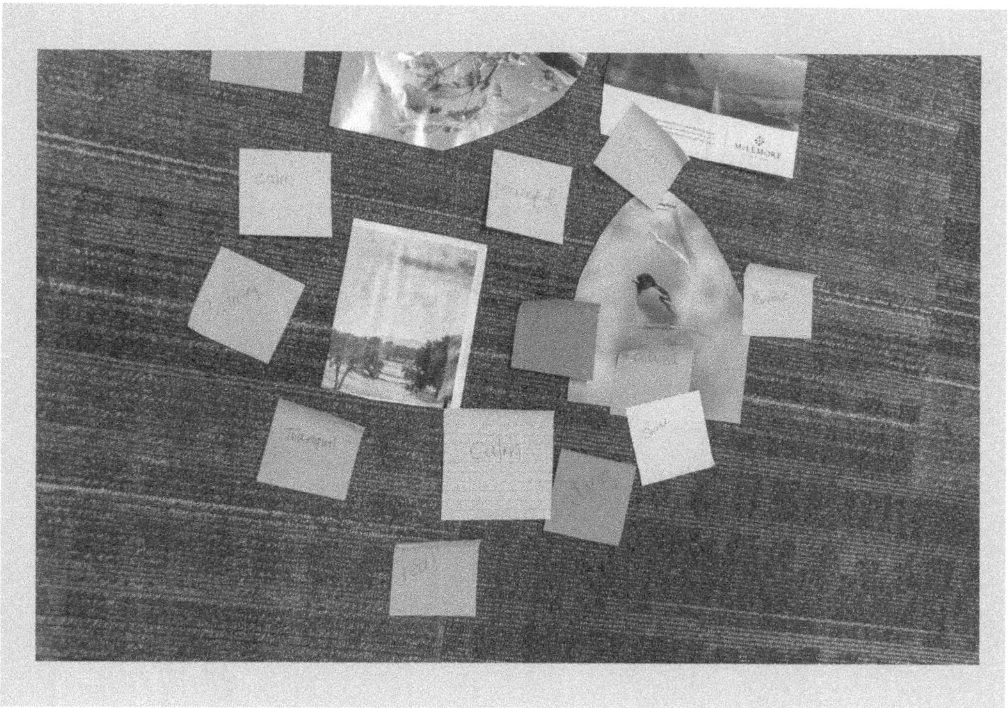

8. Discuss as a class the individual piles of images and the mood words they associated with each pile.
9. Have students make inferences about each pile of images. Ask them if they were images from greeting cards, what would be the message based on the images in each pile.
10. Discuss as a class.

When to Use It

- When you want students to focus on words that evoke mood.
- As a way to connect images and pictures to feelings, tone, and mood.
- When you want students to have a pictorial representation of a specific mood.
- As a way to address vocabulary in a low-stakes setting.

Why It Works

- It starts with images so students are able to have a visual example of a specific mood.
- Using greeting cards is a real-world connection that students can see outside of school.
- Because students are only writing individual words on their sticky notes, it makes the task more manageable since they are only writing words instead of extended responses.

Modifications

- Instead of using greeting cards, use images from magazines.
- Provide students with a mood word bank to use as they describe each pile of images.
- Use silent movie slips instead of cards or images.
- Use paint strips to record words that are related to specific moods.

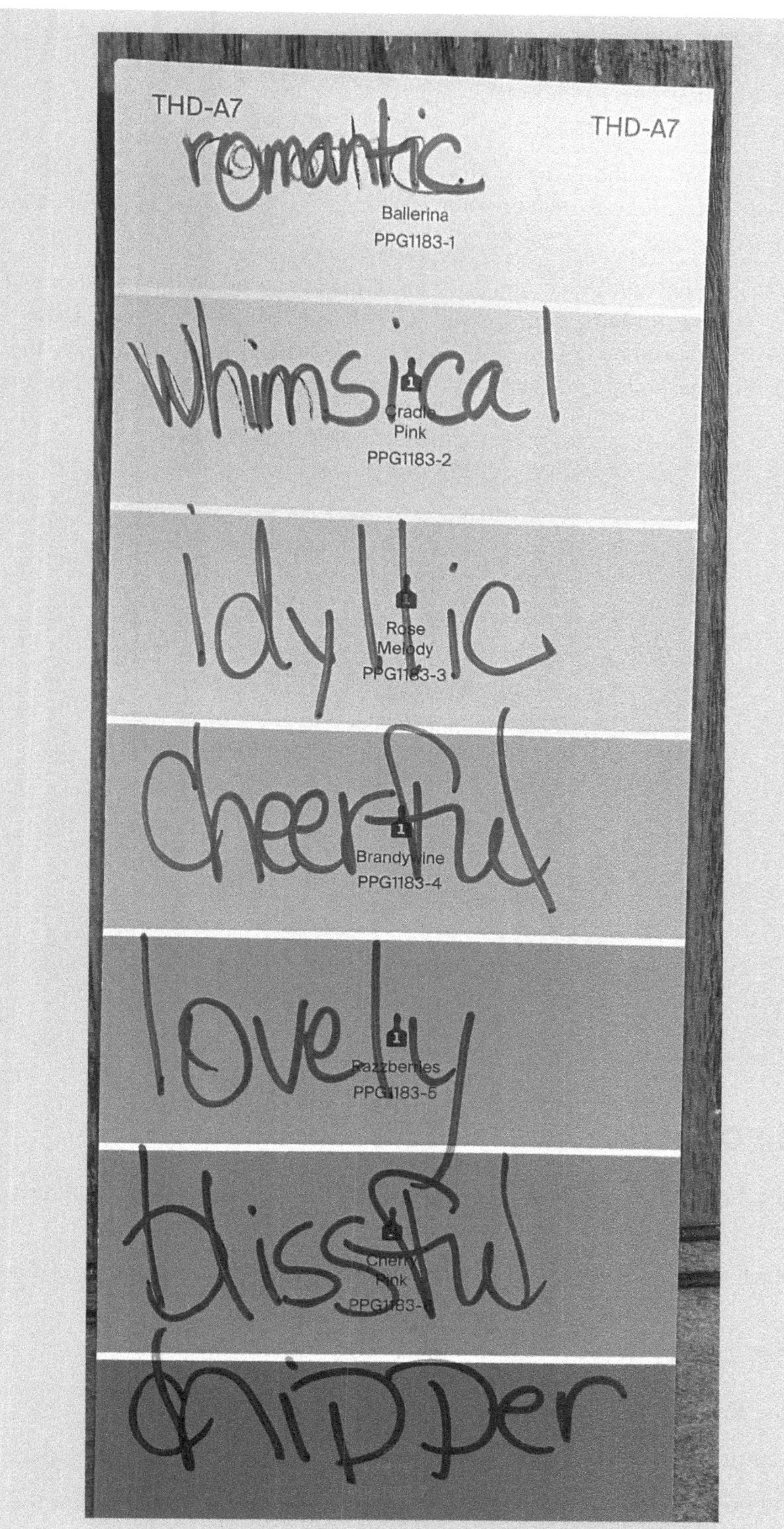
THD-A7
THD-A7
romantic
Ballerina
PPG1183-1
whimsical
Cradle
Pink
PPG1183-2
idyllic
Rose
Melody
PPG1183-3
cheerful
Brandywine
PPG1183-4
lovely
Razzberries
PPG1183-5
blissful
chipper

Extensions

- Have students find additional images that might go with the piles of images that the students created.
- Get students to choose one of the images, and based on the mood of the image, have them write a greeting card message that could accompany the original image.
- Instead of having students create piles of images based on the mood provoked, pass out the cut-out greeting cards as students walk into the room. Half of the class should receive the images and half of the class should receive the greeting card message. Have students find a matching message for their image.

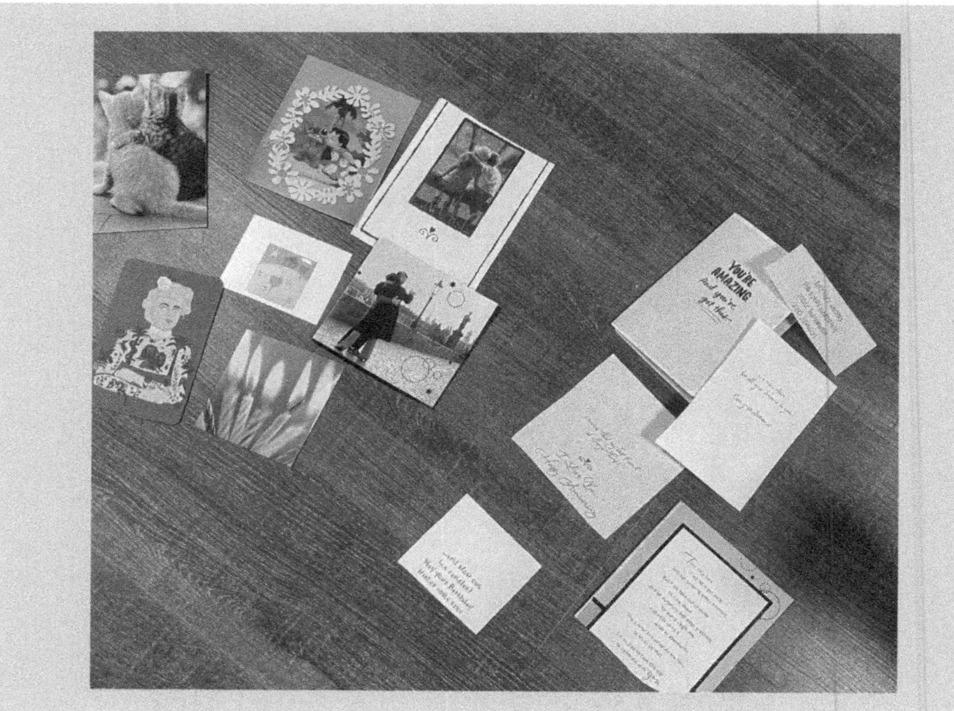

Digital Direction

- Use PicCollage or Canva to group images that belong together. Add text boxes of mood-related words.
- Have students brainstorm mood-related words using a program like Jamboard.

Lesson Lead-Ins

- Use this as a lead-in for lessons on voice and tone.
- Connect this to lessons that focus on sensory details such as NVA^2 on page 66.
- When completing culminating assessments, use this lesson to review the overall mood of a specific novel or work of literature.

CLAIMS AND EVIDENCE MATCHUP

Writing a solid argument takes some time and skill. To craft an effective argument, one must have a clear understanding of claims, supporting evidence, counterclaims, and rebuttals. Yet it is not enough to know the basic definition of each of these components; students need to understand how each of these components works in concert with each other. To gain proficiency in this sophisticated genre of writing, practice and attention must be given to all components. However, before students learn to make moves with evidence or address the counterclaim, they must learn how to first write strong claims that are supported with effective evidence. The Claims and Evidence Matchup strategy focuses on this foundational skill.

This should not be the first time that students have ever written a claim. Rather, it should be an opportunity for them to practice and develop claims based on material in prior lessons.

Putting It to Work

1. Provide students with two different colored long paint strips attached with tape along the long end (so the color blocks match up side by side).
2. Give students a specific topic that they will be writing about. Ideally, students should already have adequate background knowledge on these topics so they are not starting from scratch. In fact, this strategy works best when students have read multiple sources about a specific concept.
3. Provide students with a brief review of claim writing. Again, this engagement should not be the first time they have written a claim but rather be a skill builder.
4. Have students draft several claims on one of the paint strips. Students should write one claim per box on the strip.
5. Provide students with articles or sources that can be used to support the claims developed.
6. Using the second paint strip, students jot down supporting evidence for each of the claims on the initial paint strip. Each claim should have one piece of supporting evidence.
7. Share with the class.
8. Use the evidence to write extended compositions based around the claims drafted on the paint strips.

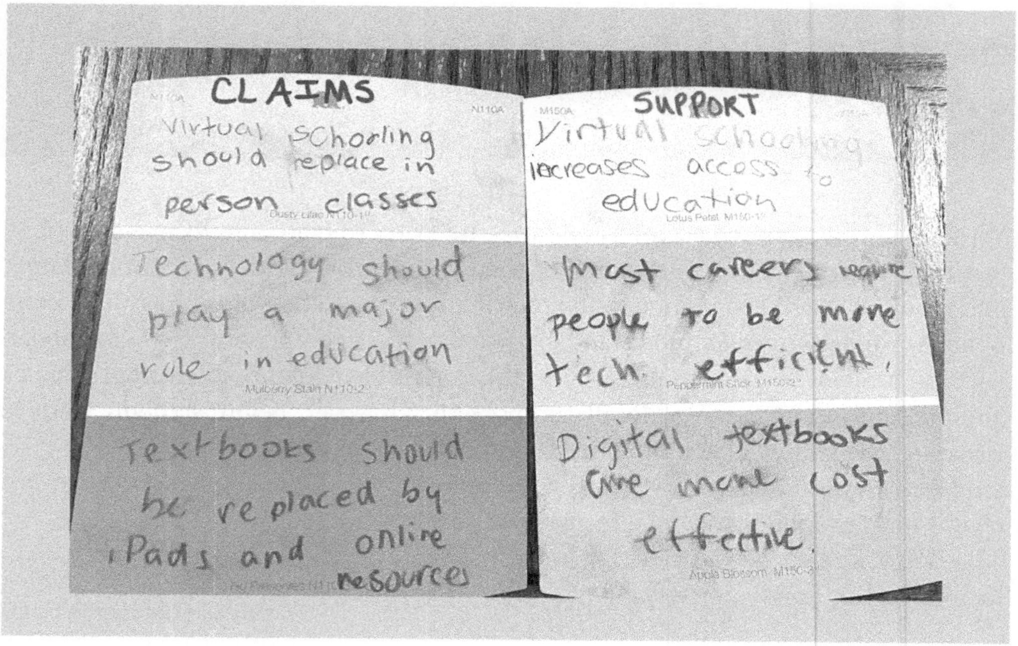

When to Use It

- Use this strategy when students are writing arguments or other writings that focus heavily on textual evidence.
- Use this strategy to help students organize evidence from multiple sources that need to be synthesized as support for argumentative claims.
- Have students use this strategy as they are working on crafting thesis statements.

Why It Works

- Using paint strips that are taped together, students are easily able to see which evidence matches which claim.
- Since paint strips have a specific number of sections/blocks, students know how long the assignment needs to be.
- It has a clear and distinct focus: claims and evidence.

Modifications

- Assign a specific claim to students. Have them look for evidence that supports the provided claim.
- Have students draft claims in one lesson and then in a follow-up lesson, have them locate supporting evidence for the claim.

Extensions

- Use multiple sources for claim support. Assign a specific color paint strip for each specific source. Stack the paint strips so that each claim has support from multiple sources.
- Have students use the textual evidence to draft fully involved argumentative essays with supporting evidence.

Digital Direction

- Use a digital tool like Miro to create a mind map of the claims and evidence.
- When working on textual evidence practice, have students create a web quest that takes their user to online sources that support their initial claim.
- Have students share claims and evidence online using a program like Jamboard, Miro, or Sketchboard.

Lesson Lead-Ins

- Use this strategy as a lead-in for units on argumentative writing.
- Connect this to the Mix and Match Remix on page 146.

STOP/GO SOURCES

Teaching the skill of source credibility is something that all students must master if they plan to be effective academic writers. Knowing how to critique a source for credibility can help students determine what material should be included and utilized in their writing.

As more and more students turn to the internet for research material, it's more crucial than ever to address the nature of credibility and how to critically examine sources. Plus, with so much material available instantaneously, knowing which sources are the best ones to use for a specific topic or genre can aid writers in developing well-planned and developed compositions. One way to do this is through targeted training that focuses on credible and noncredible sources by providing students the opportunity to critically examine a source for bias, check the author's expertise, and more. Stop/Go Sources can help!

Putting It to Work

1. Display a research topic on the board or somewhere for students to see.
2. Put students with a partner so they can complete this collaboratively.
3. Allow students to use technology (phones, laptops, iPads, etc.) to run a quick search on the topic listed. Give students sticky notes to record their results.
4. Allow about 5 to 10 minutes for students to look for websites and sources that would have information on the class topic.
5. Have students share with the class any of the sources they found. Record them on the board or somewhere for the class to see.
6. Begin the discussion of credibility. Ask students questions about credibility:
   - How do you determine if a source is credible?
   - What should you look for?
   - What are some red flags when examining sources?

(You may consider providing students with the Credibility Checklist on the companion website to help them sift through the recorded sources. Visit **resources.corwin.com/WritingWorkouts.**)

7. As a class, begin to classify which of the sources that the class located would be considered credible and which ones would not.

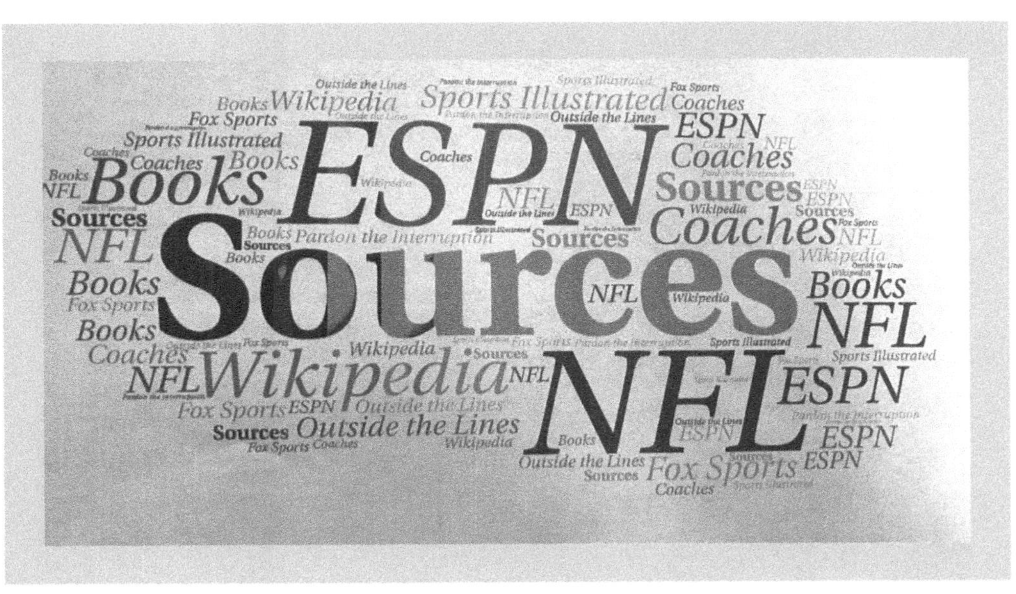

8. Once the class has determined which sources are credible and which ones aren't, provide students with a list of five to seven new topics. These should be topics that students either have seen before or topics they will encounter at a later date. This helps give this strategic lesson purpose, serving either as an opportunity for revisiting something or prepping for future learning.

9. Give each pair of students two paint strips—one that is red and one that is green. Use configurations like the ones shown here for best results.

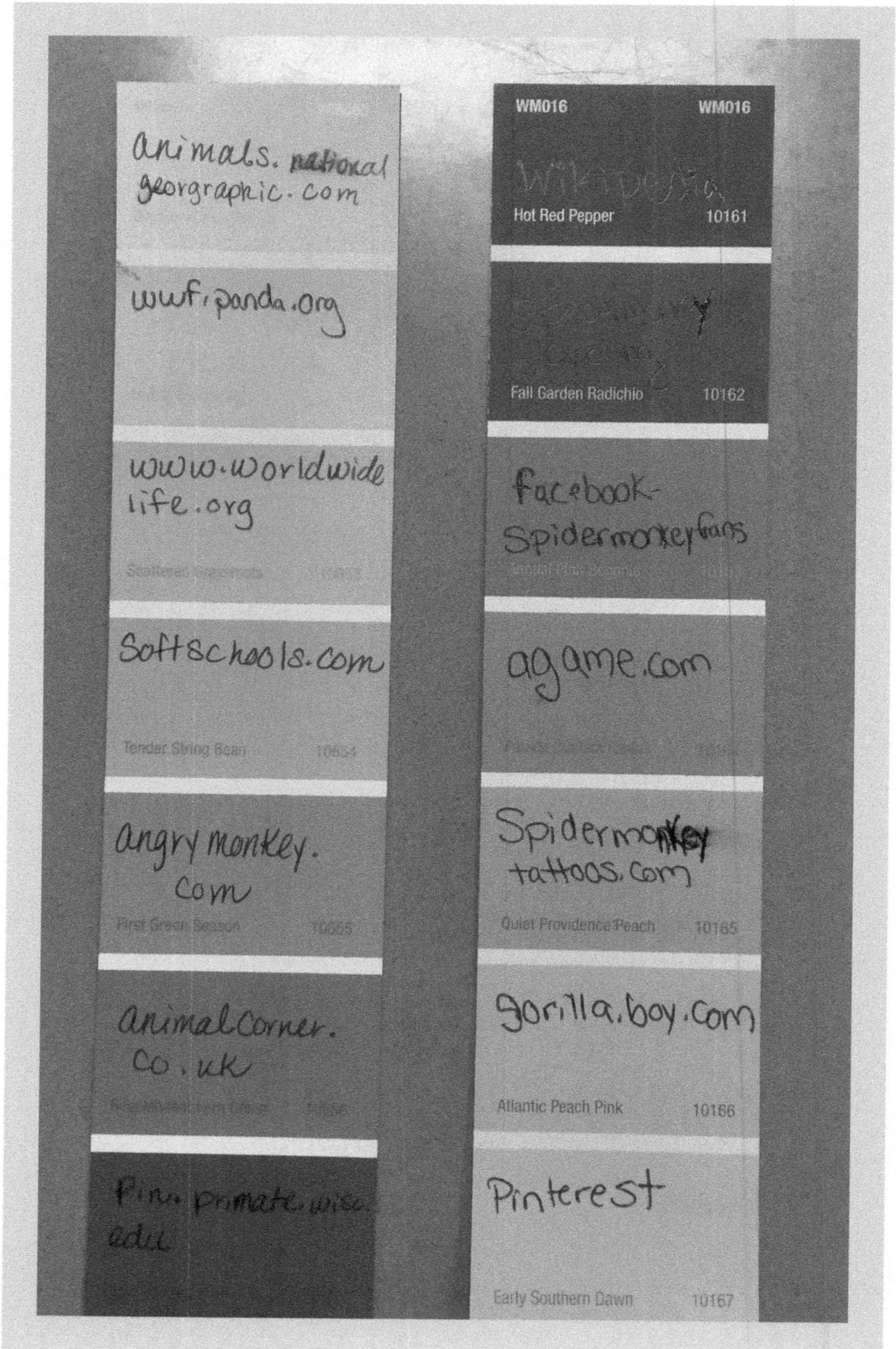

animals.national georgraphic.com
wwf.panda.org
www.worldwide life.org
Softschools.com
Tender String Bean 10654
angry monkey. com
First Green Season 10655
animalcorner. co.uk
Pin. primate.wisc. edu

WM016 WM016
Hot Red Pepper 10161
Fall Garden Radichio 10162
facebook-Spidermonkeyfans
agame.com
Spidermonkey tattoos.com
Quiet Providence Peach 10165
gorilla.boy.com
Atlantic Peach Pink 10166
Pinterest
Early Southern Dawn 10167

10. Have students choose one of the topics from the provided list and complete a web search of the topic. Using the Credibility Checklist, have students list credible sources on the Go Paint Strip (the green one) and sources that are not credible on the Stop Paint Strip (the red one).
11. Have students share their findings.

When to Use It

- Use this when students are working on research writing or genres that require them to integrate textual evidence into their compositions.
- When you want students to evaluate and critique a variety of sources.
- Use this as a strategy lesson for research writing and argument.

Why It Works

- Because students are focusing on a specific skill, it is easier to determine if a source is a Stop Source or a Go Source.
- By using a list of criteria for each type of source, students can easily evaluate selected sources.
- Because you use paint strips to collect the information, students automatically know how many sources they need to include.
- Color coding the sources helps students remember which ones go where.

Modifications

- Divide the class into two groups. Have half of the class locate Stop Sources and half of the class locate Go Sources.
- Have students start with Stop Sources and then progress to Go Sources.
- Provide students with a yellow paint strip as well. This can be used to collect any sources that they are not sure about and need assistance determining if they are credible.

Extensions

- Extend this to research writing on the sample topics provided in the initial lesson. Because students have already done a research dig on the topic, they can refer back to the Stop/Go Sources to determine where to start.
- Have students add a second paint strip that is a different color to collect facts from each of the credible sources.
- Extend this to the Mix and Match strategy (Harper, 2022).

Quick Tip!

This type of lesson works well with extended research writing because it preempts comments or challenges with students who tell you they can't find any information or they do not know whether a particular source is credible or not. Since this research dig was done prior, you can always refer them back to the Stop/Go Sources for assistance.

Digital Direction

- Use a computer program like PowerPoint, Google Slides, or Prezi to collect the different types of sources.
- Create a mock Pinterest Page of credible and noncredible sources by using a computer application like PicCollage, Glogster, or Canva.

Lesson Lead-Ins

- Use this as a natural lead-in for lessons that focus on research or integration of textual evidence.
- Connect this to lessons that focus on the quality of textual evidence in the form of Stop/Go Sources (Harper, 2017).

MUSICAL TRANSITIONS

Music is certainly an engaging way in which to incorporate literacy skills and strategies. Part of this is simply because most students listen to music in their daily lives and have extensive experience with it. Students do not have to be musicians to learn from and enjoy music. Even students who are not musically gifted or take part in any kind of musical extracurricular activities listen to the radio and personal playlists, or they hear music when watching television shows and movies.

I recently noticed that a song playing on the radio was a mashup of multiple songs that seamlessly transitioned into the next. The first song's last lyric served as the connector to the second song's first sentence. This continued until the mashup ended, and it prompted me to think about how this was a tangible, auditory example of transition sentences.

Have you seen the movie *Pitch Perfect*? If not, watch the Riff Off scene where the a cappella groups have to sing songs based on a category, but then smoothly transition from song to song without missing a beat. These are transitions at their best! In other examples of mashups or riff offs, participants stick with a theme and all songs must relate to that theme. No matter how you do it, Musical Transitions is another great opportunity to incorporate music into a literacy task.

Putting It to Work

1. Play students the Riff Off scene from *Pitch Perfect* or share with them an example of a music mashup that connects multiple songs with a common transition. You can find examples of these online, and they are frequent residents of satellite radio morning shows. The goal is to provide students with an auditory example of multiple works that are connected by a transition.
2. Have students listen to or watch the clip once just to experience the text. For the second go-round, ask them to specifically listen for ways the artists are transitioning from song to song.
3. Allow students to discuss in small groups the transitions they noticed and why/how they were effective.
4. Connect this concept back to writing by reminding students that transitional phrases help writers connect thoughts, ideas, and paragraphs.
5. Provide students with a word bank of transitional phrases. (Check out the companion website for a sample Transition Word Bank.)
6. Using the same writing sample, have students use their word bank to add transitional phrases to appropriate sections of the writing. Model an example for the students so they can see what this process and revision task would look like.

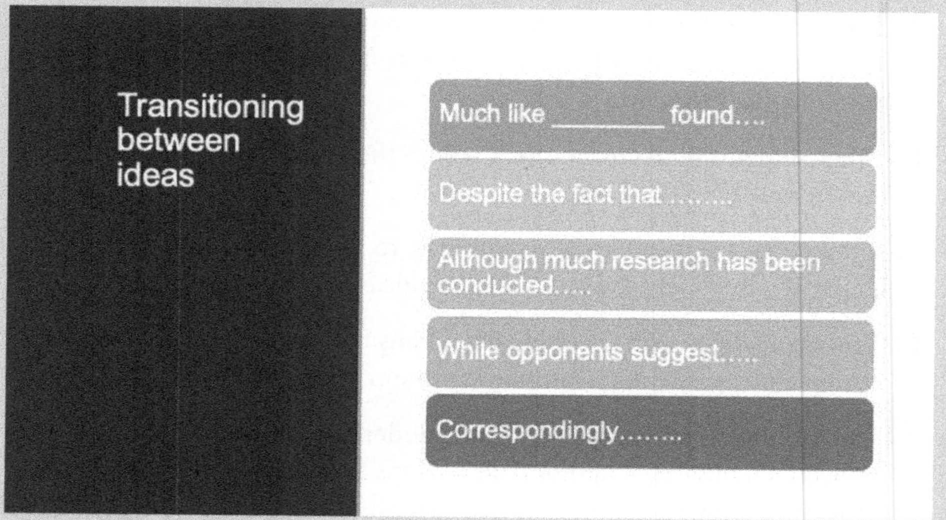

Transitioning between ideas

Much like ________ found....

Despite the fact that ....

Although much research has been conducted.....

While opponents suggest.....

Correspondingly........

7. Discuss the changes as a class.

8. Next, have students look at one of their own extended, multi-paragraph writings. Using the same word bank, have them revise to include transitional phrases in their own writings.

When to Use It

- To connect music back to revision and writing.
- When you want students to have a tangible, real-world example of transitions in writing.
- When you are working on multiparagraph compositions where transitional sentences should be employed.

Why It Works

- Since music is used as a mentor text, it offers students yet another example beyond the traditional.
- Using a word bank of phrases can aid students as they revise for this specific purpose. This way, they have a list of possibilities that might be employed.

Modifications

- Divide the transitional phrases into different types: ones that indicate sequence of events; ones that indicate shifts from concept to concept, etc. This can help students determine which ones they should use where.
- Put students into collaborative groups with their own separate paragraphs. Have them draft transitional sentences that would connect each group's paragraph to another.
- Use image cards instead and have students write transitional sentences that get the reader from one image to the next.

Extensions

- Use this as an extension to the Four Block Writing (Harper, 2017).
- Have students connect this to the Prepositional Phrase Poems on page 251 by having them write a Transitional Phrase Poem.
- Ask students to collect additional transitional phrases that could be used in their writings.
- Connect certain phrases to specific genres so students know which ones work best where.
- Extend this to the Wordless Picture Books writing on page 107 by having students revise to integrate transitional phrases.

Digital Direction

- Have students collect transitional phrases using a Wordle program like https://www.wordclouds.com/ or https://www.mentimeter.com/.
- Collect transitional phrases and add visual or pictorial examples using PicCollage, Canva, or Glogster.

Lesson Lead-Ins

- Connect this to lessons on multiparagraph compositions.
- Use this as an easy introduction to revision because it focuses on the integration of a specific phrase or sentence.

WORDLESS PICTURE BOOKS

Wordless picture books are not just for primary classrooms. Instead, they are valuable resources that can be used in middle and secondary classrooms as well. Plus, some wordless books often have sophisticated illustrations that warrant careful examination and many times have complex story lines that require students to reread sections to fully understand the message.

In primary grades, there are literacy standards that address a student's ability to match words to illustrations. Students in upper grade levels can benefit from using picture books to craft solid sentences and extended paragraphs that correspond to the images presented in the work. Using wordless picture books for the creation of extended written responses allows students to start with a low-stakes text (wordless picture books) and expound on them as they develop solid, extended written compositions. Plus, they can move beyond simply making sure that the words and images match but that each sentence matches the one that comes before and the one that comes after.

Putting It to Work

1. Use a wordless picture book as a mentor text for this lesson. Some of my favorites are:
   - *Flotsam* by David Wiesner
   - *Unspoken: A Story From the Underground Railroad* by Henry Cole
   - *Journey* by Aaron Becker
   - *Pancakes for Breakfast* by Tomie dePaola
   - *Tuesday* by David Wiesner
2. Purchase two copies of the mentor text you plan to use. (Two copies are needed since most publishers print on the front and back of the page.)
3. Cut the pages out so that the story is now in separate pieces. Put each page in a protective plastic sleeve.
4. Number each page so you will know the order of the entire book if page numbers are not already printed.
5. Show the students one of the pages on a document camera.
6. Provide them with a notecard or sentence strip.

While some may argue reading a wordless picture book isn't really reading, it actually is. Because reading is about meaning making and understanding, when students read images and develop a story or create meaning based on what they have seen, they are reading. And remember, texts are not restricted to books that have words. Texts can be images, pictures, dramatic interpretations, and more.

Quick Tip!

Don't want to cut up the book? Purchase multiple copies and put students in groups with specific pages as their focus.

7. Instruct students to look at the image and draft a sentence that describes what is occurring in the sample image.

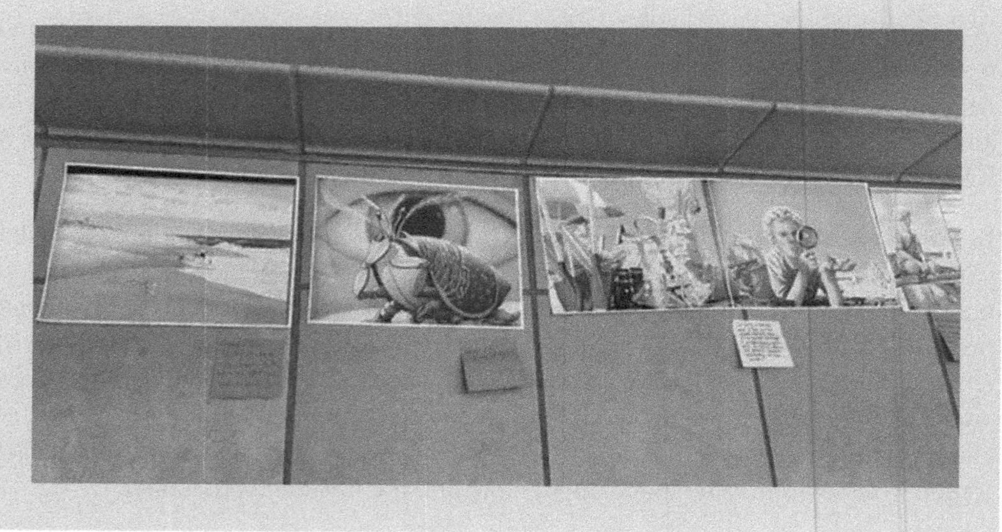

8. Share with the class. Note how some of the sentences might vary despite the fact that everyone used the same image.
9. Pass out one individual page per student. (Each student should get their own unique page from the book.)
10. Have students repeat the activity they did earlier. They should draft a sentence that depicts the image they have been given.
11. Once students have written their sentence, start building the story again.
12. Call out the page numbers starting from page one. Have students lay their images on the floor in the hallway or classroom and put their sentence right below it.

13. Repeat this for the entire book.
14. Once the entire story has been rebuilt, divide students into groups.
15. Have each group walk out into the hallway and read the story. When doing this, they should look at the images and the accompanying sentences. Provide them with a notecard or sticky note to make notations of sentences that need revisions, don't work where they are, or any other noticings.
16. Once everyone has viewed the entire story, discuss their observations as a class.
17. Remind students of the whole class activity they completed before they started the activity. In that example, students were only responsible for looking at their specific image and drafting one sentence that supported that image. However, once they rebuilt the story, not only do the sentences have to match the individual images, but they also have to match the sentences that came before and after. Thus, building a coherent story relies on much more than simply matching words to images.
18. Ask students if there are certain pages or sections that should be revised. (These should have been recorded on their notecards or sticky notes).
19. With a partner, have students choose which image's sentence they plan to revise.
20. Give them a blank notecard and have them revise the target section.
21. Once the revisions are complete, have the class go back into the hallway, and reread the story with the revisions.
22. Discuss with the class.

When to Use It

- As a way to incorporate literature in the classroom.
- If you have striving readers in your class who are reading below grade level, as well as students learning English as a new language.
- When you want to get students up and moving.

Why It Works

- Because it starts with an illustration or images, students are not limited by their alphanumeric reading proficiency.
- Since it is a wordless picture book, students may feel less intimidated by the writing.
- It gets students up and moving.
- It teaches a variety of skills including drafting and revision.

Modifications

- Use a book that has words and black out the words. Have students write their sentences and then compare them to the original ones from the text.
- Instead of using an entire wordless book, use scenes from a book or divide the book into parts so it is completed in sections.
- Have students draft words for each picture first and then progress to sentences.

Extensions

- Have students create their own wordless picture book using photos or images.
- Use scenes from silent movies for students to create accompanying scripts.
- Extend this by having students complete the NVA^2 from page 66 for the image before they write their sentences.

Digital Direction

- Load the individual pages into Google Slide or PowerPoint and have students draft their sentences using the digital program.
- Have students record their sentences over their presentation using a program like Vimeo.
- Brainstorm possible sentences on Miro, Jamboard, or Stormboard.

Lesson Lead-Ins

- Use this as a lead-in for NVA^2 on page 66.
- Connect the revision aspect of this lesson to strategies in Chapter 6.

SOCIAL MEDIA PROFILE SLIDE

If you examine social media, you can find a lot of information about an individual on their bio or "About me" page. Dating profiles are some of the best sources for facts (or loosely based facts) about an individual. Think about some of the information that different social media sites ask about an individual. Typically, they include

- Name
- Interesting facts
- Things they like to do
- Images related to them
- Background information
- Career info

While this is not an exhaustive list, you get the idea. This is where people get a snapshot of who an individual is. Fortunately, this real-world application is a perfect model for writing in the real world and can work beautifully in the ELA classroom. Writing a Social Media profile slide about a character can help students connect with characters more deeply, which can help not only with reading comprehension but also in writing character studies, researching about historical figures, and providing more detail about a topic or theme.

Putting It to Work

Note: It would not hurt to model this entire activity as a whole class to ensure success.

1. Share a variety of social media platforms with students. Focus specifically on the sections that address the user's profile or bio.
2. Ask students to consider the items included in those components.
3. Show students the example Social Media template on the companion website.

Albert Bandura

Picture of Theorist

- Known for social cognitive theory, social learning theory, self efficacy
- Most likely to advocate for children
- Would enjoy hanging out with Bobo dolls
- Violence is not my jam.
- The last book I read was...Be Kind
- When I am not working to help children, you'll find me self reflecting while traveling.
- Swipe right if you like being showered with personal **attention, retention** of all your likes and dislikes, like **repeat** dates, and would enjoy a partner who **motivates** you.

4. Explain that you will be using this template for the creation of a Social Media slide for a character in a novel or extended work. Depending on your class, you might choose to have your students replicate the profile slide of a specific social media site or you may use a more generic approach.
5. Provide students with a topic list of characters or concepts.
6. Have students choose one from the list to create their own Social Media slide.
7. Using the provided template, students should complete the slide for their chosen character/topic.
8. Share with the class.

Quick Tip!

Use this as a fact-finding mission for characters, historical figures, or concepts. You can also focus on types of characters (protagonist, antagonist, etc.).

When to Use It

- As a way to connect real-world research and fact representation to the academic setting.
- When you want students to practice the skill of research in a low-stakes setting.
- As a quick drop in writing task that addresses a specific purpose/skill.

Why It Works

- Using a ready-made template with the requirements already listed can help students as they begin their writing on the character or research on the topic.

- It has connections to the real world that many would be familiar with.
- Due to its short nature and purpose, students can complete the task in a shorter amount of time.

Modifications

- Have some ready-made facts available for students. Allow them to choose which ones to include.
- Use a fact bank that individuals can pull from if needed.
- Have students create their own profile slide first so they can practice the writing.

Extensions

- Have students extend this by drafting posts or comments for the user.
- Get students to connect with their peers by using the profiles to determine which characters would be social media friends and which ones would be blocked.
- Create connected hashtags for each profile.

Digital Direction

- Have students design their slide using a program like Canva.
- Upload the slides to Google Classroom and have students comment on their peers' creations.
- Have students locate examples of effective and eye catching social media profiles and use those as mentor texts from the web.

Lesson Lead-Ins

- Use this as a low-stakes introduction into research and fact finding.
- Connect this to writing engagements like biographies, memoirs, and autobiographies.
- Work this in as an opener for character studies.

POP-UP POEMS

Poetry, for some, including myself, is a little intimidating. Yes, there are fewer words included on the page, but coming up with the right ones? Sometimes it is easier said than done. Plus, for whatever reason, many are conditioned to think that all poems must rhyme, which, of course, is not true. There are so many different types and formats of poems and considerable examples that can be used as mentor texts. Since many students have written exclusively in prose, offering opportunities to interact and engage with different genres of expression can be a welcome change of pace.

Utilizing art and peer collaboration, the Pop-Up Poems lesson offers a unique approach to drafting poetry by progressing through several experiences: reading aloud, listening, observing, and drafting. Students are not simply creating a poem, but they are experiencing it as it emerges on the page, framed by a visual image that inspired the word creation and selection. Pop-Up Poems can help nurture the poet in all students.

Putting It to Work

1. Open the lesson by showing students a photograph. Give students a sticky note and have them write a word that describes or is related to the displayed image. Stick these words on an adjacent piece of chart paper. (You will come back to this opening activity in a bit; stay tuned.)

2. Start by reading students a descriptive text. This needs to be an excerpt with rich detail, lots of adjectives, and highly descriptive sentences. Some of my favorites are children's books by Diane Sibert including *Mojave*, *Sierra*, *Heartland*, and *Mississippi*. Other options are:
   - *Red Sings from Treetops: A Year in Colors* by Joyce Sidman
   - *Green on Green* by Dianne White
   - *A Gift for Amma: Market Day in India* by Meera Sriram
   - *Southwest Sunrise* by Nikki Grimes
   - *Saturdays and Teacakes* by Lester Laminack

Read the story or excerpt twice. The first time, you want students to simply hear the story. When they hear it a second time, they can pay closer attention and think about what to draw.

3. Don't show the students the pictures if you are reading them a picture book.

4. Instruct students to draw what they hear. You might offer an example, like, "For example, if I hear details about a field with sunflowers, I would draw that on my paper."

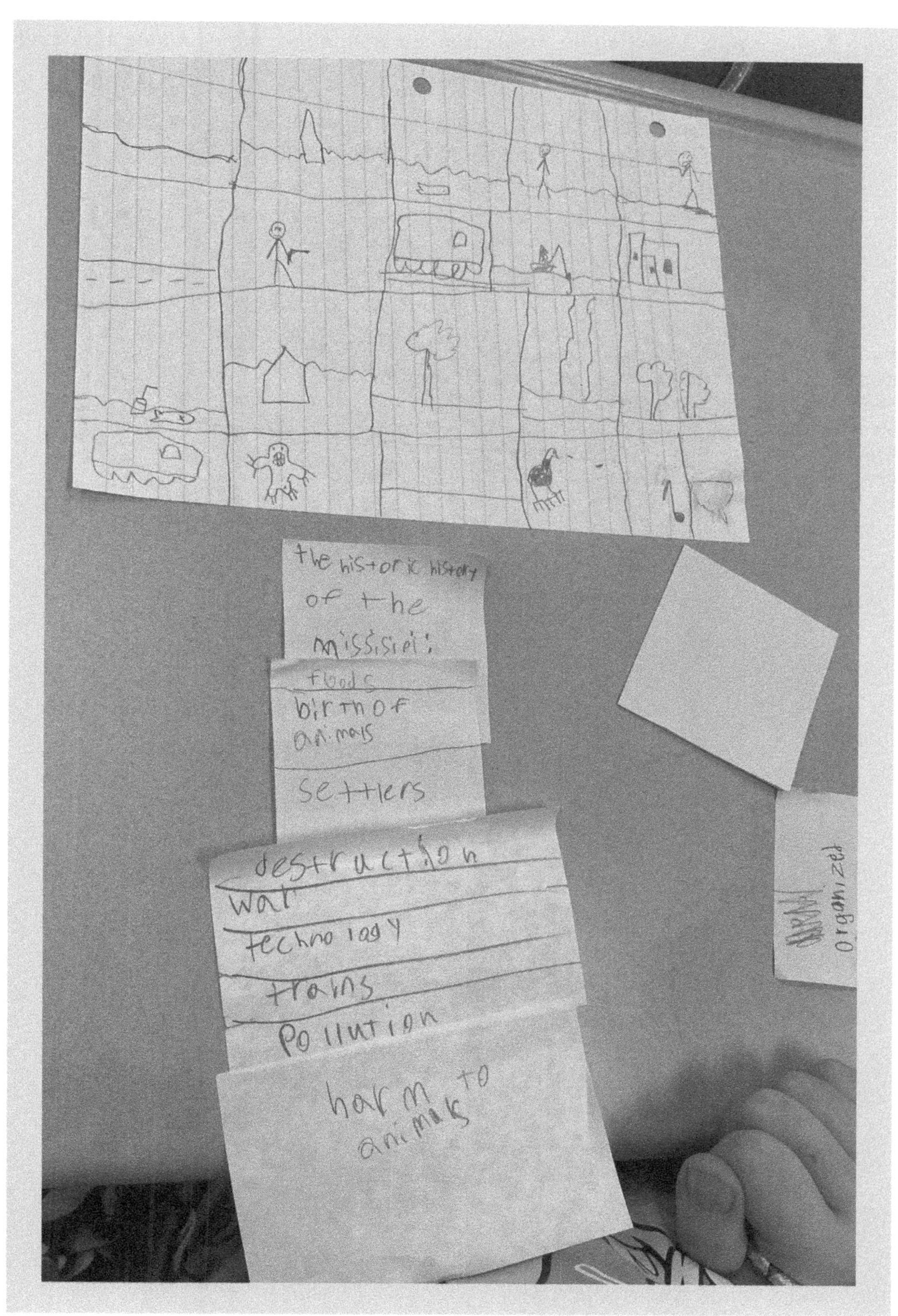

5. After you finish reading the story aloud, have students finish up their drawings and then clear their desks of everything but their drawings.

6. Give each student a stack of sticky notes.

7. Inform students that they will circulate around the room, looking at each of their classmate's artwork.

8. As they observe, they should write a descriptive word on a sticky note and stick it on their classmate's desk. The word they choose should describe or relate to the image drawn.

9. After students have circulated and seen all the art in the classroom, they will return to their desks. At their desks they should now have a collection of words written by their classmates.

Quick Tip!

Make sure you spend a few minutes reminding students of what is considered appropriate and what isn't. For this lesson, students are not critiquing each other's work but rather are helping them develop a word bank from which their peers can use as starters for their writing.

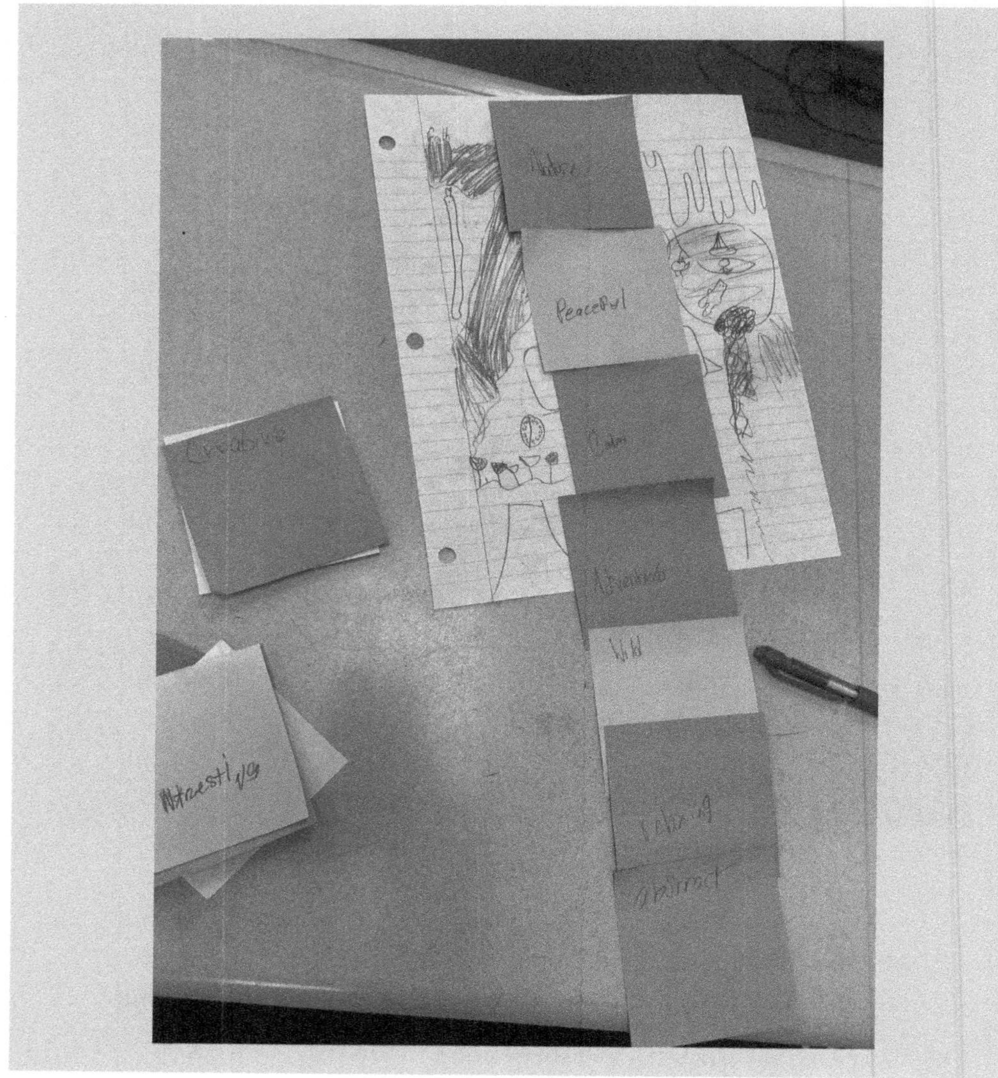

10. Using the words provided by their classmates, students will now construct a poem.

11. Before students begin constructing their own poems, model how this might be done with the sample photo you opened class with in Step 1.

12. Using the words students wrote on sticky notes in Step 1, model how a writer might construct a poem using the word bank. You don't have to use all the words, but try to use as many as possible. If you need to add filler words, record those on a different color note so you can see which were originals and which ones were added.

13. Have students use the words at their desks to construct their own poems. Follow the same procedure with filler words by providing them with additional blank sticky notes in a different color.

14. Share with the class.

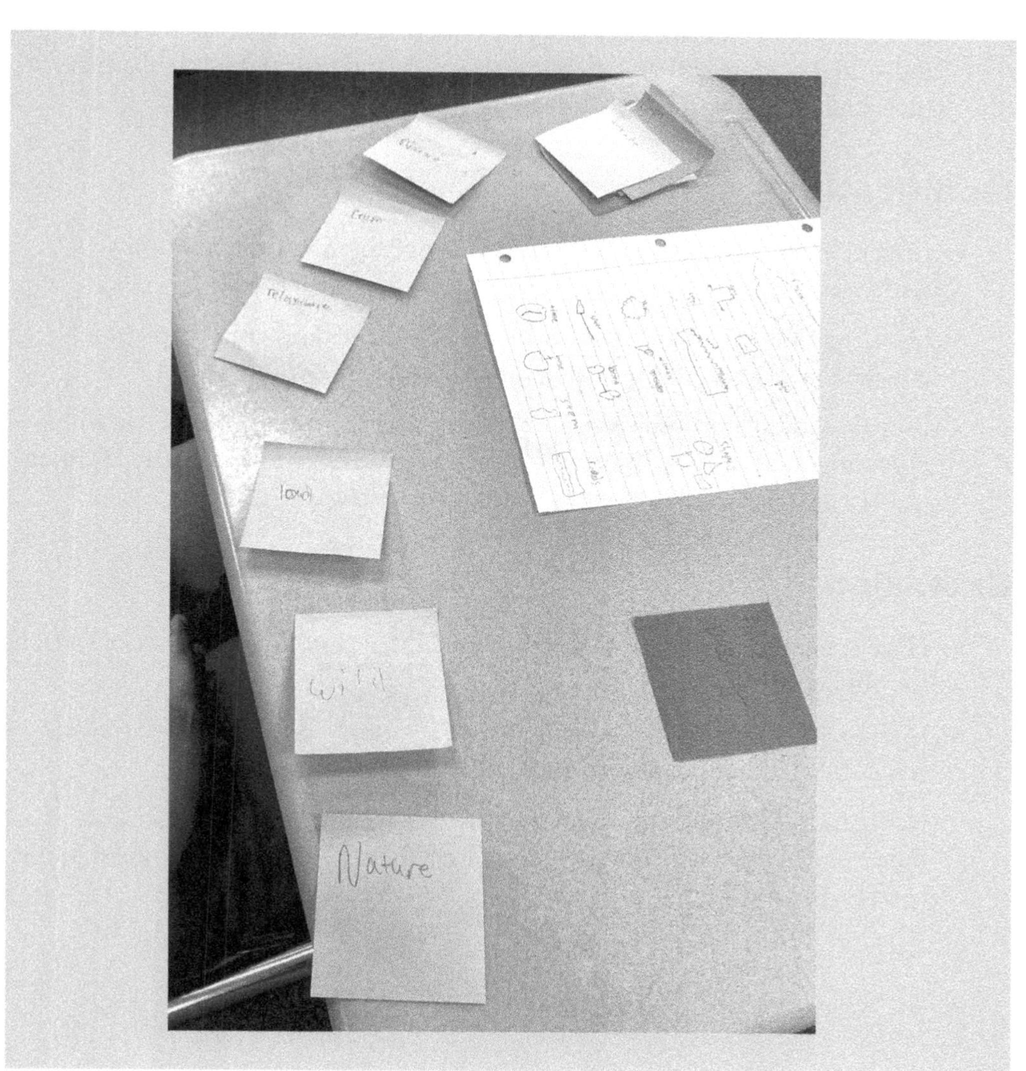

When to Use It

- As a way to connect art to poetry and capitalize on art integration.
- When you want students to practice constructing poetry in a low-stakes setting.
- As a way to focus on visualization and description when reading and writing.

Why It Works

- Having students draw as they listen can promote the skill of visualization, which can help improve comprehension.
- Using a word bank of phrases can aid students as they write for this specific purpose.
- High interest literature that is richly descriptive can help students construct a solid visual representation of the material.
- Comparing the different artwork that students create demonstrates how individual readers and writers interpret words and texts differently based on their individual background knowledge.

Modifications

- Instead of having students write a poem, have them write a descriptive sentence.
- Have students use old magazines to cut out images and create a pictorial collage that represents the material presented in the reading.
- Provide students with some example descriptor words they might use when observing their peer's writing. You might use Paint Strip Vocabulary (Harper, 2017) as a connected strategy for this lesson.

Extensions

- Have students group/classify the class-generated word bank by parts of speech (nouns, adjectives, verbs, etc.).
- Encourage students to collaborate with a partner to create a poem in two voices like the Partner Poems on page 254.
- Have students display the artwork in the classroom and then redistribute their created poems. See if the classmates can match the correct poem to the correct drawing.

Digital Direction

- Use a program like PicCollage or Canva for students to create their own digital collage.
- Have students use a virtual drawing application like Sketchpad for students who want to draw digitally.

Lesson Lead-Ins

- Use this as an opener for the NVA^2 activity on page 66.
- Connect this to the Wordless Picture Books lesson on page 107.
- Use this as a lead-in to lessons that focus on visualization for comprehension.

HIGH INTENSITY TRAINING

When it comes to physical fitness, high intensity training is definitely a staple in an effective workout regime. Those high intensity days get your heart rate up, make you sweat, and certainly make you sore the next day! However, not every workout day can be a high intensity day; if it was, the majority of us would not go back to the gym!

When training students to be healthy writers, the same applies. If students experience too many writing days that idle on seventy-five, chances are, many will crash. For students to have overall writing wellness, they need to have days where they stretch, days for rest and revision, warmup opportunities, and high intensity days. Mixing writing engagements that vary in intensity can help build stronger, more capable writers. Plus, it can help prevent writing burnout.

While every day doesn't need to be a high intensity day, there are benefits to this type of writing. First, much of the assessment-based writing that students complete requires them to write extended, fully developed compositions in a short amount of time. Similarly, other writing tasks require students to develop fully involved, well-developed compositions that are rather lengthy and are created over an extended portion of time. Though these are both different types of tasks, they are both high intensity due to the nature of the final product. Offering students opportunities to train for these demanding types of writing tasks can set up students to be as successful as possible in more high-stakes settings.

How often have you taught students who never turn in their final drafts? How about ones who address multiple components of the prompt but fail to address something else, which results in severe grading penalties? As a middle-grades teacher, I often had students who I saw writing and working daily on an extended writing task (a persuasive essay, historical fiction narrative, informational essay, etc.), but sometimes on Day 4, they didn't have their rough drafts, had lost all their research, or couldn't find an important part of their paper. I also had students who did all the work up front—they completed the research, drafted their arguments, stated their claims—but never turned in the final essay. As a result, they received a failing grade on the full assignment even though they had completed several components of the writing task. Writing tasks that require multiple days to complete involve significant revision and feedback throughout the process. Longer writing assignments also require stamina, appropriate pacing, and ongoing feedback. High intensity training can help prepare students for these aspects of an assignment.

Training for different types of tasks at varying intensities *AND* offering students spaces and places to receive validation for the work they completed (when possible) can help build writing communities that nurture and grow writers. And while as a literacy educator, I am constantly striving to build this type of writing community for my teachers and students, every so often, I am stopped in my tracks with something that gives me pause and offers an opportunity for more reflection on instruction.

Consider this real-world example. Recently I attended my girls' first long-course swim meet of the season. During this meet, several of the swimmers on our team competed in the 200-meter butterfly. Now, if you have never seen this race in action, you know it is grueling—arms flying out of the water, chests lurching up to the sky, and feet kicking in perfect symphony. It is beautiful, but it is hard. It is the perfect example of a physical endeavor that is demanding and highly complex, requires proper pacing during the race, and involves training for stamina.

While several of our swimmers completed this race successfully, many did not. A few were disqualified for illegal strokes, and some swimmers made it to the 100-meter mark and got out of the pool. That's right; they quit and got out of the pool. Couldn't and wouldn't complete another lap.

In this example, part of their ability to complete this strenuous task was directly related to the training they received that prepared them for this difficult race. Those who successfully finished the race were most often the ones who had trained for it in practice, executed drills that were extended and high intensity, and integrated training days that allowed their bodies to recover from a grueling practice routine. Those were the successful swimmers, the ones who were able to finish, disqualified or not. Notice that the disqualified swimmers are included in the group of successful swimmers. Why? They completed the task, and that should count for something, right?

Now what about those kids who got out of the pool in the middle of the race. After 100 meters they threw in the towel. Is there no hope for them to be successful in the 200-meter fly? Of course not, but they need to train for it and be ready to perform this high intensity race that requires a sophisticated cocktail of strength, stamina, technique, and mental preparation. They must take part in training that helps them get to the end goal of completing that race. This might mean focusing on completing the 100-meter fly at their next few meets and then moving to the 200 meter. Progressive training can help their performance by building strength, experience, and confidence.

But there is yet another component that affected the outcomes. Those who made it to the end, disqualified or not, had something that those who got out of the pool may not have had on that day. They believed they could do it. It might have been ugly; it might not have been legal; but they were mentally focused on finishing. They did not quit. How many students have you taught who may struggle, but they always try? They don't give up. It makes a difference on their performance, doesn't it? They've got grit.

Here's something else worth noting. One of the swimmers was disqualified at the very end of the 200 fly for taking three freestyle pulls before he finished the race. He subsequently climbed out of the pool and threw up on deck. He finished, legal or not. There was no doubt that kid had given it his all even though he got disqualified. He saw the task through to the end.

Now, I have thought a lot about that one kid's race. He successfully completed 195 meters of the butterfly, but on the last five meters, he deviated from the requirements of that race, and as a result, nothing he did in the 195 meters prior counted. Nothing. One hundred ninety-five meters of crushing physicality was erased by three quick freestyle pulls.

How does this compare to writing, you might ask? What about our students who do work on 4 out of 5 days, but do not perform on the fifth, which happens to be an assessment day? Do they get credit for the work they completed those 4 days? Sometimes, yes. Most often, no. Like the swimmer who swam 195 meters of fly and then did three freestyle pulls, all their effort on those prior days can be erased by one assessment, one grade. So as writing teachers, how do we make those 195 meters count?

First, let's look at how we assess. If you recall, we've talked about how all writing tasks don't need to be graded. In fact, a significant portion of what kids do in daily writing is really done to help them understand content, process material, and think through their lessons. When developing extended writing engagements that are high intensity due to the time devoted to the task, thinking through ways you might assess can help make certain that those 195 meters count. When we design writing tasks that build up to a crescendo, teachers can create daily assessment opportunities so that all those writing pieces do count. For example, when looking at the day-to-day progression of many of these lessons in this chapter, there are opportunities for assessment daily. Many times, if students can see that what they are doing today matters—and let's face it, sometimes grades are what matters—it's more likely that they will complete at least part of the task.

This chapter looks a little bit different than the others in this book because the focus is on extended, fully involved writing tasks. As a result, you will see that each writing lesson is completed over several days. Extended writing tasks don't just happen in one class period; instead, they build on each other over time. Adding on to each bit of writing that is completed every day can help students manage writing engagements that are more demanding and require multiple components for successful completion. Building from day to day can ease the anxiety that some students feel when presented with writing longer, more involved writing compositions. Plus, when lessons progress, students are not required to reinvent the wheel every single time they sit down to write. Instead, they are adding to a composition that they are already familiar with.

Now, some of these lessons and strategies could be pulled out and used as Targeted Training days as well. Likewise, there are some Targeted Training lessons that could and should be dropped into these High Intensity Days. As a result, you'll find a table of related Targeted Training lessons at the end of each High Intensity writing piece. That way, you can easily determine what strategies and lesson ideas would best be integrated with the extended pieces described here.

While there is a day-to-day schedule included, don't hesitate to modify the time limits. If your students need 2 days to complete one part of the task, take 2 days. If you find that you can combine 2 days' worth of instruction into one, by all means, do so. Similarly, if there are days you skip totally or replace with another lesson, that is perfectly fine. You do what is best for your students.

Remember also that high intensity doesn't just mean tasks that take multiple days. In fact, some of the cold start lessons might be considered high intensity for some students, and some of the stretch lessons might feel that way for some. The point of this chapter is to provide you with some ready-to-teach lessons that are extended to allow students the opportunities to write on the same topic for multiple days.

DESCRIPTIVE WRITING WITH CALENDARS

When working on writing tasks that are descriptive in nature, an emphasis on showing over telling is important. Sometimes, it is easier for writers to get into the habit of using stale descriptors or not fully diving into the topic while employing multiple descriptive writing tactics, which may include visual imagery, sensory components, figurative language, and more.

Working on descriptive writing tasks in chunks and adding more detail at different points of the writing can aid writers in creating rich compositions. Plus, sometimes it works best for students to start off with some ideas from a word or sentence bank to develop solid writing pieces. One of my favorite ways to integrate descriptive writing in my classroom started with the NVA^2 strategy using images from old calendars. By extending the writing over the course of a few days, students were able to develop extended descriptive writing pieces in a setting that was flexible and inviting, and Descriptive Writing With Calendars was born.

Putting It to Work

Day 1

1. Collect a variety of photos for this type of writing. Photos from old calendars work well for this. (If you do not have access to old calendars, simply locate images online using one of the image repositories listed in the NVA^2 strategy on page 66.)
2. Start by completing the NVA^2 strategy on page 66. This entire strategy serves as the Day 1 lesson. This lesson has students focus on using nouns, verbs, and adjectives from a student-generated word bank to write a descriptive sentence of an image.

Consider starting each day with a read-aloud that is highly descriptive. This can offer yet another example of what the writing students are creating might sound like. Here are some suggestions:

- *Night in the Country and The Relatives Came* by Cynthia Rylant
- *See the Ocean* by Estelle Condra
- *Salvador Late or Early* by Sandra Cisneros
- *The Salamander Room* by Anne Mazer
- *Crown: An Ode to the Fresh Cut* by Derrick Barnes

Day 2

1. Have students go back to the image they used for their individual writing on the NVA^2 strategy. Remember, these images should be very different. Some students might have fall scenes, some have images of a circus, others have images of a sporting event. The point is to make certain they have different types of images.

2. Provide them with a notecard.
3. Have students write multiple sentences using their word bank so that they have an entire paragraph on their notecard.
4. Post each student's image on the wall in the classroom.
5. Take up the notecards and redistribute them to different students.
6. Have students circulate around the classroom to see if they can match up their written description to the correct image.

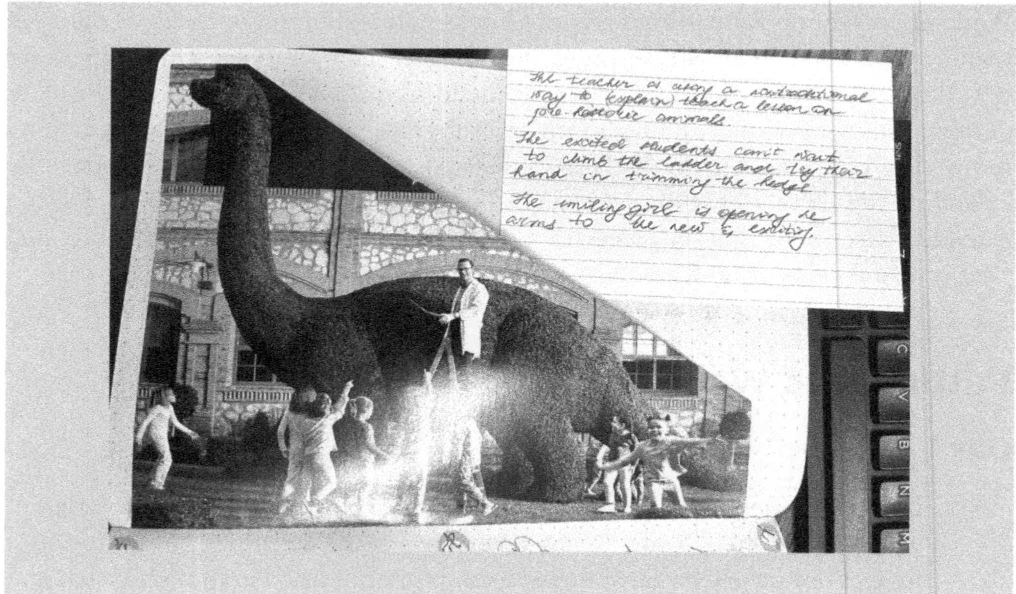

Day 3

1. Repeat the NVA² activity on page 66.
2. This time, give each student a similar image. For example, you might focus on only winter scenes, images from a football game, wildlife scenes from Africa, and so on. Simply make certain that everyone is writing about similar images.
3. Give students a notecard and have them repeat Steps 2 through 6 from Day 2.
4. Once students have located their matches, have them write on the back of the notecard which details were most helpful when determining which image went with their notecard.
5. If any students are unable to locate their appropriate match, have them meet with the writer and offer suggestions for revision that would add the detail needed to determine which picture is the companion.

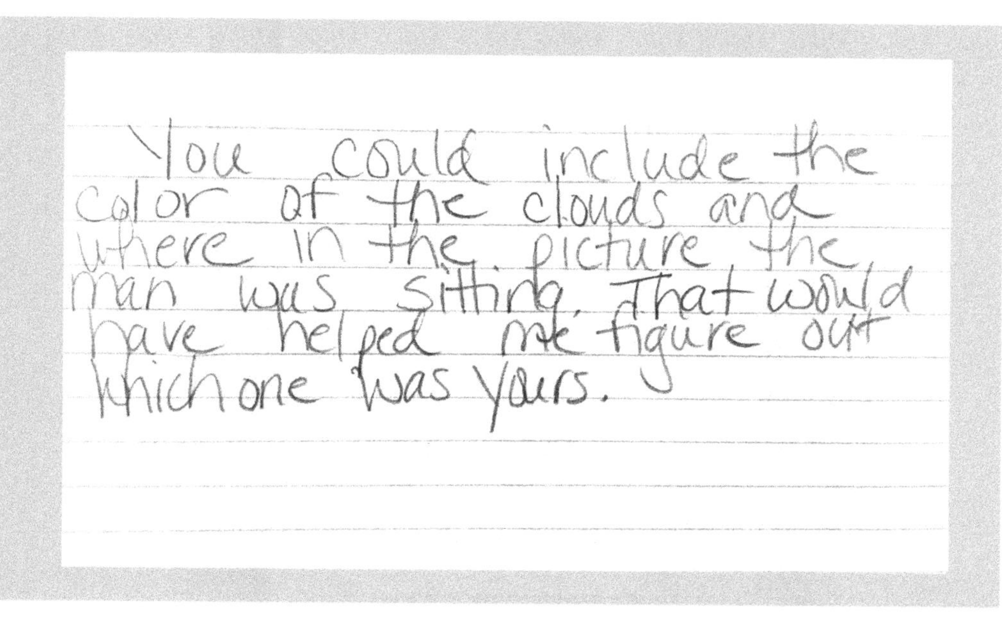

You could include the color of the clouds and where in the picture the man was sitting. That would have helped me figure out which one was yours.

Day 4

1. Have students revisit the notecard descriptors they wrote on Day 3.
2. Complete the Candy Revision activity on page 219. With sensory details in mind, this revision assigns a color of candy to a particular sense. (See the companion website for a template.) In other words, the students should have sentences that represent every single sense, and thus have all five colors represented in their papers.
3. Using their color-coded, annotated paragraph, have them separate their original sentences by sense.
4. Provide students with five new notecards—one per sense.
5. Now, students transfer each sentence to the appropriate notecard for that sense. (For example, all blue sentences go on one notecard, all yellow on another, etc.)
6. Use the NVA[2] word bank to add new sentences for the senses that are under-represented.
7. Have students staple the five notecards together so they create a five-paragraph descriptive writing sample.
8. Attach them to their original image.
9. Share with the class.

Were wemon important in the 1700's? yes, they were. One amazing women was Mercy Otis Warren. She made a huge difference. She helped during a time where most people would not espesualy women.

Mercy was born in 1728. In 1771 her brother was declared insane! Mercy's first book was published in 1772. Her brother died in 1783 because of being stricked by lightening. Her husband died in 1808. Finally Mercy died in 1814.

M O W

Mercy Otis Waren had many qualities. One of her qualities was her love of learning. She learned to live in a place surrounded by war. She was also very smart. Finally Mercy was interested in politics. held meetings in her house.

Mercy had many obstacles. First her brother was severely injured in battle and died soon after. Next her children all died before her. She could not sign her work because people would not aprove womens work. They belived ONLY men could write!

Mercy is remembered for many things. One thing she is remembered for is holding meetings. Another thing Mercy was remembered for is her poems. One more thing she is remembered for is going to school when most women didn't.

We would not be as strong of a nation if Mercy hadn't inspired us to do more! She inspired our nation

When to Use It

- As a way to integrate descriptive writing into instruction that also addresses grammar and peer revision.
- When you want students to integrate what they observe in the Sensory Revision read-aloud example in their own writing.
- As a way to model ongoing revision by revisiting the same composition throughout the week.

Why It Works

- It starts with a list of words that gets extended into complete sentences that are then extended into paragraphs.
- Students revise for a specific purpose on Day 4, and this gives them the opportunity to extend their writing into a multiparagraph composition.
- Using a picture as a starter can help students generate ideas for writing.

Modifications

- Have students complete a "pass it along" writing. To do this, have each student write one sentence on the notecard using their NVA^2 word bank. Pass the image, the word bank, and the notecard to the next student for them to add a sentence. Do this until there are five sentences on each notecard. Return it to the original owner.
- Skip Day 3 and move directly to Day 4. Put students in groups of five and have them choose one of their images to complete the sensory revision task. Each group member should be responsible for focusing on one sense and revising based on that one sense.
- On Day 4, have students choose one sense that they will add to their paper. Revise for that one sense.
- Instead of using an image of a setting, use images of characters.

Extensions

- Extend this into writing about a setting in narrative compositions.
- Use the same images to write Post-it Poems from page 114.
- Change the genre to persuasive by having students write to persuade the reader to visit the place they described.

CHAPTER 1 Writing Fitness
CHAPTER 2 Writing Warmups
CHAPTER 3 Targeted Training
CHAPTER 4 High Intensity Training
CHAPTER 5 Cold Starts and Cooldowns
CHAPTER 6 Rest, Recover, Revise
CHAPTER 7 Stretch Day
CHAPTER 8 A Balanced Diet of Reading and Writing

- Have students shift to a comparison and contrast writing by partnering up with a peer whose picture is distinctively different. Compare the similarities and differences of both images.

Digital Direction

- Write the sentences directly on an uploaded image using PicCollage.
- Create a slide presentation of all the images with student voice-overs of the writing using PowerPoint, Google Slides, or Visme.
- Have students use Movie Maker or iMovie to create a class movie compilation of their descriptive images and narration.

Lesson Lead-Ins

- Use the NVA^2 lesson as a lead-in for this extended writing composition.
- Connect this to the lesson on Pictures for Mood on page 90.

Tandem Training

Lesson Name	Focus
NVA^2 on page 66.	Adding descriptive details
NVA^2 strategy on page 66	Describing images and photos; writing descriptive sentences
Pictures for Mood on page 90	Using images to evoke mood
Cast the Character on page 82	Visualizing a character from a text

PAINT STRIP ARGUMENTS

Sometimes one of the biggest challenges for young writers involves organizing their words and thoughts. Finding ways to make organizing information easier and more manageable for students can help them become successful when writing in multiple genres.

Crafting arguments is a skill that is often utilized across grade bands and content areas. Yet arguments require sophisticated skills, including the ability to integrate appropriate evidence that solidifies the claim. Plus, writers must address the counterclaim and provide a rebuttal for such. Young writers can develop skill with all these components (organization, integration of evidence, counterclaims, rebuttals, and more) by drafting arguments on paint strips. Doubtful? Wait till you see how this unfolds in the classroom.

Putting It to Work

Day 1

1. Start by discussing the genre of argument and what this type of writing entails.
2. Have students brainstorm a list of possible topics that they might use for writing in this genre. Have some backup suggestions in case any students have trouble coming up with a topic. These might include topics like:
    - Year-round school
    - Human trafficking
    - Health care access
    - Uniform/dress code policies
3. Once students have come up with a list of topics, begin this writing task with the Stop/Go Sources activity on page 98. Use this strategy as the starting point for this task.

Day 2

1. Using the sources generated in the first day's lesson, have students focus on a certain number of sources to investigate; this number will depend on your students' skill level, the genre, and the number of days you want to devote to this task, but typically three to five sources is a good starting place.

In the weeks' prior to starting this lesson, make sure that some of the read alouds, text excerpts, or other texts that students engage with are from the argumentative genre. Before students start writing arguments, they need to have read several.

> **Quick Tip!**
>
> Keep in mind that the Mix and Match strategy, a big part of this portion of the activity, takes a few days on its own, so the more sources you require, the longer the overall lesson will be.

2. You might also consider giving students a specific purpose when they are collecting their notes from each article. For example, "Look for any evidence of health conditions caused by environmental factors." Setting a purpose for reading and note-taking can help students locate the appropriate evidence.

3. Complete the note-taking portion of the Mix and Match activity (Harper, 2022). For this, have students use their paint strips to collect notes from each article. Make sure students use different colored paint strips for the different articles and model how to take notes from the article.

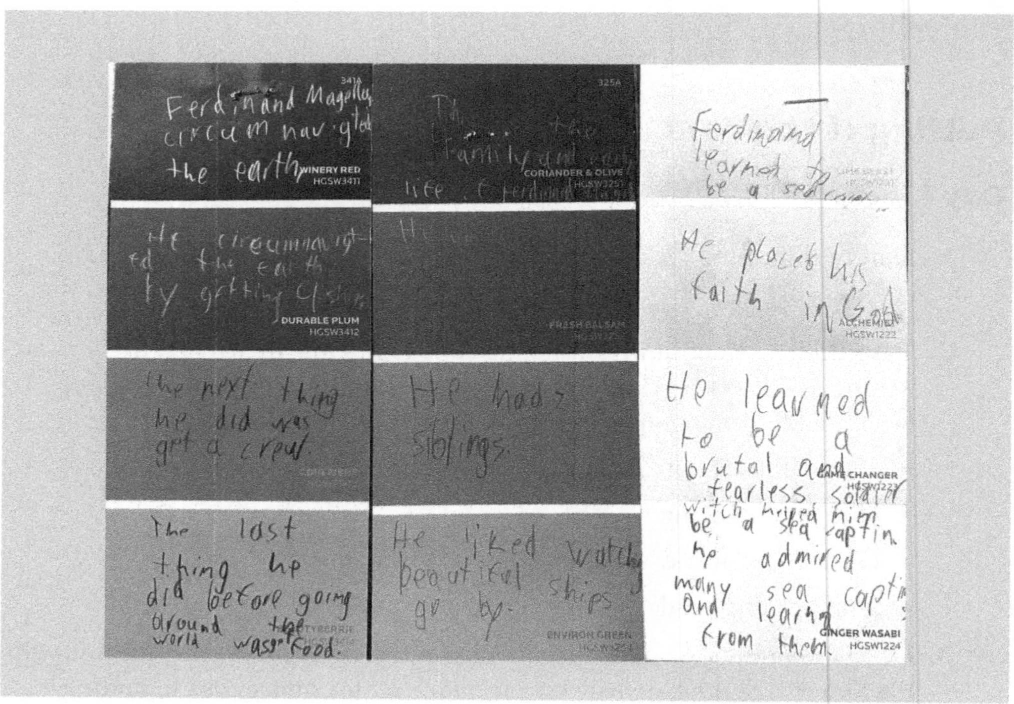

Day 3

1. Based on the information students gathered in the Mix and Match strategy, have students draft claims for their arguments.

2. Have students complete the Claims and Evidence Matchup strategy on page 95.

Day 4

1. Have students cut the paint strips from the Mix and Match activity into individual pieces.

2. Get students to group their evidence by topic. Have them remove any evidence that does not support their overarching claim or is part of the counterclaim.

Make sure you model claim construction first. Check out the National Writing Project's C3WP resources at https://sites.google.com/nwp.org/c3wp/home

3. Once students have grouped their evidence by topic, give students some sticky notes.

4. Have them label each group of evidence based on the topic so they know what their topic sentence should be when writing this in paragraph form.

5. Next, provide students with only green paint strips. While you are only giving out green paint strips, I would suggest you give out different shades of green so that students will know what goes where.

6. Students should organize their evidence and rewrite it in complete sentences to create a paragraph using their first green paint strip. Continue with each subsequent paint strip.

7. By the end of this day's lesson, students should have the body of their argument written on the green paint strips.

8. Students should tape the green paint strips together so they create a vertical extended essay.

How many green paint strips should you pass out? That depends on how many paragraphs you want the argument to be. Because each new green paint strip represents one paragraph, you would want to give students with as many needed to achieve the paragraph requirement.

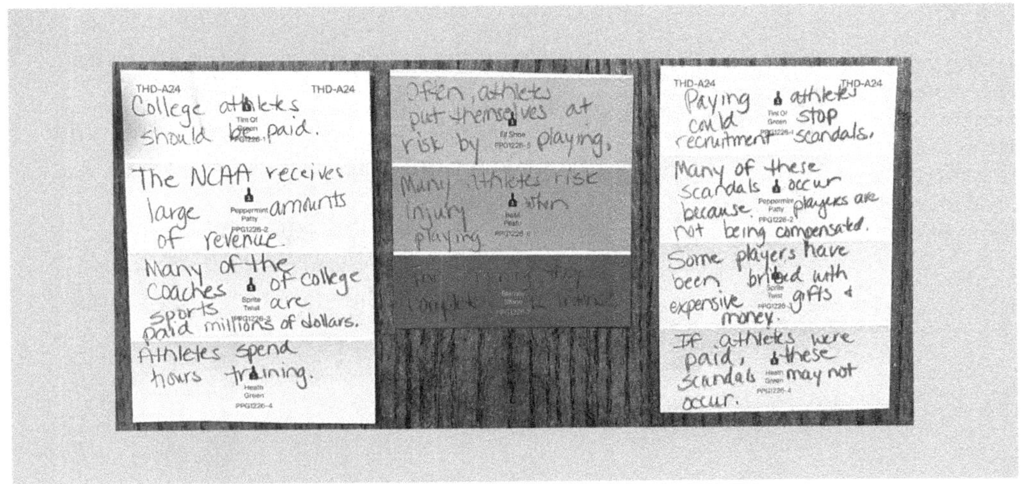

Day 5

1. Have students revisit the evidence they eliminated on Day 4 that did not support their claim or was part of the counterclaim. Make sure you model this before you set students free to do this on their own.

> **Quick Tip!**
>
> If there is no clear counterclaim in the material eliminated, have students revisit the sources they used originally, this time only looking for counter claims.

2. Provide students with one red paint strip.
3. Include the counterclaim on the red paint strip and evidence that supports the counterclaim.
4. Tape the counterclaim to the last green body paint strip.

Day 6

1. Have students focus only on the red paint strip that includes the counter claim and supportive evidence.

> **Quick Tip!**
>
> Why color code? Green means go and it serves as a reminder for information that supports the student's claim. Red serves as "Stop! Here's what the opposing side says."

2. Provide students with a yellow paint strip.
3. Have them only respond to the counterclaim on the yellow strip.
4. Use any leftover evidence from Day 4 to address the counterclaim.
5. Record on the new paint strip.

Day 7

> **Quick Tip!**
>
> Why are you using yellow here? Because you don't want to end on the counterclaim without addressing it. The color designation can help students remember whether they have completed all parts of the assignment. End on yellow? You addressed the counterclaim. End on red? You forgot to address it.

1. Have students revisit their paint strip argument and reread the entire composition.
2. Provide students with two yellow paint strips.
3. Using the information addressed in the body, have students draft an opening paragraph and a closing paragraph on the yellow paint strips.
4. Attach the opening paragraph to the beginning of the essay and attach the conclusion to the end of the composition.

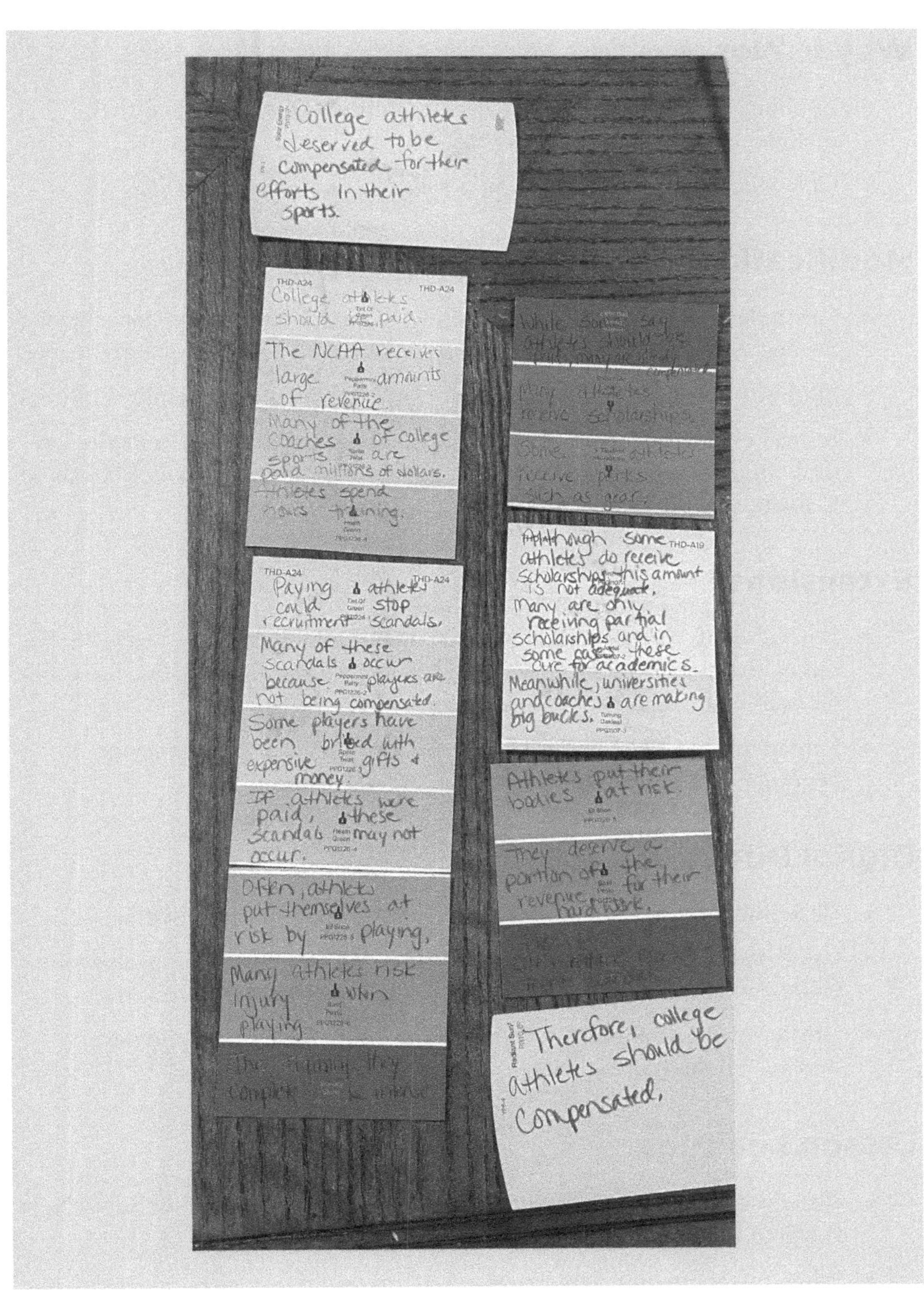

When to Use It

- Use this as a natural progression from persuasive writing to arguments.
- When you want students to incorporate research into their writings.
- As a way for students to connect to topics that are relevant to their lives and interests.

Why It Works

- Building on this lesson day by day helps students complete a task that includes multiple components.
- Color coding the material can help with organization.

Modifications

- Get students to swap with a partner who is writing about the same topic but with the opposing claim. Have them draft the counterclaim for their partner's paper.
- Start with one source for evidence in Day 2 and progress to multiple sources.
- Instead of having students write entire opening and closing paragraphs, have students draft opening and closing sentences first on sticky notes. Stick these to the rest of the essay.

Extensions

- Have students connect this to the Resource Roundup lesson on page 45. For this connection, you may have them just focus on completing one brief slide for each of the outlined components.
- Extend this to a Continuum Debate (Harper, 2022) by partnering up opposing arguments and conducting an oral debate.

Digital Direction

- Have students use Padlet to respond to their classmate's arguments.
- Use PowerPoint or Google Slides instead of the paint strips for organization. Color code the slides green, red, and yellow to mimic the paint strips.
- Create a paint strip template in PowerPoint or Google Slides and have students fill them in digitally.

Lesson Lead-Ins

- Use this along with the Expert/Know Nothing List on page 33 or Sticky Note Paragraphs on page 137.
- When integrating research writings, use this lesson to work on research tasks.

Lesson Name	Focus
Stop/Go Sources on page 98	Identifying credible sources
Mix and Match Strategy (Harper, 2022)	Locating information, researching using multiple sources
Claims and Evidence Matchup on page 95	Finding evidence for multiple claims
Resource Roundup on page 45	Utilizing multiple sources to answer prompts

STICKY NOTE PARAGRAPHS

Sticky notes offer students the ability to write on small pieces of real estate, but build out extended writings in a low-stakes manner. Since there is a specific amount of room on which they can write, and in most cases, this space is about nine square inches, using sticky notes can make writing slightly less intimidating.

Why paper and pencil or pen? Writing on paper taps into visual motor skills, which focus on the ability to interpret visual information and respond with some type of motor action (i.e., writing, completing revision tasks by moving sentences around physically.) Plus, how often have you been composing on your laptop only to be interrupted by the ding of an email? That doesn't happen when you only have paper and pencil at your desk!

Yet one of the other benefits of these sticky squares of paper is their ability to be easily moved and manipulated to different parts of a student's paper. In this case, revision is easily completed because students can pick up a sticky note, move it in front of or after another one, and determine if that revision works. If not, they simply move it back. There's no erasing or rewriting. Instead, students simply pick up notes and put them down. Even if they write a sentence that might be off topic, they only need to relocate it to the far corner of their desks for revisiting later in case it ends up fitting with their completed composition. Plus, you'll often find that students will write more when they write in this manner.

And yet another fantastic benefit? Sticky note paragraphs can be modified for students at varying skill levels and for multiple grade levels. Primary students can use sticky notes to build sentences, upper elementary students can build *a* paragraph, and middle and secondary students can build multiparagraph compositions.

Putting It to Work

Day 1

1. Have students brainstorm potential persuasive topics they might write about. (Have a backup list of possible topics ready in case students don't generate enough topics.)

2. Choose one topic to practice with as a class.

3. Provide students with sticky notes that are a certain color.

4. Instruct them to write a topic sentence that is in support of the class topic.

5. Once they have written their topic sentence, have them come up with three examples of evidence that supports their topic sentence.

> **Quick Tip!**
>
> This evidence should be pulled from their prior knowledge. In later lessons, students will conduct research to locate reasons from sources.

6. Place one of the topic sentences on the white board or on display for students to see.
7. Ask students to share one of their reasons/evidence that supports.
8. Stick the evidence notes on the white board.
9. Ask students to give another reason that is different from the one already posted. Repeat with the third reason.
10. Next, ask students if anyone has additional evidence that is related to any of the reasons posted.
11. Build the reasons out with the sticky notes that students share. As you do this, you will actually begin to build out the body paragraphs of the essay using sticky notes.

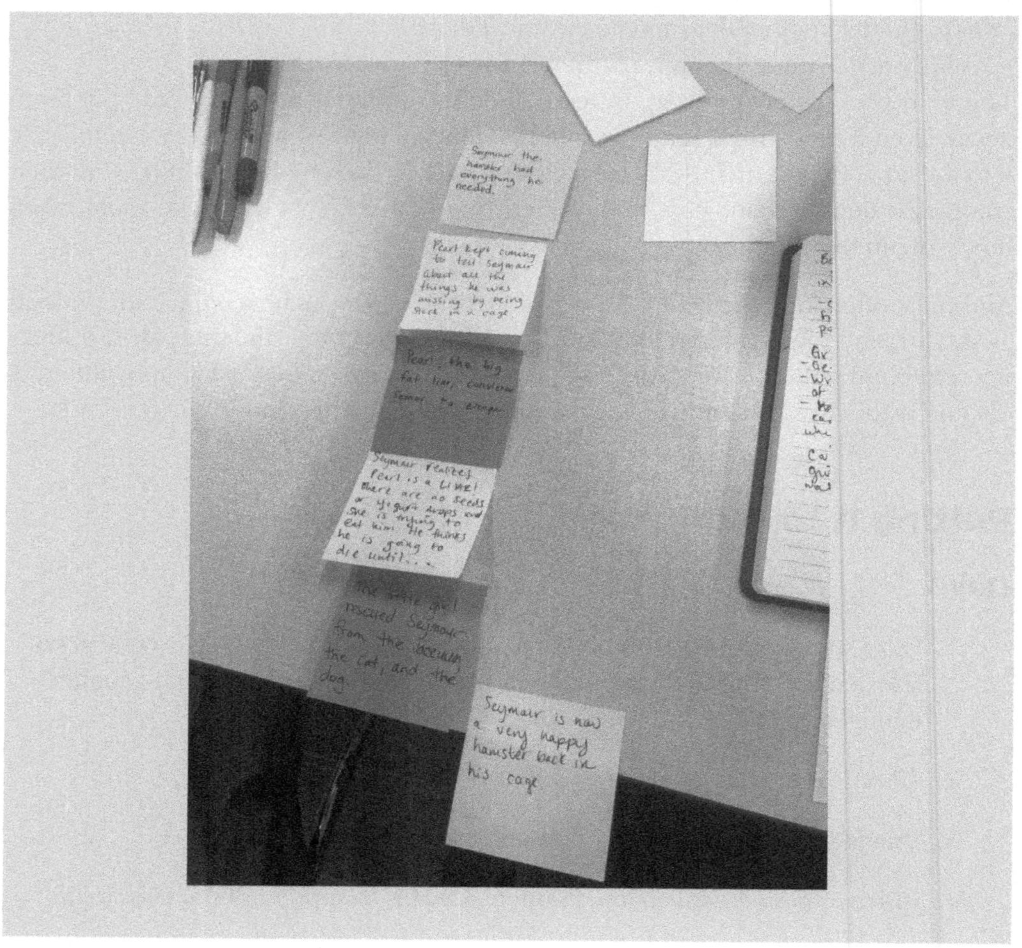

12. Have students revisit their topic sentence. Provide them with another sticky note so they can draft a conclusion.
13. Stick it at the bottom of the board.

Day 2 Two

1. Have students revisit the same topic from Day 1.
2. Give students sticky notes that are a different color than what was used on Day 1.
3. Repeat Steps 4 through 13 from Day 1—only this time, students should write a sentence against the topic (a counterclaim).

Days 3 Through 5

Note: This portion of the lesson, Day 3, will likely take multiple days. Plan on 2 to 4 days for this part of the lesson.

1. Revisit the topics from Day 1.
2. Have students choose their topic from the class-generated list.
3. Instruct students to determine whether they are in support of the topic or if they are against it.
4. Have students complete the evidence collection component of the Paint Strip Arguments on p. 131, using different colored sticky notes instead of paint strips.

Make sure you have a variety of sources available on each of these topics. These can be print, digital, or a combination of both.

5. Using the evidence they collect from the teacher-provided sources, have them build their composition with sticky notes just as they did on Days 1 and 2 in Steps 4 through 13.

Day 6

1. Revision time! Implement the Candy Revision strategy on page 219, the Bless, Press, Address strategy on page 194, or the Level Up strategy on page 212.

Day 7

1. Have students complete their revision tasks or use this day for more peer or teacher conferencing.
2. Once students have completed the entire task, have them take a picture of their sticky note essay for submission.

Remember, students complete the entire writing using only sticky notes! They don't have to transpose or rewrite a *final* copy.

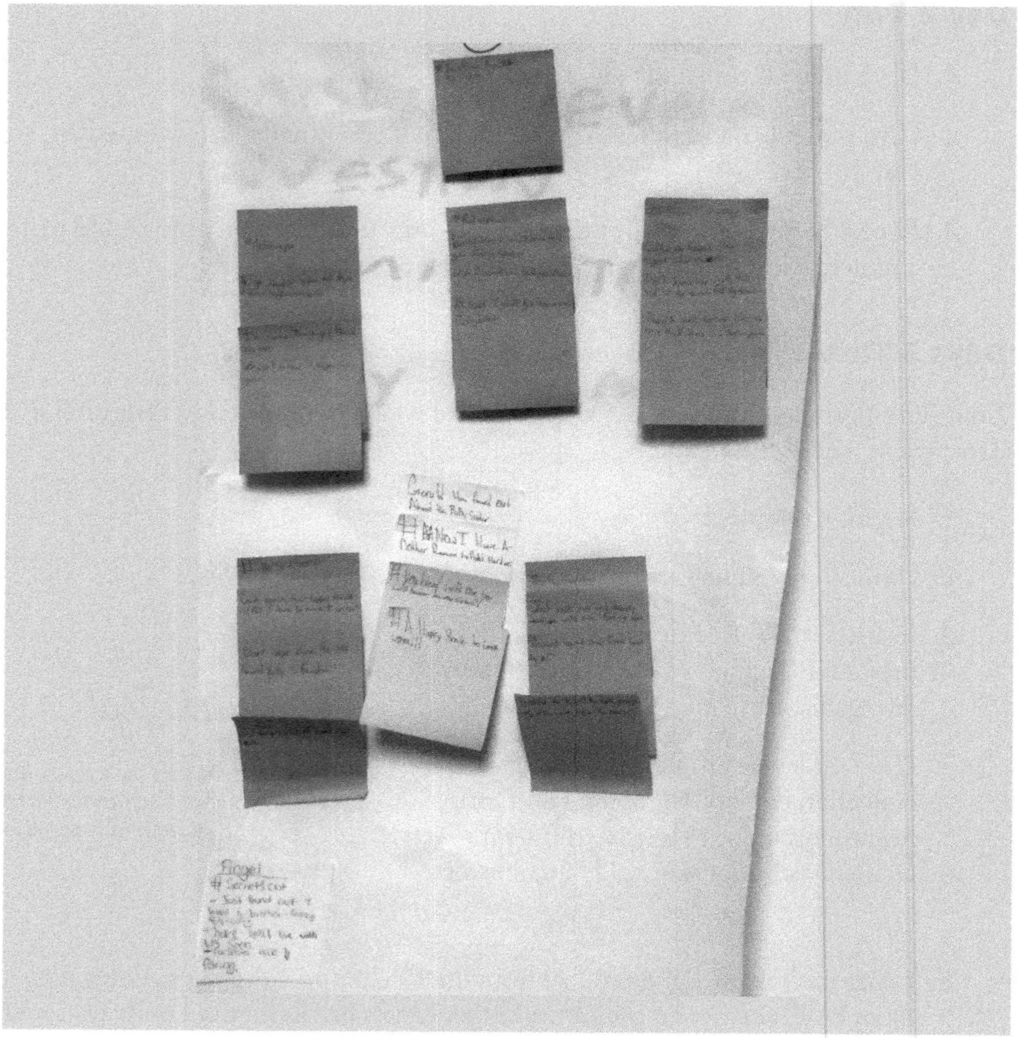

When to Use It

- To ease in to multiparagraph compositions.
- When you want students to complete a fully involved essay without the intimidating essay feel.
- To easily model ongoing revision.

Why It Works

- Using sticky notes can help students see immediate success because they are able to easily include enough information to fill up that small area of space.
- Building out paragraphs becomes much more manageable because students can count the sticky notes to determine where they need additional details.
- Organization becomes easier since students can group like details together simply by making piles of sticky notes.

Modifications

- Have students collaborate on this task and complete it with a partner.
- Instead of focusing on the persuasive genre, start with a personal narrative or an informational piece of writing.
- Place students in small groups and have them build their essay together using the reasons they each drafted individually.
- Provide students with ready-made evidence examples and have them sort them into the appropriate paragraphs.

Extensions

- Merge the material from both sides of the topic into one argumentative essay.
- Have students orally debate their topics using a Continuum Debate (Harper, 2022).
- Using the evidence they locate in their research, have students rank their evidence from strongest to weakest.

Digital Direction

- Use Jamboard to complete this engagement using digital sticky notes.
- Have students create visual paragraphs (Pinterest Paragraphs, Harper, 2022) with a program like Canva or PicCollage.

Lesson Lead-Ins

- Use this as a gateway engagement for extended writing compositions.
- Connect this to the Paint Strip Arguments writing on page 131 as a means to draft that research or to the Resource Roundup on page 45.

Tandem Training

Lesson Name	Focus
Stop/Go Sources on page 98	Identifying credible sources
Mix and Match Strategy (Harper, 2022)	Locating information, researching using multiple sources
Candy Revision on page 219.	Adding more detail
Resource Roundup on page 45	Utilizing multiple sources to answer prompts
Level Up on page 212	Checking language for formality

IN-SYNC SOURCES

In many middle and secondary classrooms, students are often required to answer constructed responses that include information compiled and synthesized from multiple sources. Plus, several of the prompts require students to address multiple questions in one specific prompt. Therefore, students must not only break the prompt down into the specific questions that are being asked but also look across multiple sources to create the composition. Sometimes these sources are traditional passages, but others include different forms of texts like tables, images, political cartoons, and more. For students to get prepared for these high intensity assessment tasks, time must be allotted in class for students to practice these types of writings.

Putting It to Work

Day 1

- Begin this lesson with the Resource Roundup on page 45. This strategy helps students collect pertinent information from multiple sources using the template available on the companion website at resources.corwin.com/WritingWorkouts.
- Make sure when you create the questions that students use on Day 1 that you lift them directly from the constructed response prompt they will answer for this task.

Day 2

- Have students choose one of the questions from their Resource Roundup template.
- Provide them with a paint strip for their first question. Make sure you color-code these based on the question.
- Have them visit the sources they identified on Day 1 that would answer the question.
- Record the information on the paint strip.

From a management perspective, divide the class into the same number of groups as you have questions. For example, if students on Day 1 focused on three questions, create three groups, one for each question. This will help eliminate overcrowding at the resource stations.

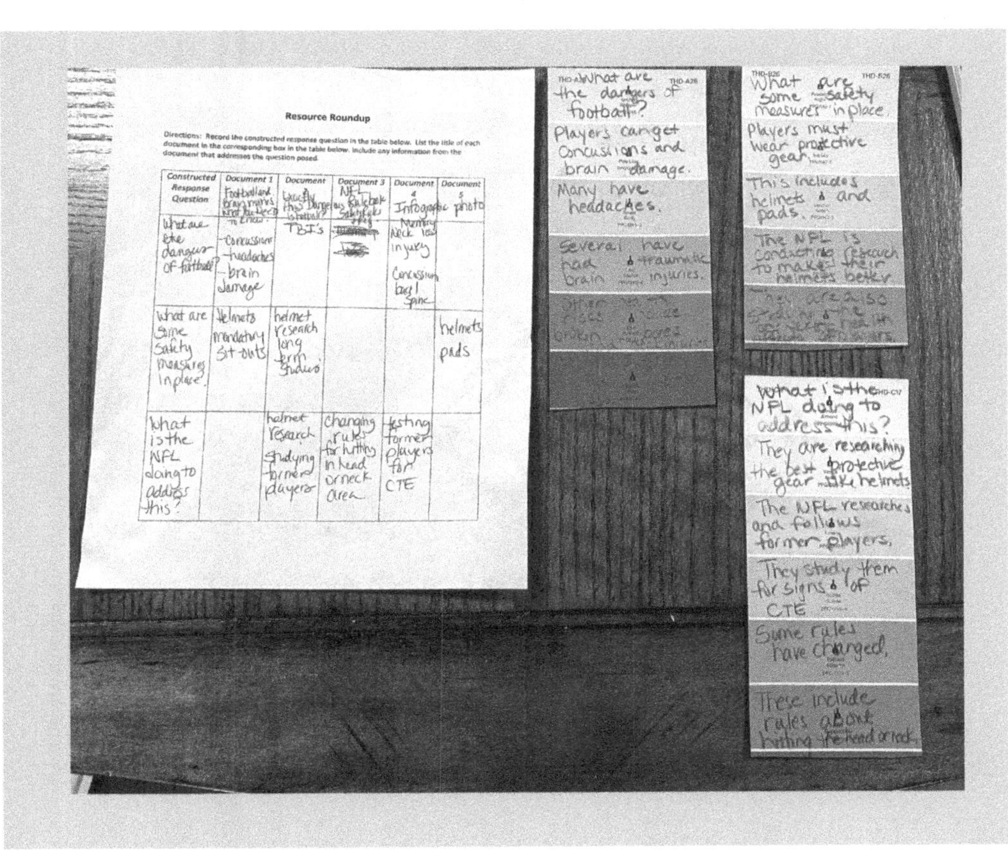

Day 3

1. Repeat the procedure from Day 2, but have students focus on a different question by rotating the groups.

Day 4

1. Repeat the procedure from Day 2, but have students focus on a different question by rotating the groups.

Day 5

1. Provide students with notecards. Using the material from each paint strip, have students write the information in sentence format on their notecards. Make sure to model this before students complete this on their own so they can see how material from their notes is transferred into complete sentences.
2. Staple the notecards together into one long vertical line.

Students should use one notecard for each paint strip; these will translate into individual paragraphs.

How did the Indains respect people? There are many examples. They lived in houses together. Also they helped each other with their hair. Children got their food first. They shared their food with each other. They helped fight other trides. This is how they respected the people.

Indians respected animals in a lot of ways. They didn't practice on animals. They didn't kill horses. They turned the animal skin inward. They made animal fur into clothes. They made jewelry with elks teeth. Also they made headdresses with bison skulls. Horses were used as the drowry when a young man paid for this bride. This how the Indains respected animals.

Indains respected the land in a lot of ways. The prairie people grew corn and other crops. The Prairie People grew corn, squash, beans, and other crops. They hung corn and meat. They up their lodges for the tipi. This is how they respected the land.

Day 6

1. Have students use the information from the body paragraphs to create introductory and conclusion paragraphs.
2. Draft each of these on a new notecard.
3. Staple the introductory notecard to the beginning of the assignment and the conclusion notecard to the end of the assignment.

When to Use It

- To break constructed responses down into multiple parts.
- To integrate writings that utilize multiple sources for research.
- To connect different subject areas into the ELA classroom.

Why It Works

- Getting students up and moving can increase engagement.
- Using different types of texts and sources can address varying ability levels in the classroom.

- It helps students see that questions can be answered through the examination of multiple types of sources.

Modifications

- Start with a few sources and only one question. This can help students ease into multipart constructed responses with multiple sources.
- Complete Days 2 through 4 in one day by dividing students into groups and assigning one question to each group. On the next instructional day, create new groups composed of one student from each question group. Have them collaboratively answer the full constructed response.

Extensions

- Have students locate an additional source that could be used to answer the question.
- Using the sources provided, have students develop a constructed response that could be answered with the sources.
- Have students rate the sources based on the quality of information provided.

Digital Direction

- Use QR codes to direct students to resources that are located online.
- Instead of having resource stations laid out physically, create a digital web quest where students must go to multiple sources online of information.

Lesson Lead-Ins

- Connect this to the Annotate, Plan, Write strategy on page 168.
- Use this after students have practiced other extended pieces like the Sticky Note Paragraphs on page 137.
- Connect this to the P.E.N. strategy on page 201.

Tandem Training

Lesson Name	Focus
Stop/Go Sources on page 98	Identifying credible sources
Mix and Match Strategy (Harper, 2021)	Locating information, researching using multiple sources
I.N.K. strategy on page 197	Adding more detail
Resource Roundup on page 45	Utilizing multiple sources to answer prompts
Annotate, Plan, Write on page 168	Writing on demand

MIX AND MATCH REMIX

Writing responses that utilize information collected from multiple sources is a staple in multiple classrooms across grade levels and content areas. Revisiting the Mix and Match strategy (Harper, 2022) offers another way that students can use paint strips and multiple sources to write extended compositions. This time, instead of answering a variety of constructed response prompts, students use material from the multiple sources to develop an extended written composition that is organized by concepts.

Putting It to Work

Day 1

1. Start by discussing the genre of informational/research writing and what this type of writing entails.
2. Have students brainstorm a list of possible topics that they might use for writing in this genre.
3. Once students have come up with a list of topics, begin this writing task with the Stop/Go Sources activity on page 98. Use this strategy as the starting point for this task.

Day 2

1. Using the sources generated in the first day's lesson, have students choose a certain number of sources to investigate. You can set parameters based on how many days you want to devote to this task. Keep in mind that the Mix and Match strategy takes a few days on its own, so the more sources you require, the longer the overall lesson will be.
2. Complete the note-taking portion of the Mix and Match activity (Harper, 2022). For this, have students use their paint strips to collect notes from each article. Make sure you use different colored paint strips for the different articles and model how to take notes from the article. Students should have one fact/detail per block on the paint strip.

Consider giving students a specific purpose when they are collecting their notes from each article. For example, "Look for any evidence of health conditions caused by environmental factors." Setting a purpose for reading and note-taking can help students locate the appropriate evidence.

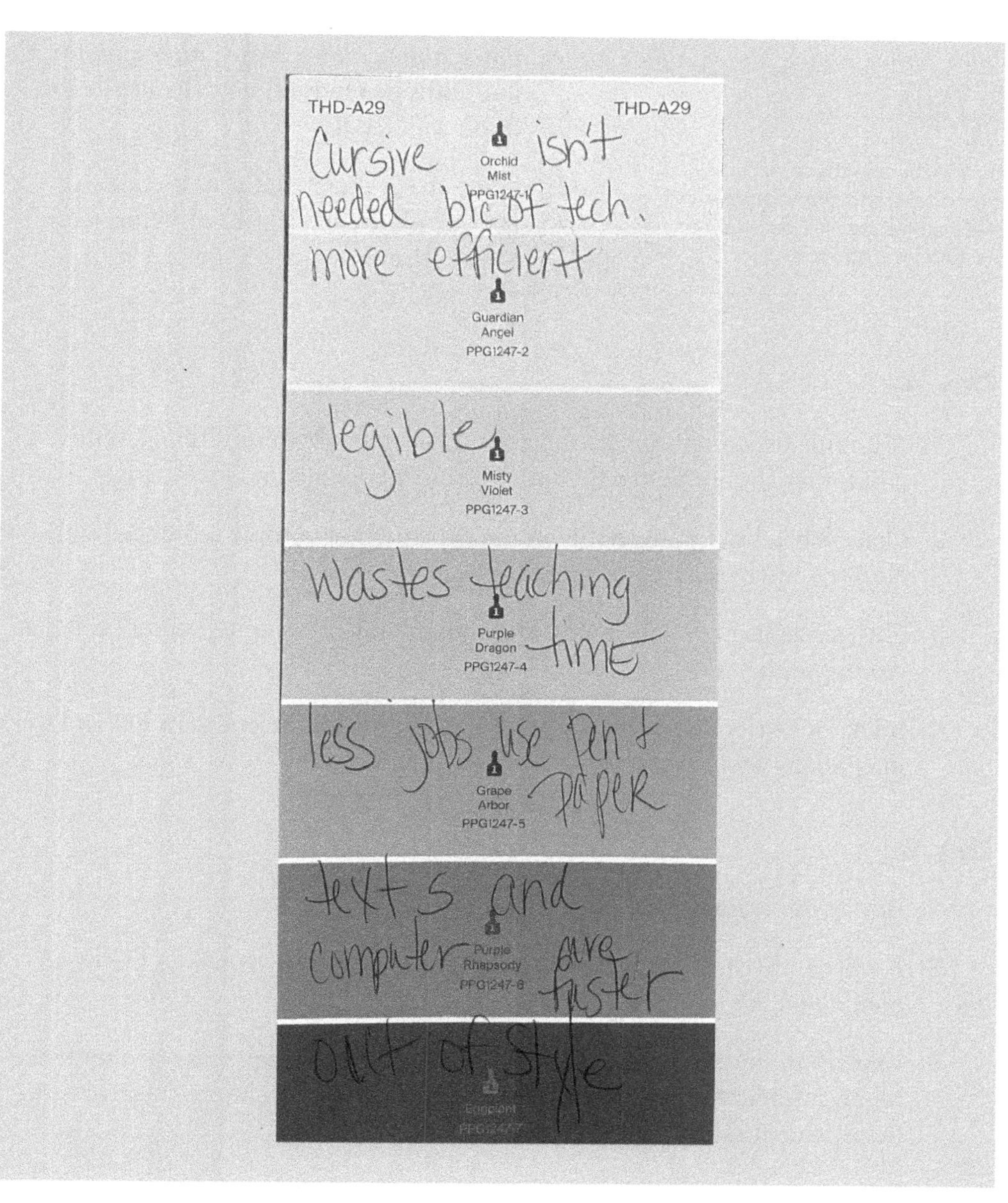

Day 3

1. Have students cut their paint strips into the individual blocks.
2. Start shuffling the evidence into piles based on the evidence that belongs together.
3. Give students sticky notes and have them label each of these piles with the overarching topic.
4. Show students how to construct a topic sentence based on the sticky note label they created for each of their piles of evidence.
5. Model for students how to take the information that is written in note form on their cut-up strips and construct complete sentences.

6. Give students notecards. The number of notecards depends on how many piles of evidence they have.
7. Have them construct a notecard paragraph for each pile of evidence. Staple the notecards together in a vertical line.

> **Quick Tip!**
>
> Don't be tempted to skip these parts. Modeling how to take shorthand notes and create complete sentences is necessary to ensure successful compositions.

Day 4

1. Ask students to consider what is missing from their composition. (At this point, they should notice they are missing an opening and a closing.)
2. Complete a brief mini-lesson on the construction of topic sentences and closing sentences.
3. Give students two sticky notes. Have them draft an opening sentence and a closing sentence.
4. Stick the correct new sentence to the beginning of the composition and to the end. Now students have a complete composition.

Day 5

1. Revisit the composition once more.
2. Focus on the sticky note introductory and conclusion sentences that were completed the day prior.
3. Explain to students that while in some cases it is enough to write a sentence for an introduction or conclusion, in extended compositions, these need to be expanded into paragraphs.
4. Refer to the body of the composition for material that can be added to the opening. For example, encourage students to pull the main idea from each body paragraph to use as part of the opening.
5. Model how this might be done.
6. Give students two notecards.
7. Have them draft a complete introductory and conclusion paragraph.
8. Attach each to the body of the essay already completed with the notecards.

> **Quick Tip!**
>
> Modeling is super important. Make sure that students see how you might fully develop an entire paragraph based on material in the body of the composition.

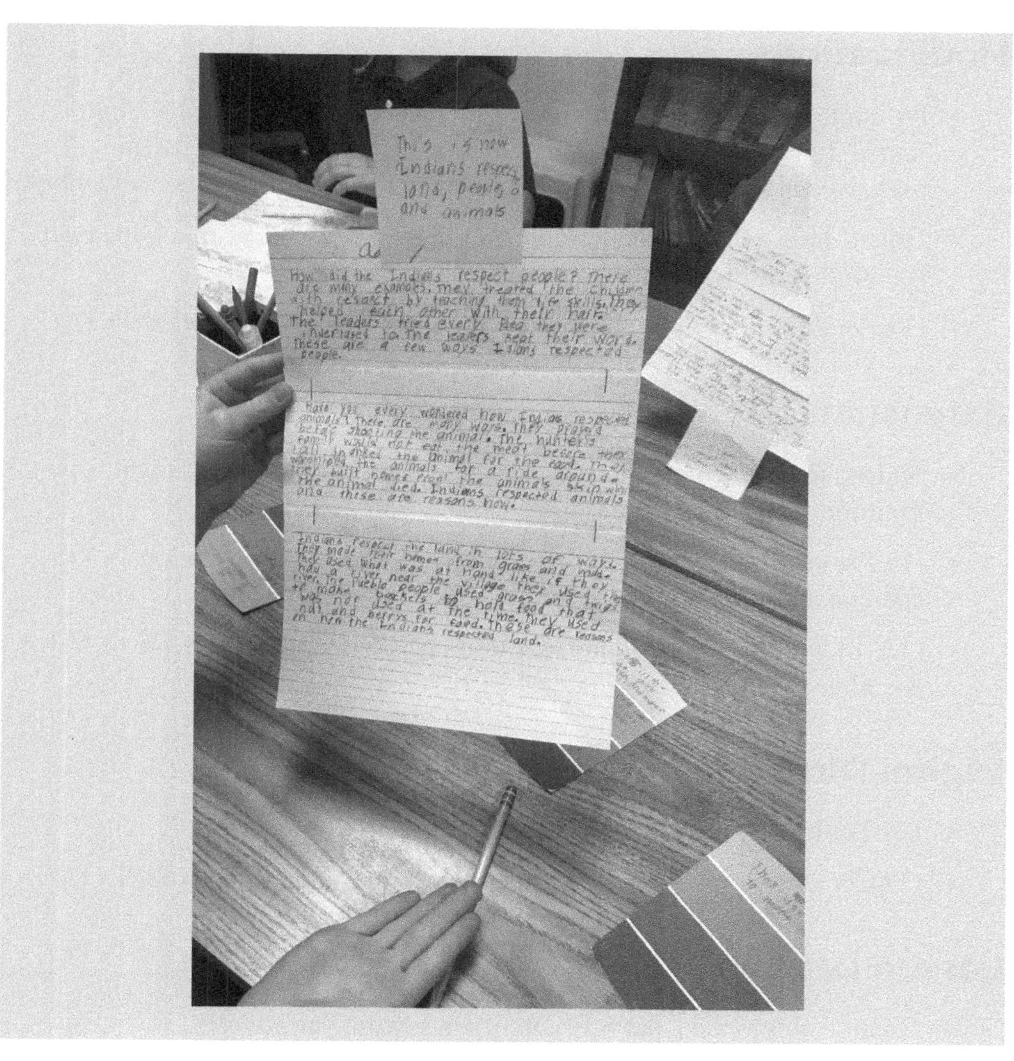

When to Use It

- When you want students to write an extended composition using multiple sources.
- To effectively organize content based on a specific topic.
- When you want students to utilize more than one source when writing compositions.

Why It Works

- Color coding the sources can help students track where they found the information.
- Cutting the paint strips into pieces can help students group like details together since they can physically manipulate the evidence.
- As students find more information on their topic, they can easily add to their notes.

Modifications

- Put students in collaborative groups and have each group focus on one source. Jigsaw the groups on the following day and have them use the material collected across sources to collaboratively complete the written task.
- Utilize different configurations of paint strips based on how much material you want students to collect.
- Use colorful sticky notes instead of paint strips for evidence collection.

Extensions

- Address the implementation of transitional phrases with the Musical Transitions lesson on page 103.
- Have students locate images that can be added to the composition as additional information.
- Get students to locate additional sources for their topics and create their own Resource Roundup.

Digital Direction

- Use Jamboard to collaboratively brainstorm topic ideas.
- Collaboratively write this multiparagraph composition using Google Docs.

Lesson Lead-Ins

- Connect this to the Paint Strip Arguments writing on page 131.
- Use this as a lead-in to any writing that requires students to develop multi-paragraph compositions using multiple sources.

Tandem Training

Lesson Name	Focus
Stop/Go Sources on page 98	Finding credible sources
Resource Roundup on page 45	Using multiple sources to conduct research
P.E.N. on page 201	Revising to include additional details
Level Up on page 212	Modifying words based on formality and audience
Musical Transitions on page 103	Employing transitional phrases

PK/NK (PRIOR KNOWLEDGE/ NEW KNOWLEDGE)

When conducting research, it can be difficult to determine what you knew before you started the task and what you learned as part of the research activity. In many instances, students often know a lot about a topic, but when they start writing about it, they might now cite their sources. How often have you had students write information in a research report that is factual, but they did not back up with information from sources? When pressed, did they tell you they already knew that? Many of my middle grades students offered me the same explanations when I asked them where they got their information. One strategy that can help students locate new information, while finding support for the information they already know, is the PK/NK strategy.

Putting It to Work

Note: This strategy works best when students have already chosen research topics and have located some sources related to their topics.

Day 1

1. Provide students with a source based on a topic that students have some background knowledge on.
2. Give students two different colored highlighters.
3. Have students highlight any material they already knew with one color highlighter (PK).
4. Have students highlight material they did not know with the other highlighter (NK).
5. Compare the two.
6. Discuss how the new material can be used in their research writing through the integration of direct quotes.
7. Show students how they can use the material highlighted as prior knowledge as support for material in their research that they already knew.

Day 2

1. Have students apply the PK/NK strategy to any sources they are using for their research.
2. Annotate all sources by highlighting the text based on Prior Knowledge and New Knowledge.

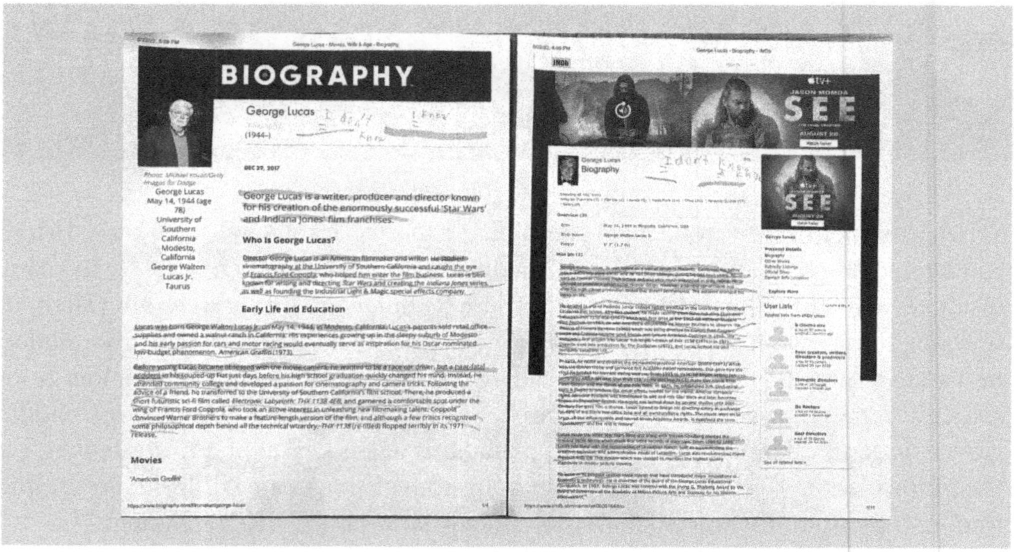

Day 3

1. Have students revisit their research they have written prior.
2. Using the information annotated in the PK/NK strategy, have students integrate any new evidence or material in their writings. For any material that students already knew and included in their writing, use the pertinent highlighted PK material as supporting evidence.

When to Use It

- When you want students to classify what they already know about a topic and what they are learning about a topic.
- To help find supporting details from sources for information students already know.
- As a tangible and visual measure of prior knowledge and new knowledge.

Why It Works

- Students have a specific purpose for reading: prior knowledge and new knowledge.
- It aids them in locating new material to include in their writings while finding support for what they already know.

Modifications

- Have students record their PK/NK on paint strips or sticky notes instead of highlighting the original article.
- Instead of having students highlight the entire article, have students find a specific number of details that are new and ones that count as prior knowledge.

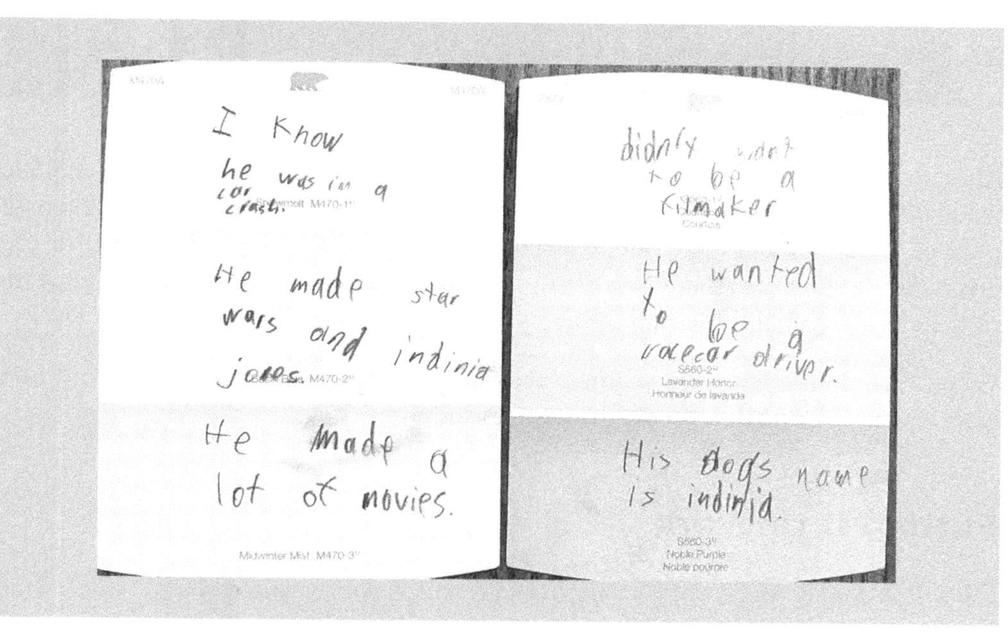

Extensions

- At the end of the research project, have students revisit their sources again to see how their amount of knowledge has changed.
- Have students locate additional sources that support their topic.

Digital Direction

- Annotate the sources using a digital application like Diigo.
- Have students locate two additional sources: one that includes information they already know and one that has a significant amount of information that is new material.

Lesson Lead-Ins

- Use this as a lead-in for any writing task that involves the research genre.
- Connect this to the Expert/Know Nothing List on page 33.

Tandem Training

Lesson Name	Focus
Stop/Go Sources on page 98	Finding credible sources
Resource Roundup on page 45	Using multiple sources to conduct research
Expert/Know Nothing List on page 33	Locating topics for research/writing

PAINT STRIP PARAPHRASE

Another focus in research and informational writing involves a writer's ability to effectively integrate information gleaned from several sources using direct quotes and paraphrased texts. Sometimes, students copy directly from their sources and fail to give credit. Yet at other times, students change one or two words in a direct quote, copy the rest, and believe that this counts as paraphrasing.

When completing research writing, spending time addressing how to cite and integrate sources is time well spent. Paint Strip Paraphrase does exactly this.

Putting It to Work

Day 1

1. Open the class by showing students an excerpt from a source that would be used for research writing.
2. Together as a class, pull out relevant facts and direct quotes based on the established purpose. Students should record these on individual sticky notes.
3. Choose an example fact and model how you would rewrite the direct quote into your own words.
4. Discuss as a class how writers can translate direct quotes into their own words, but remind students that credit still must be given to the source.
5. Provide students with a source related to the material that they will be researching.
6. Give them a paint strip to record their information and facts they collect from the source.

Day 2

1. Once students have recorded their direct quotes, give them another paint strip that is a different color.
2. Have them translate each individual direct quote into a paraphrased statement on the corresponding paint strip in the correct block.

Make sure that you establish a purpose for reading. In this example, it is a good idea for you to utilize sources that address the same topic idea so a uniform purpose can be established for all the articles included. Purpose will shift based on the material you choose. Just make sure that you establish a purpose before students start completing the opener.

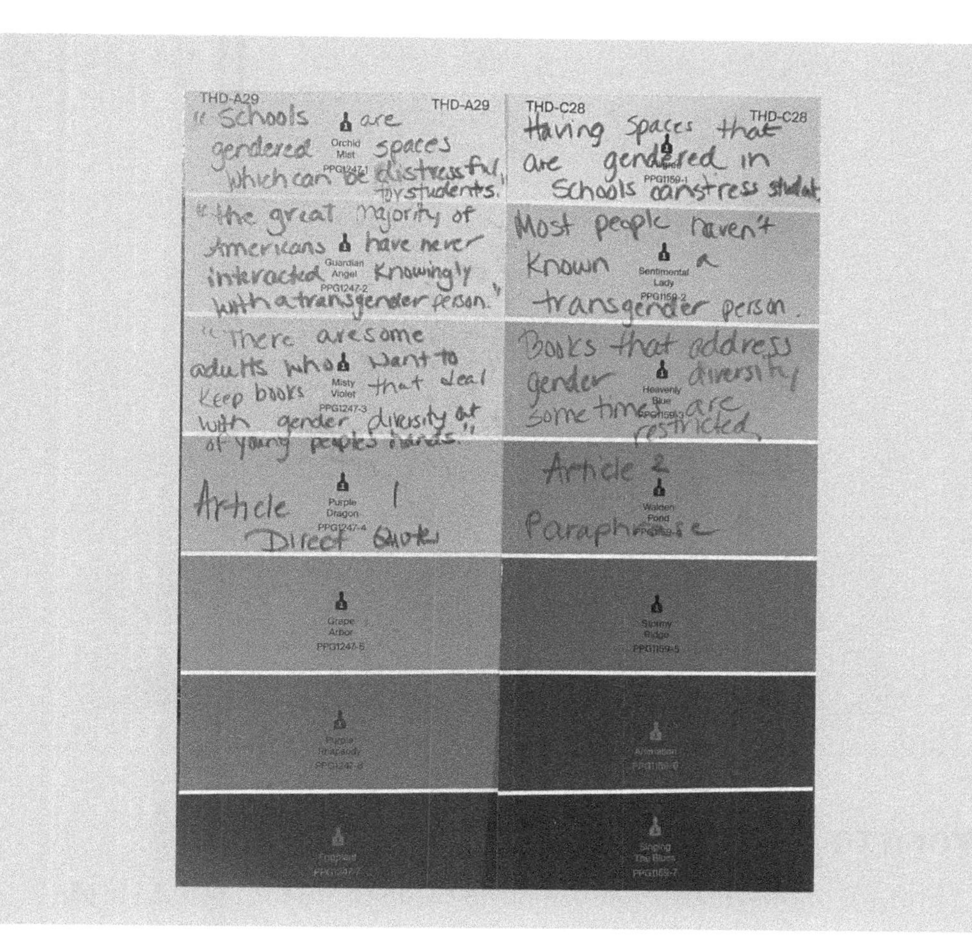

"Schools are gendered spaces which can be distressful to students."
Having spaces that are gendered in Schools
"the great majority of Americans have never interacted knowingly with a transgender person."
Most people haven't known a transgender person.
"There are some adults who want to keep books that deal with gender diversity out of young people's hands."
Books that address gender diversity sometimes are restricted.
Article 1 Direct Quote
Article 2 Paraphrase

Day 3

1. Once students have completed their first two paint strips, have them get with a partner and swap paint strips with them.
2. Give each student another paint strip and have them evaluate each direct quote and paraphrase their partner drafted.
3. On the corresponding block of the new paint strip, they should record a note that explains their partner did paraphrase correctly, or offer suggestions or observations for ones that were not paraphrased.
4. Discuss as a class how students can employ this tactic in their own research writing.

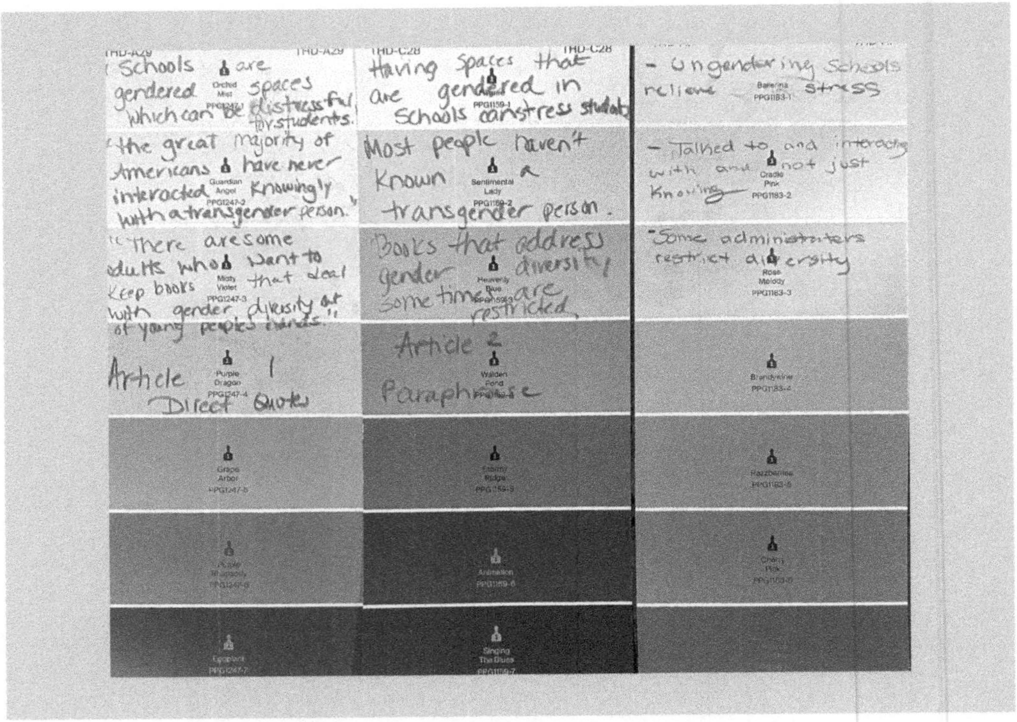

When to Use It

- Use this when students are completing writings that require them to cite sources.
- As a way to connect peer conferencing to research writing.
- When you want students to see how a direct quote varies from a paraphrased statement.

Why It Works

- Since students have a specific focus during each phase of the strategy, the task can be more manageable.
- Comparing the direct quotes to the student's version of the paraphrased excerpt can aid peers in offering specific and focused feedback.
- Because paint strips have a specified number of sections, students know the length and duration of the assignment up front.

Modifications

- Instead of having students work with a partner, have them self-evaluate their direct quotes and paraphrases.
- Provide students with a prefilled paint strip of direct quotes from the source. Have them focus on constructing a paraphrase only.

- Create prefilled paint strips with direct quotes and paraphrases. Pass these out to students and have them determine which direct quotes match each paraphrase.

Extensions

- Have students reread the same article for a different purpose and collect additional direct quotes based on this new purpose.
- Instead of having them write about whether the quote was appropriately paraphrased, have students self-evaluate by explaining how they modified their sentences.
- Have students look at their extended research writings and determine when they should utilize direct quotes and when they should employ paraphrased information.
- Build the entire research composition using a combination of direct quote paint strips, paraphrased paint strips, and filler sentence paint strips.

Digital Direction

- Use a thinking map digital application like Miro Mind Maps to collect the information digitally.
- Have students upload the Paint Strip template (Harper, 2022) and digitally record their quotes and paraphrases using a digital writing pen like Logitech Crayon.

Lesson Lead-Ins

- Use this as a lead-in for textual evidence lessons.
- Offer this as a review for integrating evidence from sources into extended writings.
- Connect this to the Claims and Evidence Matchup on page 95.

Tandem Training

Lesson Name	Focus
Say, Say, Say on page 19	Finding multiple ways to write the same phrases
Resource Roundup on page 45	Using multiple sources to conduct research
Claims and Evidence Matchup on page 95	Finding textual evidence for claims
Level Up on page 212	Modifying words based on formality and audience

COLD STARTS AND COOLDOWNS

This chapter is dedicated to strategies for writing that focus on cold starts and cooldowns. Integrating writing cooldown strategies into instruction as well as focusing on ways in which to prep students for those writing tasks that don't offer them the opportunity to complete a thorough warmup or cooldown can improve their overall writing fitness and skill.

What's a Writing Cold Start?

Physical workouts that don't include warmups are often called cold starts, which have a lot of similarities to what students are expected to do when they write on demand, especially in assessment scenarios. Cold-start workouts jump right into the real task without any preparation or planning for the exercises to come. As a result, the body gets warmed up during the actual workout instead of before it begins. Sometimes students must write without the luxury of extra time for limbering up.

In an ideal classroom setting, there would always be time for ample warmups, construction and reconstruction of writing products, and reflection, but today's classroom is anything but ideal. Just like in a physical workout, sometimes writing tasks don't include time for a proper warmup and rely on a cold start. In fact, most writing on demand engagements force students to be good stewards of their time and require them to shave off some of their planning minutes in lieu of actual drafting and revision. In most instances, cold starts are the way that writing assessments or writing-on-demand tasks are structured. Because many of those performance assessments are timed, students don't have a lot of expendable time to get warmed up and prepped before they move into the actual writing task. (And they sure don't have time for cooldowns!)

When working with teachers, many often share that when presented with writing-on-demand tasks that are timed, their students sometimes struggle with allocating the appropriate amount of time for each component of the writing task. In some instances, students spend too much time brainstorming and prewriting only to find that they don't have enough time to finish the entire task. Plus, if students have been shown how to complete a prewriting task only using bubble maps, replicating that type of brainstorming on a computer can be difficult. Yet another challenge is directly related to how the final product is constructed and presented. Because so many writing-on-demand assessments are completed on the computer, typing also becomes a barrier. This is frustrating not only for the students but also the teacher, especially when the students know how to complete the task but don't manage their time appropriately.

Giving students opportunities to write from the start without warmups can help prepare them for the cold and somewhat sterile nature of assessment writing. Utilizing a variety of strategies that capitalize on cold starts can help students better prepare for writing-on-demand tasks and increase the likelihood that they will be successful with timed writing engagements.

In the sections below, a variety of strategies that can be used to promote cold-start writing are detailed: Fun Way/Test Way; Out of the Gate Annotate; Annotate, Plan, Write (A.P.W.); and ACDC. Working some of these in throughout the school year is a great way to help students practice and prepare for the mandated assessments that almost every student must take.

What's a Writing Cooldown?

A cooldown after a physical workout allows the body to regulate heart rate and release lactic acid from muscles, among other benefits. In writing, a cooldown provides opportunities to reflect, regroup, and process.

One item that is significant has to do with the intensity of the activity. For example, when completing an HIIT (High Intensity Interval Training) routine, not completing a cooldown can have significant physical effects. Yet not completing a cooldown after a routine abdominal workout or a yoga routine may have fewer negative effects due to the intensity. However, a yoga routine is one in which a warmup is almost always necessary due to the flexibility tasks associated with those routines.

Similarly, when students are completing writing tasks that require a significant amount of stamina and are high intensity, these definitely warrant writing cooldowns so students have the time to process, reflect, and think through the material presented in the lesson. Think about how beneficial writing breaks and written conversations can be when dropped in during lessons that include especially dense and difficult material. A writing cooldown allows students to:

- Stop and think about the material presented.
- Articulate questions they might have about the material.
- Make connections to the lesson.

- Determine what items are clear and what items need clarification.
- Reflect on their learning.

Even though cooldowns in a workout might get skipped to conserve time, cooldowns in writing are extremely beneficial and can offer one more opportunity for students to practice the craft of writing. Plus, because they are typically quick and easy to drop in at the end of a lesson, there is not a whole lot of planning when adding them to your instructional routines. Cooldown strategies featured in this chapter include Exit Slip Variations; Top Ten Plays; and Writing Wordle.

What About Time?

Now, I certainly am guilty of skipping the warmups and cooldowns many days when completing a workout. Part of this is simply because sometimes I need to save time. However, this time saver can result in less-than-optimal performance. Skipping a warmup can have adverse effects on mobility and performance. Skipping a cooldown doesn't allow your heart rate to slowly return back to normal and can sometimes result in injuries or other physical symptoms like dizziness, nausea, and trouble breathing.

But in the classroom, the reality is that there might not be time for students to complete a cooldown for every writing task, and they may not even need one depending on the task. When students are completing a writing engagement that they are familiar with or one that involves material they are well versed in, a specific cooldown might not be necessary. But when new, dense content is the focus or there is an extended difficult writing task that students must complete, cooldowns are just good practice. Giving students time to reflect on their learning in small quick bursts can help aid them as they work on self-assessment tasks through reflections on their learning. These can have big payouts when it comes to fostering student autonomy and individual agency in the classroom.

When planning writing lessons and determining if a warmup or cooldown is needed, consider the following:

- Is this the first time students have written in this genre?
- What about the material they are writing about? Is it complex and difficult?
- Do students have adequate background knowledge about the content?
- Is this an extended writing engagement?
- Will students be expected to revisit this work at a later date?

Thinking through items like those listed above can help teachers make certain that the supplemental writing tasks (warmups, cooldowns, etc.) are well matched and can leverage instructional time for optimal performance.

FUN WAY/TEST WAY (COLD START)

One question I often get from teachers is how to transfer the fun writing activities using sticky notes, paint strips, and address labels into the traditional demands of state-mandated assessment tasks. In this case, a functional chart, much like the AKA charts (Harper, 2017) or the Leveled Words charts (Harper, 2022), can help students draw connections between the cool, fun ways we write in class and the more traditional and structured writing seen on assessments. Transferring what is done in the nontraditional writing assignments to the structured test confines can help ensure that students don't get stumped when they don't have a stack of sticky notes or paint strips to use on the assessment.

Putting It to Work

1. Use chart paper to create a class T Chart that includes a heading titled Fun Way and a second heading titled Test Way.
2. As you introduce strategies like the ones from this book that employ alternative modes for drafting (sticky notes, address labels, paint strips, etc.), include the strategy name and a sample on the side of the chart labeled Fun Way.
3. Use examples of traditional graphic organizers that are like what is produced with the nontraditional examples. For example, sticky note paragraph organizers are similar to the traditional five-paragraph graphic organizer.

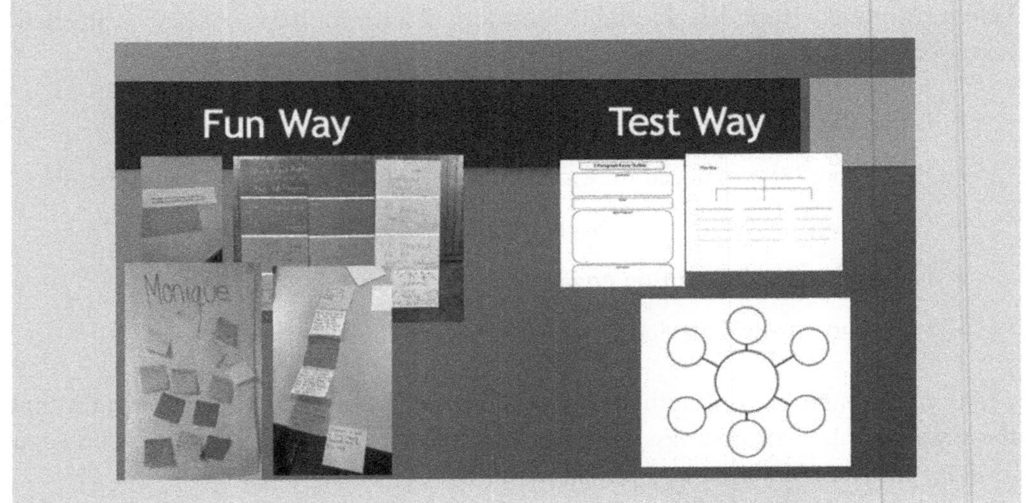

4. Paste those onto the side of the chart labeled Test Way.
5. As the school year progresses, continue to add tangible examples of the fun strategies and the traditional ones.
6. Refer back to the chart on a regular basis and encourage students to add to it on their own.

When to Use It

- Use it throughout the year to document and collect examples of different strategies and graphic organizers that can be used in class and on the assessments.
- Post this chart as a reminder of all the strategies and ideas that have been incorporated throughout the year.

Why It Works

- It serves as a tangible reminder of all the types of writings that students have completed during the entire year.
- Showing students how to transfer the nontraditional, low-stakes types of writing from class to the assessments can help them be more successful in their higher-stakes assignments and assessments.
- Making connections between the fun classroom strategies and the traditional ones can help students make the transition from the novel strategies to the ones tests demand.

Modifications

- Have students complete their own T Charts to reference in their personal notebooks.
- Organize the chart by genre so students can determine which types of brainstorming charts work best with certain types of genres.

Extensions

- Have students look online to find additional types of graphic organizers that can be added to the chart.
- Also include a sample of writing that was developed using the nontraditional and traditional method of organization.
- Have students make a list of all the genres that might work for each organizational method.

Digital Direction

- Have students record PSAs about each type of organizational item. This can serve as a how-to for other students and also reinforce the learning.
- Create these charts using a collaborative Google document instead.

Lesson Lead-Ins

- Use this as an anchor chart to support review lessons for assessments.
- Connect this to genre studies and lessons on planning and drafting.
- Use this as an informal way to document learning in the classroom over the course of an extended period of time.

OUT-OF-THE-GATE ANNOTATE (COLD START)

Many writing tasks that are present on assessments include multipart questions or prompts. Sometimes, students focus on completing one part of the prompt when in fact, answering the question fully might involve answering multiple questions and can even require students to collect evidence across multiple sources. Having students annotate and examine the prompt before they begin their drafting and planning can help students determine what is required for completion of the writing task. Out-of-the-Gate Annotate helps students pay attention to what is being asked of them before they begin writing.

Putting It to Work

1. Start by providing students with a sample on-demand prompt to use as practice.
2. Have students annotate by making markings on the prompt that would be feasible during a test. Don't have them color code or highlight because these tools are probably not going to be available on the assessment.
3. Encourage students to annotate by circling, underlining, double-underlining, or making some other notation that can be replicated on the test. (*Note*: Don't have them color code or highlight as these tools are probably not going to be available on an actual assessment.)
4. Once students have marked up the question, have them write out to the side what they need to do to answer the question.

Make sure you model this first. To do this, take a sample writing prompt that is displayed for the whole class. Together as a whole group, annotate the sample before moving on to the next ones.

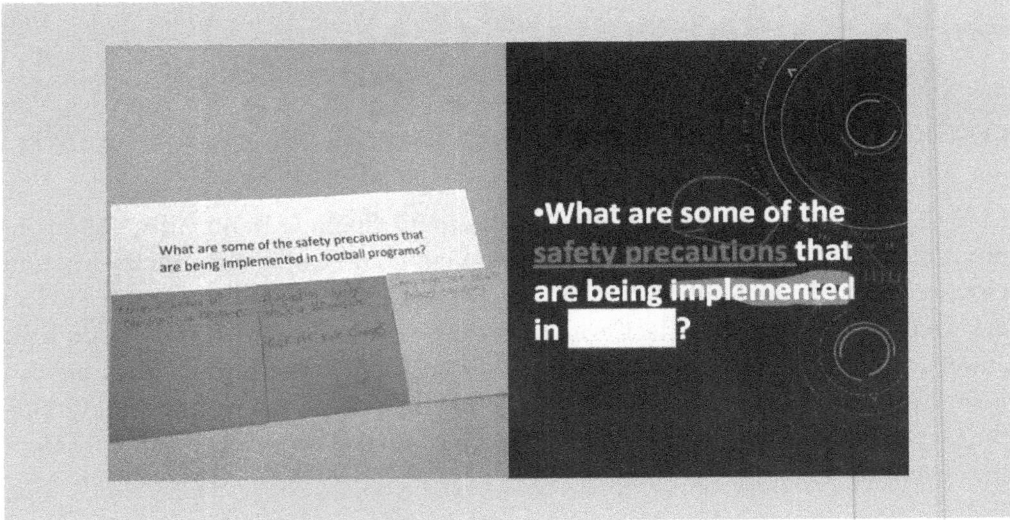

5. Have them make a list of the tasks/requirements they will have to complete to answer all parts of the question.

When to Use It

- Use this strategy throughout the year so that students get practice completing prompts that are cold starts.
- Connect this to constructed responses in other subject areas to help strengthen compositions and understanding.

Why It Works

- It mimics a real instructional demand that students must complete.
- It starts by having students pay attention to the prompt first, which is the first step in developing solid constructed responses.
- Preparing students for the demands of assessment ensures that students will be adequately prepared for success.

Modifications

- Have students start by orally annotating and sharing what each part of the prompt requires.
- Break students into groups and have them practice annotating in a group setting first and then move on to solo annotation.

Extensions

- Extend this cold start strategy into the fully involved Annotate, Plan, Write (APW) lesson on page 168, Paint Strip Arguments lesson on page 131, Sticky Note Paragraphs lesson on page 137, or the Mix and Match Remix lesson on page 146 where students do use a color-coding technique to annotate.
- Continue this lesson with multiple sources and have students begin drafting the constructed response.
- Connect this lesson to the Resource Roundup on page 45.

Digital Direction

- Have students use a collaborative tool like Jamboard to record their annotation noticings.
- Use Diigo to digitally annotate the prompt for online environments.

Lesson Lead-Ins

- Lead this into the strategy Resource Roundup on page 45.
- Use this strategy as an opener for multipart constructed response work.
- Share this strategy throughout the year, but especially during testing season and review times.

ANNOTATE, PLAN, WRITE (APW) (COLD START)

Part of writing an effective constructed response not only involves the ability to determine what the question is asking the writer to do but also relies largely on the planning and execution of the task in a short, confined time. The Annotate, Plan, Write (APW) strategy takes the Out-of-the-Gate Annotate strategy a step further by helping students plan their writing and then begin drafting for their writing on demand piece. Practicing this strategy can help students successfully complete their on-demand writing tasks.

Putting It to Work

Of course, it is important for you to model this as well. You might encourage students to create an APW chart like the one included as a template to make notes as they go along.

1. Start by providing students with a sample on-demand prompt to use as practice.
2. Have students annotate by making markings on the prompt that would be feasible during a test; avoid color coding or highlighting as these tools are probably not going to be available on the assessment. This is the A part of the strategy.
3. Encourage students to annotate by circling, underlining, double-underlining, or making some other notation that can be replicated on the test.
4. Once students have marked up the question, have them plan out their writing. Students should consider adding a specific amount of time for each part or include a ballpark number of sentences. They might do this part as a storyboard or list, or they might use a traditional graphic organizer from the Fun Way/Test Way chart. This serves as the P part of the strategy.
5. Once they have annotated and planned out their procedure, students should begin writing. This is the W part of the strategy.

When to Use It

- Use this strategy throughout the year so that students get practice completing prompts that are cold starts.
- Connect this to constructed responses in other subject areas as a way to help strengthen compositions and understanding. Help students get those extra "stamps" in their literacy passports!

Why It Works

- It mimics a real instructional demand that students must complete.
- It starts by having students pay attention to the prompt first, which is the first step in developing solid constructed responses.
- This strategy moves a step further by having them plan their writing task before they move into the actual writing.
- Preparing students for the demands of assessment ensures that students will be adequately prepared for success.

Modifications

- Have students start by orally annotating and sharing what each part of the prompt requires.
- Put students into different groups for annotating and planning. Have the A group annotate the prompt and the P group plan the writing.
- Break students into groups and have them practice annotating in a group setting first and then move on to solo annotation.

Extensions

- Extend this cold start strategy into the fully involved Mix and Match Remix on page 146 where students do use a color-coding technique to annotate.
- Have students add the letter S to the acronym and have them summarize their process.
- Continue this lesson with multiple sources and have students begin drafting the constructed response.
- Connect this lesson to the Resource Roundup on page 45.
- Connect this lesson to the Fun Way/Test Way charts so students can get ideas for planning their writing.

Digital Direction

- Have students use a collaborative tool like Jamboard to record their annotation noticings.
- Use Dabble to plan out their drafts.
- Use Diigo to digitally annotate the prompt for online environments.

Lesson Lead-Ins

- Use this strategy when you are introducing multistep writing prompts.
- Practice this strategy throughout the year, but highlight it during assessment and write-on-demand season.

ACDC (COLD START)

No, this isn't the rock band that gave us such great hits as "Thunderstuck" and "Back in Black." Instead, this is another cold-start strategy that uses an acronym for students to remember. ACDC stands for Assess (the question), Craft (your position), Determine (evidence), and (develop a) Conclusion. This particular strategy works best with prompts that require students to collect evidence and craft their position for writing. Argumentative essays, writings with textual evidence, and research: These work best with this particular strategy.

Putting It to Work

1. Start by providing students with a sample on-demand prompt to use as practice. Use on-demand prompts that focus on argumentative writings and/or ones that focus on research and utilize the integration of textual evidence.
2. Have students Assess the question by reading the prompt and making notations about what the prompt is asking them to do.
3. Encourage students to annotate as they assess by circling, underlining, double-underlining, or making some other notation that can be replicated on a test.
4. Once students have assessed and annotated the question, have student Craft their position. This might be in the form of a thesis statement or a claim.
5. After students have written their claim or position, have them Determine what evidence they will need from the text to support their thesis or claim. They can list these items out on the ACDC template on the companion website.
6. Use the claim or position statement that was drafted in Step 2 to develop a possible Conclusion for the writing composition.

When to Use It

- Use this strategy throughout the year so that students get practice completing prompts that are cold starts.
- When working with prompts that require textual evidence, supporting research, or focus on the argumentative genre, this is a great go-to strategy.
- Use this to ease into compositions that include thesis statements.

Why It Works

- Each step has a specific focus and requires the students to pay attention to different parts of the writing task.
- This strategy is tailored specifically for a certain type of writing prompt so it isn't necessarily a one-size-fits-all approach.
- Preparing students for the demands of assessment writing ensures that students will be adequately prepared for success.

Modifications

- Focus on one part of the acronym at a time. For example, because crafting a position or making the claim might be more difficult for some students to articulate, spend extra time working through that section.
- Have students play around with drafting different positions and claims. Then have them make determinations about what types of evidence would best support each claim.
- Break students into groups and have them work through this strategy initially in a cooperative setting.

Extensions

- Have students add the letter D to the end of the acronym (ACDCD) and have them start drafting their composition.
- Continue this lesson with multiple sources and have students begin drafting the constructed response.
- Connect this lesson to the Resource Roundup on page 45 by having students rotate around the room as they determine what evidence is needed.

Digital Direction

- Have students use a collaborative tool like Jamboard to record their annotation noticings.
- Use Padlet for students to have video discussions about their claims and evidence.
- Use Diigo to digitally annotate the prompt for online environments.

Lesson Lead-Ins

- Use this strategy when you are introducing multistep writing prompts.
- Focus on this strategy when working on prompts that focus on writing arguments, making claims, drafting thesis statements, or incorporating textual evidence in writing.

EXIT-SLIP VARIATIONS (COOLDOWN)

Exit slips aren't new in classroom instruction, but there are new ways to integrate this old-school, proven cooldown that aids students in reflecting on their learning. Exit slips offer teachers one more opportunity to quickly assess learning, and they allow students the ability to process, reflect, and think through the lesson material once more. Plus, exit slips are quick writing activities that can be dropped in just about any lesson. However, maintaining a fresh rotation of exit slips can prevent exit-slip burnout and can help you plan and modify future instruction based on what information is presented by the students.

Here you'll see a variety of exit-slip options, following a standard set of procedures, when to use them, benefits, and lead-ins. Since the overall frame of when and how to use exit slips shouldn't get altered much, look for a variety of exit-slip options after the procedural section.

Putting It to Work

1. Based on the content of the lesson, determine what type of exit slip you might want students to complete. For example, when presenting new content, you might want to incorporate an exit slip that includes a component where students can include any items of confusion or misconception.
2. Either post the chosen exit-slip for students to see, or use one of the premade templates found in the appendices section on the companion website.
3. Give students two to three minutes to complete the exit slip.
4. Collect and then share with the class at the beginning of the next class session, or use the information gained to plan the next instructional lesson.

When to Use It

- When you are introducing new material or continuing instruction on a concept to measure student understanding.
- As a way to check in with students in an informal manner.
- When you want to ease students into daily writing by providing opportunities for them to reflect and process information through a written modality.

Why It Works

- Exit slips serve as quick, informal ways to gauge and assess students learning in an informal manner.
- They incorporate a quick burst of writing that can aid students in processing information, clarifying any misconceptions, or extending their thinking.
- Most are completed on small pieces of paper (those small pieces of real estate), which can be less intimidating for many students.
- There is no major focus on grammar, spelling, or sentence construction, so students can feel free to write without penalty.

Modifications

- Use these not only at the end of a class period but also at the end of an instructional task. For example, add an exit slip when students complete a lab activity, movie clip, or collaborative task as a way to check in on their learning.
- Have students collaboratively complete exit slips with a partner. For some students, talking through the material as they plan how to complete the exit slip can improve their understanding.
- Depending on the exit-slip format, switch them up and use them as entrance slips or tickets in the door.

Extensions

- Redistribute the exit slips to the class on the following day. Make sure you don't give students back their own exit slips. Have their peer respond to part of their exit slip.
- Take questions raised from the exit slips to extend into research possibilities.
- Based on the material gathered in the original exit slip, use the data to construct purposeful, small-group engagements or teacher-led stations.
- Post the exit slips in stations throughout the room. Have students rotate through and read what their classmates wrote. Then have them draft an overarching memo or reflection based on their review of the exit slip data.

Digital Direction

- Use digital applications like Jamboard, Padlet, or Flipgrid for students to record their information.
- Use the Collaborate feature in Nearpod for students to post their material.
- Try Backchannel Chat as a way for students to have a live, digital conversation about their learning.
- Use Socrative to collect exit-slip feedback.

Lesson Lead-Ins

- Because exit slips are used as recaps or reflections following lessons or activities, they really function more as *lead-outs*. However, material gained from what is written in the exit slips can help you plan for future lessons.
- Use exit slips to help plan for specific and purposeful review lessons. If exit slips indicate that students have mastered a particular component, skip that when reviewing. If there is a lack of understanding on a specific section, then review lessons can be focused on that part.
- Rearrange the format and use these options as entrance slips/tickets in the door or quick writes that jump-start a lesson.

Earth, Wind, and Fire

Earth	What is one item that is solid under your feet?
Wind	What is one item that is still blowing around in your head?
Fire	What's one part of the lesson that you are on fire for?

Earth, Wind, and Fire

Earth	What is one item that is solid under your feet? Claims require textual evidence.
Wind	What is one item that is still blowing around in your head? My topic makes it hard to find unbiased sources. How do I know if my source is credible?
Fire	What's one part of the lesson that you are on fire for? I am excited about using video clips and pictures as evidence.

Triangle, Circle, Square

▲	What are three things that you learned in the lesson today?
●	What is one part that is still rolling around in your head?
■	What's one part that you have squared away?

△ 3 Things that helped me think through research
• wording of RQs → "How might ___ impact ___"
• tightening up participants (grade range, maybe "6–12" over K–12, for example
• being broader w/ participants — doesn't have to just be teachers — can be instructional coaches, interventionists, more

□ 1 Thing Squared Away
• how to take field notes

○ 1 Thing that is still rolling around
• what we are going to use as a framework

Touchdown, Fumble, Pass

Touchdown	What was your big score for the day?
Fumble	What did you not get today? What part needs clarification? Where did your understanding drop off?
Pass	What part of the lesson would you pass on?

Touch Down, Fumble, Pass Native Americans

Touch Down	**What was your big score for the day?** I learned about native tribes and how they adapted with european settlement
Fumble	**What did you not get today? What part needs clarification? Where did your understanding drop off?** I don't quite understand how information on tribes was recorded before europeans.
Pass	**What part of the lesson would you pass on?** I would pass on the knowledge that most Native American tribes lost huge parts of their land and culture due to european claiming their land.

ACDC

A (ASK)	Ask me one question about today's material.
C (CONNECT)	Connect today's lesson to another concept.
D (DRAW)	Draw an image/picture that goes with the lesson.
C *(CUES)*	What cues can help you remember today's material?

ACDC

A (ASK)	Ask me one question about today's material. What causes erors in this process?
C (CONNECT)	Connect today's lesson to another concept. Genetics traits
D (DRAW)	Draw an image/picture that goes with the lesson.
C (CUES)	What cues can help you remember today's material? telephase – talking on telephone with 2 people telephase has 2 nuclear envelopes.

Throw SHADE

S	Summary sentence
H	Hints
A	Ask a question
D	Draw a picture or Define a concept
E	Examples

Unit Rate

Throw SHADE

S	Summary Sentence However many of a certain quantity there are.
H	Hints time goes in the bottom/denominator
A	Ask a Question Can unit rates be used for decimals
D	Draw a picture or Define a concept 3 packs per bag
E	Examples cost speeD

QC²

Q	Questions
C	Connections
C	Clarification

QC²

Q	Questions after Sarah came no thought of the mom or talked about her. Why?
C	Connections My mom's mom died
C	Clarification If Sarah married Jacob.

TOP TEN PLAYS (COOLDOWN)

One of the best ways to get students to have more buy-in for writing and the whole process is to provide them with tangible examples of writing and literacy skills in the real world. One of ESPN's most popular segments, *Top Ten Plays*, profiles the top plays or moments in sports for the week. This segment is a perfect example of literacy skills used in the real world. Think about it. To create a top ten list, the events must be summarized first, a literacy skill present in multiple standard sets and content classrooms. Because many of the top plays are from different sports, the reporters and commentators also have to utilize effective transitional words and phrases so that the material makes sense. Using Top Ten Plays can serve as an effective cooldown because it requires students to reflect on multiple aspects of the lesson and develop an overall one-sentence summary of a concept.

Putting It to Work

Top Ten Plays Video

1. Show students a video clip of the ESPN segment *Top Ten Plays*. (Hover over the QR in the margin for a good example, https://youtu.be/aSzQ7FPeu98.)
2. Talk about what students notice when watching the clip.
3. Ask them how they would utilize the same ideas and premise when discussing a novel, concept, or idea. It is important to help students make connections between what is done in the video example and how it can be transferred into the ELA content.
4. When students finish a unit, novel, or concept, discuss the important parts of the unit.

Ask students questions like:

- What types of sports are included?
- How long is each numbered event?
- What accompanying information is also included?
- How do the reporters get from one sport to the next?
- What factors affect inclusion on the list?

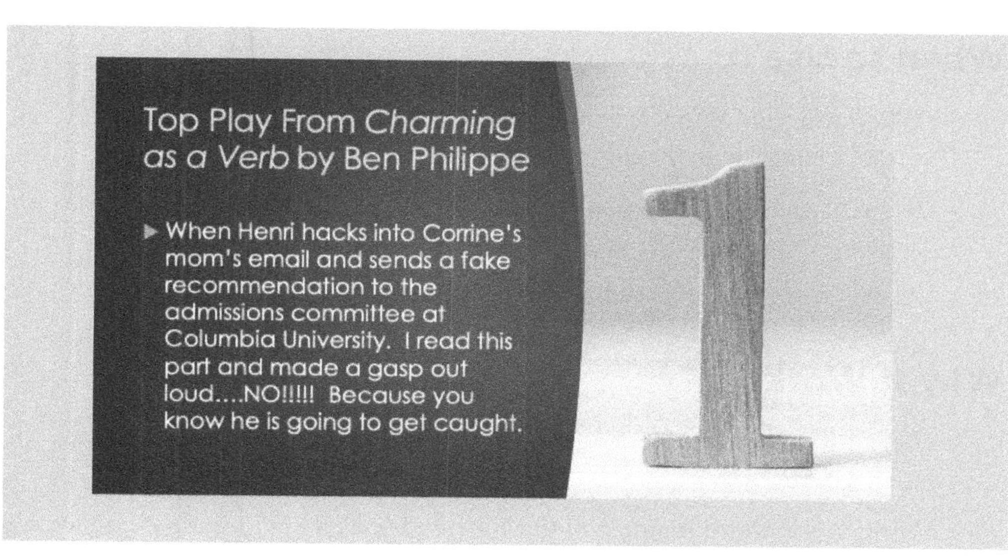

Top Play From *Charming as a Verb* by Ben Philippe
▶ When Henri hacks into Corrine's mom's email and sends a fake recommendation to the admissions committee at Columbia University. I read this part and made a gasp out loud....NO!!!!! Because you know he is going to get caught.
1

5. Make sure to hit the high points of the concept. Record these for students to see.

6. Using the template provided on the companion website, have students create their own Top Ten Plays for the concept you are studying.

Crossover
by Kwame Alexander

Top Ten Plays

Play/Event	Description	Justification
1. Josh's hair gets cut	He + Jordan bet and he loses.	Josh is obsessed w/ his locs.
2. Chuck "Da Man" Bell is their Dad.	He is a famous basketball player.	He influenced the boys to play.
3. Their dad isn't eating healthy.	They go to the Chinese Restaurant + Krispy Kreme.	This leads to his death.
4. Chuck has high blood pressure.	He goes to dr. and gets diagnosed.	This leads to his death.
5. Jordan dates Miss Sweet Tea.	Josh sees them kissing in the library	Josh had a crush on her and he's mad his brother is with her.
6. Josh does play by plays of his game.	He goes through all his moves.	It shows he is confident + obsessed with bb.
7. JB's nose is busted by Josh.	Josh throws a hard pass at his brother's face.	He is angry that he's dating Miss Sweet Tea.
8. Josh is suspended.	He gets in trouble for hitting his brother.	BB is everything to Josh.
9. Josh's dad has chest pains playing bb.	They are shooting free throws & he clutches his chest, but then he's ok.	This is foreshadowing his death.
10. Chuck Bell dies.	He has complications from a massive heart attack.	Their dad is everything to them so losing him is tragic.

7. Share with the class.

When to Use It

- When you want students to recap an extended novel, unit, or lesson by summarizing the main points.
- If you want students to use a real-world example of a summary as a model for a reflective summary lesson.
- As a quick one-sentence summary of the main points of a lesson.

Why It Works

- Because students craft one sentence at a time, it can make the task more manageable.
- Using a real-world example of the *Top Ten Plays* can help students see writing in the real world.
- Because students use a mentor text (video) as a model, they can make observations about what information should be included in their writing sample.

Modifications

- Instead of having students create the list of ten examples all at once, have them do a few each day as you work through the novel or unit. This way, they can write a small amount each day and then compile it into a full reflective document.
- Have students complete one Top Play reflection, which you compile into a class list of the Top Ten Plays.

Extensions

- Extend this cooldown into a review at a later date by revisiting the material listed in the Top Ten Plays and have students guess what the overall concept is.
- Have students use one of their Top Ten details as a springboard for completing a mock Pinterest board (Harper, 2017, 2022) with additional details including images, figures, quotes, and other pertinent information.
- Have students connect this cooldown to the Pizza Slice Summary (Harper, 2022) or summarize it further into a hashtag or tweet (Harper, 2017).

Digital Direction

- Have students recreate an actual video segment of the Top Ten Plays modeled after the mentor text video.
- Instead of initially creating their own top ten lists, have students annotate the mentor text using a video annotation program like Mote or VideoANT.

Lesson Lead-Ins

- Use this as a lead-in to any lessons that involve reviewing a concept.
- Have students use portions of their created lists as a way to connect previous concepts to ones.

WRITING WORDLE (COOLDOWN)

One of my new favorite puzzles that I complete almost daily is the *New York Times* Wordle. It's also popular with young people these days; last month I was on a field trip with high school students, and almost every single one of them completed the daily Wordle! The puzzle solving aspect that so many love whittled down to a random five-letter word. To find this random, out-of-context word, you have to utilize specific puzzle-solving skills. I am sure each person has their own method, but regardless, you can't simply guess words without a strategy and be successful.

When thinking about cooldowns in writing, using a similar activity can connect a real-world engagement with what is required in the academic setting. Making a few modifications can take these puzzles to another level by requiring students not just to guess an out-of-context word but also to connect it directly to the lesson of the day.

Putting It to Work

1. When completing a novel/story, genre of writing, or unit, have students make a list of words associated with the topic.
2. Provide students with the Writing Wordle template found on the companion website.
3. Explain to students that they will fill in the template with six five-letter words related to the concept, novel, or story the students have been reading. Make sure that you model this with students the first time around.
4. Refer back to the brainstormed list of words to see how many five-letter words were listed. Transfer those to the template first. For example, if students have finished reading *The Hobbit*, they might include these words:
   - Shire
   - Smaug
   - Bilbo
   - Dwarf
   - Jewel
5. Have students complete their template with additional five-letter words that relate to the topic.
6. Share with the class.

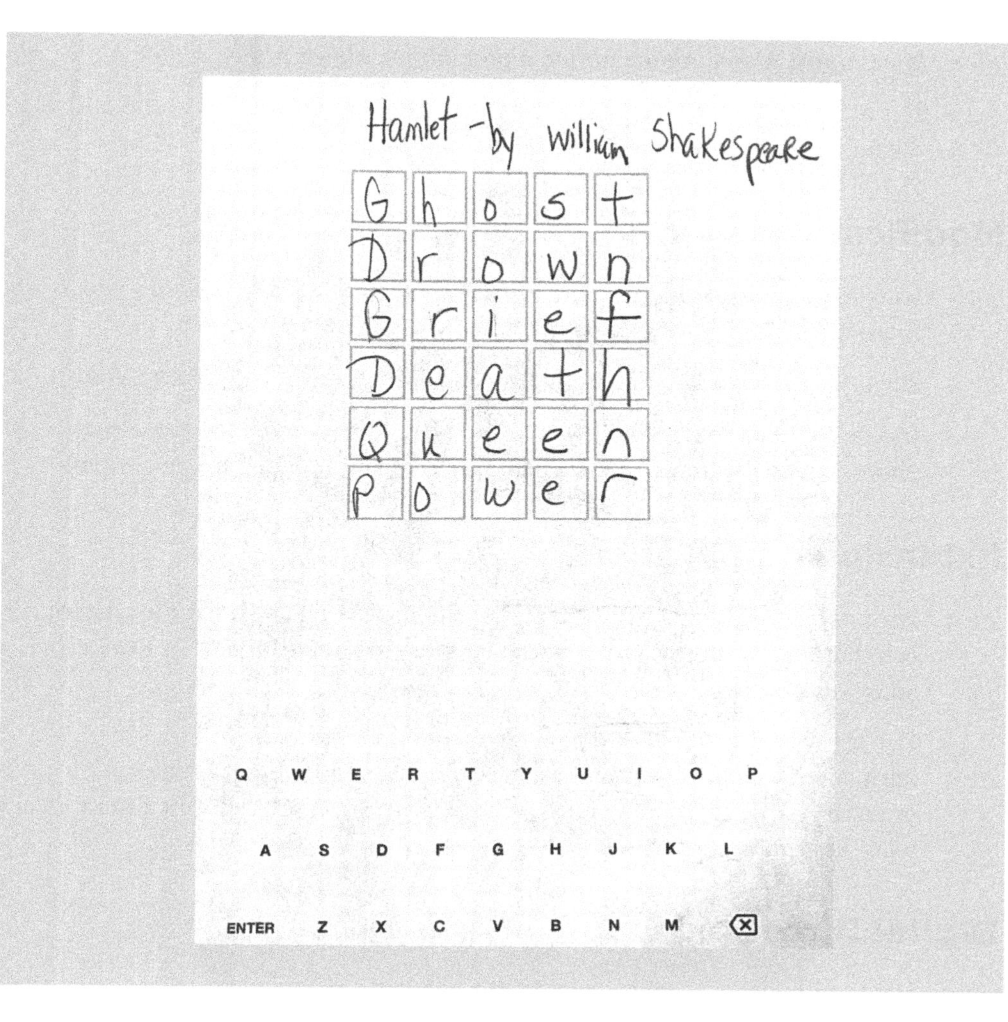

When to Use It

- When you want students to recap an extended novel, unit, or lesson by summarizing it into a few related words.
- If you want students to use a real-world example of a summary as a model for a reflective summary lesson.
- As a different way to incorporate vocabulary or words related to a reading into your instruction.
- As a way to remind students of what should be included in a particular genre of writing. For example, in the genre of argument, you might see the words *claim, prove,* and *cites* as examples.

Why It Works

- Because students focus on words related to a topic/text, the writing task is more manageable.

CHAPTER 1 Writing Fitness
Writing Warmups
CHAPTER 3 Targeted Training
CHAPTER 4 High Intensity Training
CHAPTER 5 Cold Starts and Cooldowns
CHAPTER 6 Rest, Recover, Revise
CHAPTER 7 Stretch Day
CHAPTER 8 A Balanced Diet of Reading and Writing

- It has a real-world connection to a popular puzzle game.
- It is a short, quick writing engagement that can be completed at the end of a lesson.

Modifications

- Instead of having students complete a list of six words related to a topic, have them create one word related specifically to the content.
- Have students work collaboratively to complete the entire Writing Wordle.
- Instead of requiring students to use only five-letter words, have students choose any six words, regardless of length, that are related to the content.

Extensions

- Extend this cooldown into a review at a later date by revisiting the material listed in the Writing Wordles and have students determine what work is being addressed.
- Use this cooldown the following day by redistributing the completed templates to different students. Have students add to their classmates' templates with additional words or have them write out a justification for each word originally chosen.

Digital Direction

- Have students create their own Writing Wordle online using www.mywordle.strivemath.com.
- Load the Writing Wordles into digital applications like Quizlet or Kahoot to involve the entire class in choosing the best words for a text.

Lesson Lead-Ins

- Use this as a lead-in to any lessons that involve reviewing a concept.
- When implementing class games like Taboo where students have to guess a concept without using certain words, use Writing Wordles as a way to get students thinking about the words associated with a concept.
- Connect this strategy to other word-related strategies like Survival Words or the Continuum of Words (Harper, 2017, 2022).

Chapter 6

REST, REVISIT, REVISE

Ahh . . . revision. Many students don't enjoy this part of the writing process simply because it involves revisiting something they may believe is already complete. I feel exactly the same way when a trainer corrects my form on a dead lift! Yet revision, like those subtle corrections made while working out in the gym, is where the magic happens! Much like in a physical workout, revision allows students to pay specific attention to a particular component, thus improving the overall composition. And like those corrections in the gym, sometimes revision is simple and a quick fix, and other times it involves a major overhaul. For example, keeping your elbows in while doing a triceps extension is a relatively easy fix, but executing a perfect push-up with a tight core, nonlocked arms, and a flat back? That takes a little more effort. Yet these revisions to physical form can help individuals avoid injuries and get better results. Revision can help writers clarify confusing parts, add details that lift the words off the page, and create meaningful and dynamic characters. This all adds up to building healthy writers.

One of the most vivid experiences I had with revision as a middle school teacher involved a conversation with a precious eighth-grade student who I watched copy her rough draft from another class verbatim onto a piece of fancy lined paper in her best cursive writing. Our conversation went something like this:

> "Hey, T. Tell me about your writing. What are you doing now?"
>
> "I'm writin' my final draft."
>
> "OK, so this is your rough draft?"
>
> "Mmm hmm" (and nods).
>
> "So . . . . how do you write your final draft?"

"I just copy what I wrote on this paper on the fancy paper."

"Well, how do you know what you need to fix?"

"I don't. I just copy it."

That exchange taught me a lot about revision. For one, some students don't really understand it and two, time must be built into instruction to address it. Purposeful instruction on what revising entails along with time to revisit compositions can help students solidify their understanding of a somewhat nebulous concept.

In some cases, revision is confused with general editing—you know, spelling, grammar, and what not. However, revision is not the same as editing. Revision involves a purposeful thought process regarding composition, format, structure, style, word choice, sentence structure, dialogue placement, and so on. Sometimes revision means words and sentences end up on the cutting floor, while other times revision involves relocation of paragraphs and quotes, and yet on many occasions, revision means elaboration and explanation.

What is interesting is the misconception that revision occurs at the tail end of composition creation, when really it occurs throughout. Revision is not a final destination; rather, it is a journey. While I am typing this manuscript, I am thinking through my sentences and revising as my thoughts hit the screen. This type of revision is ongoing and has a symbiotic relationship with drafting. It is a natural part of the writing process. Yet as I am drafting this manuscript now, my overall purpose is not revision, but rather composing my message. Much later, I will revisit this chapter with the sole purpose of revision, which will involve a different type of strategy and attention. During that time, I will examine this manuscript for specific revision purposes including clarity, word choice, and flow. I'll check to make sure I have provided clear instructions, that the images I chose are effective, and that my sentences are not awkward and clumsy. Do you see how *that* purpose is different than the initial purpose where I am drafting and subconsciously revising?

Despite the fact that revising for a purpose requires more strategic focus, the nature of writing and revision that naturally occurs when drafting can help students gain their confidence when they start the fully involved task of specific and purposeful revision. You might think about asking students some of these questions about their drafting process:

- Do you ever write sentences and change the words you are going to include based on your thoughts?
- Have you reread a sentence right after drafting it and made a change?
- How often do you choose the words you use based on what you know you can spell correctly?
- When you start writing, do you think about different ways to start off your paper? Correspondingly, do you think of options for conclusions?
- Do you sometimes summarize what you might say to save time when writing and use fewer words?

Questions such as these might help students begin to understand that they are in fact taking part in revision activities already, but they may not be aware that what they are doing counts as revision.

When addressing revision in writing, there are a few tips that can help make revision more successful:

- Not every piece of writing needs to be revised. This is especially important to consider for writing in the content areas. In many cases, the types of writing that are being crafted within that setting are used as a means to process material, think through content, and wrestle with meaning.
- Revision should be purposeful and focused. Having a clear focus for revision can help students craft better final products simply because they know what the expectations are for completion. Beware of the ambiguity that can result from simply telling students to read their papers and fix what is wrong or telling them to try to make it better.
- The act of revision is ongoing; it is not a final destination. Students take part in revision while they draft and when they consider specific changes and alterations when they revise for a targeted purpose.

Think about how football, basketball, swim coaches, and more get their players to improve. It's often not just with extra practice, but feedback that is focused, individualized, and frequent. Taking a page from that playbook can have big payoffs in the classroom.

- Revision takes time. While some types of revision can move quickly, sometimes students need additional time and opportunities to revisit their writing. In some cases, this means they need time away from what they wrote, because this can provide them with the distance needed to revise their writings.
- Sometimes revision needs to be completed individually but other times warrants collaborative and partner revision. Taking part in revision engagements in a variety of settings can aid students in becoming more proficient at revising in general.
- Time must be built in for revision. In today's busy classrooms, there often isn't time carved out for students to revisit their writings. Short pockets of time throughout a writing lesson or unit, as well as specific lessons focused on revision, can provide students with the time to revisit their thoughts and ideas.
- Some types of revision are not written. For example, my account of writing my mother's eulogy (Harper, 2022) is an example of revision and drafting that mainly existed in my thoughts and mental planning, yet they still count.

Quick Tip!

You may be wondering how to measure this when there is no tangible written evidence. Easy. Ask. Have a conversation with your students. Their descriptions of how they began planning and revising mentally can help teachers understand their writing processes.

I would be remiss if I did not say that for some, revision is perceived as painful. It often is equated with doing something wrong and finding errors. For example, look at this image of a small snippet of my dissertation that received no fewer than 30 track changes on page one! Yet that is only part of it. To help reframe revision as a positive part of the writing process, help students view revision as not simply criticism but rather an opportunity. While revision may not be everyone's most favorite part of the writing process, it can be quite rewarding. You see, when you start revising, it means you actually have a product drafted that you can work with and from. For me, that is already a win because it means I have words on the paper. The absolute worst sentences and paragraphs can be revised and made better, but a blank sheet of paper with nothing on it? What's there to revise? One of my favorite authors, Brod Bagert, once told a group of teachers to "write your worst." Why? Because when we tell students to try their best or write their best sentence, for many students, that seems unattainable and somewhat stressful. Yet if you tell students to write their worst? Anyone can do that! Plus, with strategic revision, the worst writing can get revisited and *become* their best!

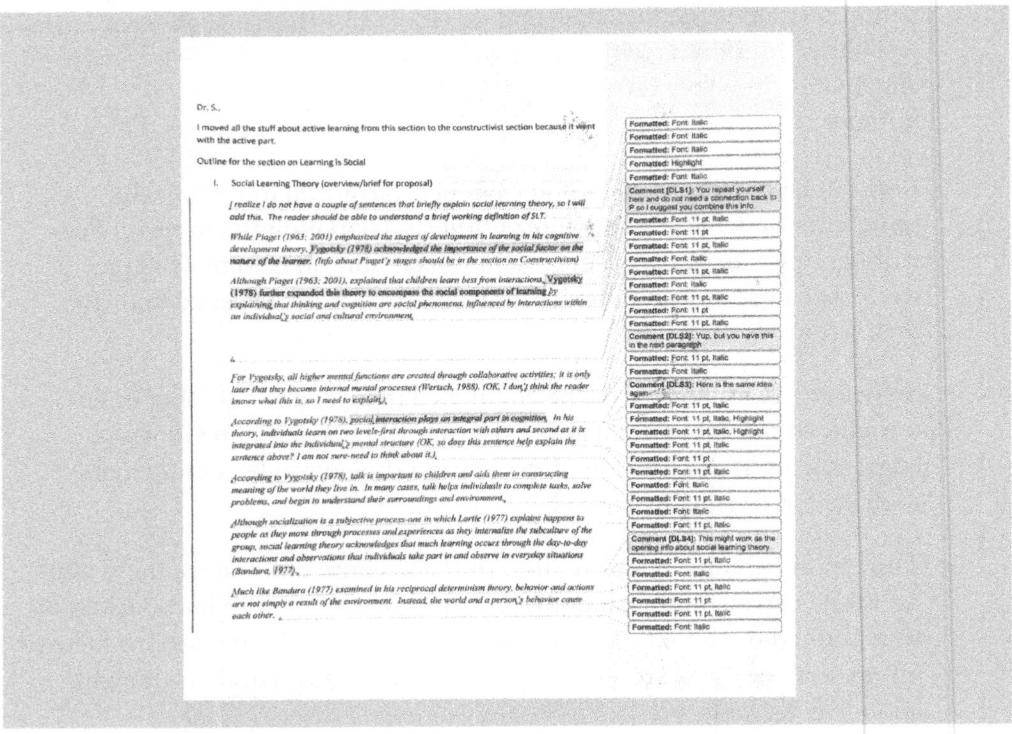
Dr. S.,

I moved all the stuff about active learning from this section to the constructivist section because it went with the active part.

Outline for the section on Learning Is Social

I. Social Learning Theory (overview/brief for proposal)

I realize I do not have a couple of sentences that briefly explain social learning theory, so I will add this. The reader should be able to understand a brief working definition of SLT.

While Piaget (1963; 2001) emphasized the stages of development in learning in his cognitive development theory, ***Vygotsky (1978) acknowledged the importance of the social factor on the nature of the learner.*** *(Info about Piaget's stages should be in the section on Constructivism)*

Although Piaget (1963; 2001), explained that children learn best from interactions, **Vygotsky (1978) further expanded this theory to encompass the social components of learning** *by explaining that thinking and cognition are social phenomena, influenced by interactions within an individual's social and cultural environment.*

For Vygotsky, all higher mental functions are created through collaborative activities; it is only later that they become internal mental processes (Wertsch, 1988). (OK, I don't think the reader knows what this is, so I need to explain).

According to Vygotsky (1978), ***social interaction plays an integral part in cognition.*** *In his theory, individuals learn on two levels-first through interaction with others and second as it is integrated into the individual's mental structure (OK, so does this sentence help explain the sentence above? I am not sure-need to think about it.)*

According to Vygotsky (1978), talk is important to children and aids them in constructing meaning of the world they live in. In many cases, talk helps individuals to complete tasks, solve problems, and begin to understand their surroundings and environment.

Although socialization is a subjective process-one in which Lortie (1977) explains happens to people as they move through processes and experiences as they internalize the subculture of the group, social learning theory acknowledges that much learning occurs through the day-to-day interactions and observations that individuals take part in and observe in everyday situations (Bandura, 1977).

Much like Bandura (1977) examined in his reciprocal determinism theory, behavior and actions are not simply a result of the environment. Instead, the world and a person's behavior cause each other.

Formatted: Font: Italic
Formatted: Font: Italic
Formatted: Font: Italic
Formatted: Highlight
Formatted: Font: Italic
Comment [DLS1]: You repeat yourself here and do not need a connection back to P so I suggest you combine this info.
Formatted: Font: 11 pt, Italic
Formatted: Font: 11 pt
Formatted: Font: 11 pt, Italic
Formatted: Font: Italic
Formatted: Font: 11 pt, Italic
Formatted: Font: Italic
Formatted: Font: 11 pt, Italic
Formatted: Font: 11 pt
Formatted: Font: 11 pt, Italic
Comment [DLS2]: Yup, but you have this in the next paragraph
Formatted: Font: 11 pt, Italic
Formatted: Font: Italic
Comment [DLS3]: Here is the same idea again
Formatted: Font: 11 pt, Italic
Formatted: Font: 11 pt, Italic, Highlight
Formatted: Font: 11 pt, Italic, Highlight
Formatted: Font: 11 pt, Italic
Formatted: Font: 11 pt
Formatted: Font: 11 pt, Italic
Formatted: Font: Italic
Formatted: Font: 11 pt, Italic
Formatted: Font: Italic
Formatted: Font: 11 pt, Italic
Comment [DLS4]: This might work as the opening info about social learning theory
Formatted: Font: 11 pt, Italic
Formatted: Font: Italic
Formatted: Font: 11 pt, Italic
Formatted: Font: 11 pt
Formatted: Font: 11 pt, Italic
Formatted: Font: Italic

In this chapter, you'll find a variety of revision strategies that can be used to teach a myriad of tasks, in both individual and collaborative settings. As you consider which strategies you want to integrate, make sure you think through the following:

- The purpose of the writing
- How will the final product look?
- Time allotment
- Connections to future writing lessons
- Writing genre
- Audience

Thinking through these simple details can ensure successful lessons and writing opportunities in every classroom. Plus, it helps both the teacher and student know what is expected in the revision task and how the task will be completed.

Quick Tip!

A shout-out to my dissertation chair, Dr. Diane Stephens, who taught me one of the best revision tips ever: When writing extended pieces, especially in the academic genre, take any sentences that don't fit yet and cut and paste them at the end of your article/document. Once you have finished writing, go back to those extra sentences that you've collected. Place them within the document as needed. The ones that are left over? Cut and paste them into a new document and name it "Extra Sentences." Later, if you need them, you'll have them. I can't tell you how many times that revision strategy has saved me!

Quick Tip!

When coaching revision, ask students nudge questions like:

- Are there items missing in any of the sentences?
- Structurally speaking, are any of them incomplete?
- What additional details might need to be added?

FIRST WORD

Habits are often difficult to break, especially bad ones! In some instances, students rely on the same sentence starters in their essays. Think about it. How often have you read a paper by a student that has sentence after sentence that starts off with the word *I*? How about sentence after sentence starting with *The*? And let's not forget the ever popular use of the conjunctions *and*, *so*, and *but*. In addition to these blatant repetitions, sometimes students rely on the same transitional phrases in extended compositions. However, when students write extended pieces that are multisentence, multiparagraph compositions, it can sometimes be difficult to weed through all those sentences to see just how many of them begin the same way. Drawing attention to the beginnings of sentences can help students make modifications to their sentences that can make their writing more fluid and effective.

Putting It to Work

Note: This strategy works best when students are drafting an extended, multiparagraph composition.

1. Provide students with a highlighter and a notecard.
2. Ask students to look at a composition of their own and highlight just the first word of every sentence.

Which Witch is Which

Cackles the witch

There once was a witch named Cackles who loved to make teachers mad. When she had gone to school she had gotten expelled. She had put a tack on the teacher's chair and then told the teacher the class pet did it. She loved to laugh but she would only play tricks on teachers. Nobody knows why but she had never enjoyed the teachers at her school.

When Cackles got an invitation to go back to school and ruin the teachers day, she knew that she had to make room in her schedule. She was so excited she knew that she had to dress fancy. She tried to look her best for the event.

Cackles lived alone with her pet frog. She liked to read and watch movies. Her favorite color was green and she liked spiders. She likes bright colors and odd outfits. She had always loved cool shoes to go with her outfit.

She wore her very tallest hat and a long cloak with spiders on it. She would ride a nimbus 2,000 to the school to go and torment the teachers. Cackles was tall and very skinny. She had straight brown hair and her skin had a hint of green. She had a few warts from touching toads on her hands. She looked creepy when she arrived at the school. She had a few rotten teeth and bushy eyebrows.

Cackles went to the school and pranked the teachers. She had a lot of fun. She was even joined by all of the students at the school. They were going to need to have Witch security now to keep the teachers safe.

3. Now have students transfer only those highlighted words on their notecards.

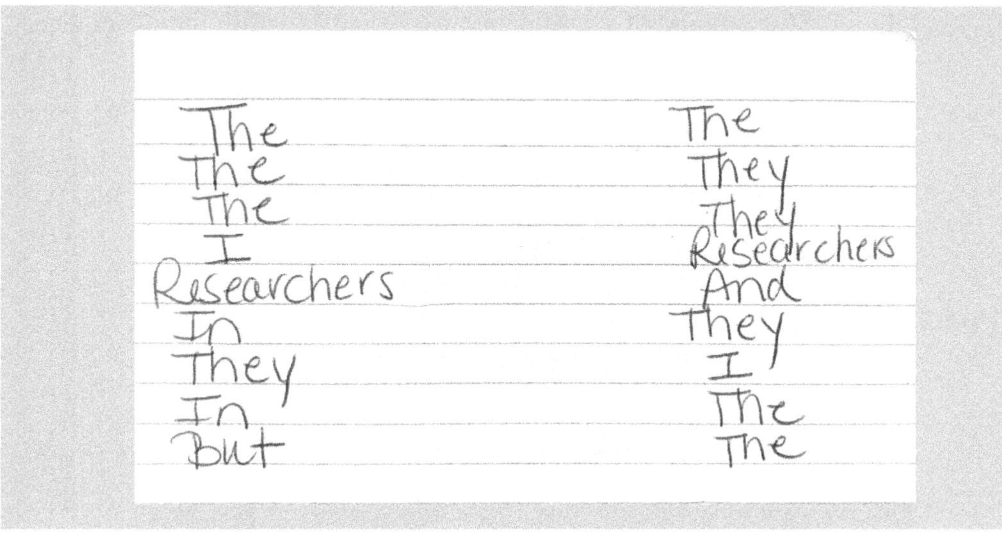

4. Instruct students to put their papers away and only look at the notecard. Doing this allows students to focus on just the beginning of each sentence. Because they have transferred the first word of every sentence on their notecard, they have reduced an entire essay down to a list of words so they can pay attention only to the beginnings of each sentence.

5. Have students discuss their list of words with a partner. Ask them to consider, based on their lists, if they have sentence structure issues (sentences that start with *and, but, so,* etc.), are they overly repetitive in their initial sentence starters, or are there run-ons present (this will be noticeable if there are only a few words listed on their notecards)?

6. Ask students to write on the back of their notecards one specific revision action they could take based on this list. This might include revising all their sentences that are indicative of fragment status or changing some of their sentence beginnings with other phrases.

7. Provide students time to make the chosen revisions.

When to Use It

- When students are working on extended pieces that can benefit from strategic revision.
- When writing personal narratives, as the tendency can be to start many sentences with the pronoun *I*.
- As a way to highlight the importance of sentence variety and overused phrases.

Why It Works

- It reduces the amount of text students are reading and gives them a strategic focus on just the first words.
- Revising the beginnings of specific sentences gives students a targeted focus for their revisions.
- It breaks the revision down into small manageable tasks: highlight, list, determine your action, and revise.

Modifications

- Students who omit punctuation and are habitual run-on offenders can highlight the end punctuation only. This can help students identify run-ons and can help students determine if they are overusing a certain type of sentence.
- Have students complete the First Word activity together as a class using the same writing sample. This can help scaffold students as they move from whole class, to collaborative, then to independent work.
- Use passages from novels as texts to examine. Have students make notes about how different authors start off their sentences and how it affects the flow.

Extensions

- Extend this from beyond the substitution of first words in the sentences to include instruction into sentence combining and sentence structure. Have a lot of short simple sentences? Try a compound one instead.
- Have students look for words they repeat throughout the essay and highlight them for revision.

You could even compare how different leveled books are structured. For example, in primary picture books, you might see that the same words are used over and over simply because of the vocabulary proficiency of a certain audience. Draw this to the student's attention because this can build an awareness regarding audience and word choice.

My sister and I ate popcorn at the circus. My mom took us to a birthday party. We saw elephants, horses, and monkeys at the circus. Going to the circus is a lot of fun. One time, we got tickets to go to the circus from a contest we won at school. We had the best time on our trip to the circus. It was late when we got home. We ate cake at the birthday party and we had fun. After we watched the animals perform we ate cotton candy we ate popcorn we rode the rides at the circus and we talked to our friends.

- Add this revision strategy to the students' revision tool belt and use it along with other revision strategies in this chapter for extended revision practice. For example, provide students with additional sample essays and have them determine which revision strategy would be best based on the needs of the essay.

Digital Direction

- Instead of print text, have students listen to speeches online and make notations of how often a speaker uses the same opening or closing.
- Have students brainstorm possible new beginnings on an application like Jamboard that can be shared with the class.
- Get students to record themselves stating the words from their notecards using a program like Padlet. Have a partner respond to their recording by making suggestions for revision based on what was said.

Lesson Lead-Ins

- Use this strategy in tandem or as a lead-in with Descriptive Writing With Calendars on page 125, or the Level Up strategy on page 212.
- Have students practice with this strategy as a springboard into suggestions for peer conferencing or self-evaluation.

BLESS, PRESS, ADDRESS

Years ago when I took part in the National Writing Project's Summer Institute at the University of South Carolina, I learned a catchy revision strategy for writing. Bless, Press, Address quickly became one of my favorite revision strategies, not just for its cool Southern inspired phrase ("Bless your heart"), but because it required students to examine their papers and determine what type of feedback was needed. With this strategy, students have to determine what type of conferencing assistance they need from a peer. Too often, students are over reliant on someone else to offer them suggestions for what is needed in their papers. Yet providing students with a strategy that can help them claim and articulate what is needed in their compositions helps them retain their ownership and autonomy over their own learning and writing, thus helping empower them as they make decisions about their work.

> **Quick Tip!**
>
> Speaking of autonomy and ownership over writing, here's a quick tip. When offering feedback to students, resist the urge to mark up their papers. Instead, write comments and suggestions on sticky notes, in the margin in a digital document, or on a separate sheet of paper. This makes it easier for students to respond and address the feedback since you haven't added any clutter to the paper—and it's nice to have a little checklist or to remove the stickies once a revision has been addressed.

Putting It to Work

1. Introduce conferencing and revision or provide a brief review.
2. Have students take out a sample of their own writings that they have completed or are currently drafting. These writing samples should be ones that are in the developed stages of drafting. Ideally, they should have a multiparagraph composition to evaluate.
3. Define each term:
   - If you want your paper *blessed*, then you will ask your conferencing partner to focus on the positives and good parts of your paper.
   - If you are not sure exactly what your paper needs regarding revision, ask your partner to help you *press* it, meaning you need help pressing the wrinkles out. Pressing often includes items such as general editing, making suggestions regarding word choice, asking clarifying questions, and so on.
   - If you know that there is a part of your writing that needs to be addressed, ask your partner to *address* the _________ of your paper. For example, you might know that your dialogue needs work, so you would ask your partner to address only the dialogue in your essay.
4. Put students with partners or in collaborative groups.

Bless, Press, Address

Bless *(Positive comments about the writing)*	your topic is interesting. The opening quote you used caught my attention.
Press *(Suggestions for improving the overall piece of writing, i.e. pressing out the wrinkles)*	FRAGMENTS - LOTS OF ANDS AND BUTS. THEY NEED TO BE FIXED.
Address *(Specific parts of the writing that need revision)*	Your ending drops off. There's no conclusion.

5. Have students take turns conferencing with their partners or groups using the Bless, Press, Address strategy. If desired, use the Bless, Press, Address template on the companion website.

When to Use It

- This strategy is best used when implementing teacher-student writing conferences and/or peer conferences.
- Use this when you want students to evaluate their overall piece of writing and make holistic observations about the entire piece.

Why It Works

- It gives students direction; because there are only three options, students are able to determine which one best meets the needs of the writing they are revising.
- The Bless option offers a safety net. If students are not quite sure what is needed in their target piece of writing, opting to have it *blessed* gives students the ability to focus on the positives of their piece. Correspondingly, the Press option gives students the ability to ask for general assistance if they do not have a specific item that needs to be addressed.

Modifications

- Instead of having students choose which purpose they want their conference partner to assume, have a Bless Day, Press Day, and Address Day where everyone focuses on those specific actions.
- Create Bless, Press, and Address stations and have students rotate through each station until they have visited all three.
- Use Bless, Press, Address as a reading discussion strategy. For example, after reading a chapter in a novel, have students Bless it by sharing parts they liked about it. Have students Press by discussing parts of the novel that they found confusing or difficult. Last, have students Address a specific event in the novel and discuss it.
- Use Bless, Press, Address as a feedback strategy for oral presentations. Instead of always using a formal rubric, have students use this strategy to offer feedback on speeches and other oral presentations.

Extensions

- Extend this from a teacher-student conferencing engagement to a peer conferencing engagement.
- Have students brainstorm different feedback stems they might use as they conference with their peers. For example, when blessing pieces, you might use phrases like, "I liked it when you . . . ," "the way you described __________ made me think of . . . ," and so on.
- After conferencing, have students write a two-sentence plan of action that explains how they plan to utilize and implement the feedback they received.

Digital Direction

- Use a discussion tool like Flipgrid for students to digitally respond.
- Use breakout rooms in Zoom for each Bless, Press, and Address station.
- Create Google documents or Jamboards for students to collectively offer feedback on a text.
- Use Google Chat for students to discuss compositions using this strategy.

Lesson Lead-Ins

- Offer this strategy as a warmup for a full conferencing period where students work with multiple partners on revisions.
- Use this strategy as a way for students to collectively evaluate a piece of writing using constructive feedback.
- Offer this as a lead-in to revision stations where students rotate through multiple revision tables.

I.N.K.

Part of effective revision often involves knowing what details need to stay and which ones need to hit the road. Depending on the purpose of the writing, more or less detail may be needed. For example, in a summary, students may find that they need less information than they would in a piece that requires an extended response. Correspondingly, the crafting of an extended composition may require additional evidence and justifications to create a solid piece of writing. Knowing the purpose for writing can help students determine exactly what they need to omit and what they need to keep. The I.N.K. strategy focuses on just that because it stands for "I Need to Kick" and "I Need to Keep."

Putting It to Work

1. Provide a writing sample for the class to critique.
2. Go over the purpose of the writing so that students are clear on why it was written and the overall purpose. Don't be tempted to skip this part because it is integral for solid understanding. If students do not know the purpose of the writing, it will be difficult to determine which details need to be kicked or kept.
3. Based on the purpose, students will determine what details need to be kept and which ones need to be kicked.
4. Provide students with a copy of the I.N.K. template on the companion website.
5. Have students work individually or with a partner to identify which details should be kept or kicked and have them record them on their template.

I.N.K.

Title of my Writing Connecting the Continental Army and french Navy

I Need to Keep (Details/Items I need to keep in my paper.)	I Need to Kick (Details/Items I need to kick out of my paper.)
Yorktown - Supplies trap	Caribbean ports, travel before and after Yorktown
Benjamin franklin Ambassador	Role as founding father Personal background
Marquis de ~~Lafa~~ Lafayette Military Service Reflection the AR = his beliefs	family background, Military commission Specific details on trip to America
General Cornwallis trapped at Yorktown Causes of Surrender	Where he went, what he did after his surrender
Valley forge Improved soldiers' capabilities Impact on french decision Time of year, location	Specific Units / states represented

6. Share with the class.
7. Once the class has collectively determined which details stay or which ones go, revisit the original writing sample and make the needed revisions.
8. Compare the newly revised sample to the original one and discuss as a class.
9. Next, have students take a sample of their own writings and work either individually or collaboratively to complete their own I.N.K. template. Easy writings to start with include summaries, personal narratives, and persuasive compositions.

When to Use It

- When you want students to examine their writing and determine which details need to be omitted and which details needed to stay.
- If students are working on developing summaries, reflections, or pulling out key ideas from sources.
- As a lead-in for peer conferencing and/or self-reflection and evaluation.

Why It Works

- The acronym can help students remember exactly what to focus on: important details and extraneous ones.
- It provides students with a directed focus for revision.
- In many cases, this strategy can be completed in a short amount of time.
- It works with a variety of genres across multiple content areas.

Modifications

- Instead of using this as a revision strategy, use this as a note-collecting strategy where students keep or kick important information from a variety of texts.
- Break down a sample paragraph into individual sentences written on notecards, sentence strips, or slips of paper. Have students physically keep or kick the sentences by sliding them into the appropriate piles for consideration.

Extensions

- Once students have determined the material they need to keep, have them come up with several hashtags (Harper, 2017) that capture the main idea.
- After students determine what they need to keep versus what needs to be kicked, extend the engagement to the P.E.N. strategy on page 201 where students expound on what they have already written.
- Connect this strategy to the Summary Sweep activity (Harper, 2022).

Digital Direction

- Have students annotate their writing samples digitally with a software application like Diigo. With this program, they can color code what should be kept and kicked.
- Use Jamboard to brainstorm collaboratively what should be kept and kicked. Use different color sticky notes on the program for easy organization.

Lesson Lead-Ins

- Use this as a starter for note-taking with a purpose, peer conferencing days, or summary crafting.
- Tie this in with the Pizza Slice Summary strategy found in *Write Now & Write On* (Harper, 2022).
- Use this strategy as a transition to the Hashtag Summaries found in *Content Area Writing That Rocks (and Works!)* (Harper, 2017).

P.E.N.

While the I.N.K. strategy focuses on the determination of important versus extraneous material, the P.E.N. strategy helps students focus on giving additional details and elaborating on material already in their writing. This is especially helpful for students when they are writing extended pieces for several purposes and learning how to cite sources to support claims and ideas. Take research writing, for example. Some students may already know a lot about a topic but might struggle with adding specific details and including summarized research from a variety of sources.

Using the strategy of Prove, Elaborate/Explain, New Details (P.E.N.) provides students with a solid framework for developing fully involved compositions. Because students sometimes might not know exactly how to add more detail, giving them suggestions like proving the statement, elaborating on the material, or adding new details can give students a targeted focus for completion and revision. Plus, because each of the components address some aspect of adding more detail to a composition, it is a natural fit for compositions that require citation of evidence and support from multiple sources.

Putting It to Work

Note: The first time you attempt this strategy, do a whole class lesson so that students can see how it works in a whole group setting.

1. Provide students with a sample paragraph or two that needs more detail and substance.
2. Go over the paragraph with the students and begin a class discussion about the overall message and topic of the paper. (Make sure to draw attention to the purpose of the composition, because this will make it easier for students to complete the task.)
3. Have students highlight sections in the paragraph that are unclear, need additional details, require further evidence, and so on.
4. Provide students with the P.E.N. template found on the companion website.
5. Have students locate details they need to prove and include them in the Prove section of the template. Do the same for the Elaborate/Explain and New Details section.

P.E.N. Strategy

Prove	Prove that students need time for physical activity. Back it up. stats?
Elaborate/Explain	Explain more about how physical activity benefits students socially & emotionally.
New Details	–class time in PE has decreased. 3.8% elem., 7.9% middle, 2.1% high } get enough PE time

6. Once students have listed those details in each corresponding box, have them use their resources to complete each task. These resources might include digital texts, print sources, or peer collaboration. This is a great opportunity to incorporate some research as well!
7. Have students choose one item from each section (P.E.N.) and add it to the existing composition.
8. Share with the class.
9. Explain how these additions improved the paper.
10. Have students apply the P.E.N. strategy to their individual compositions.

When to Use It

- If you want students to work on adding more detail to their research and informational papers.
- As a springboard for adding and citing evidence in compositions.
- When you want students to specifically focus on certain aspects of revisions (adding details, citing evidence, etc.).

Why It Works

- It offers students focused direction on revision.
- The template can be used with a variety of genres and content areas.
- Because there are only three parts to the template, students may feel less overwhelmed with the task.

While this strategy can be used with multiple genres, it works best with argument, research and informational, and persuasive. While it can be used to expand and elaborate a personal narrative, I would suggest using one of the other genres as the focus for initial instruction with this strategy.

Modifications

- For the whole class introduction, instead of having everyone do all parts of the template, divide students into groups of Ps, Es, and Ns. Have each group complete their specific letter task, then have them regroup with students from the other letter sections and share.
- Introduce one letter of the template at a time. Give students time to master each section before moving on to the next one.
- Have students choose which letter on the template they would like to use as their focus for their paper. Proceed with revision.

Extensions

- Use this strategy in tandem with the I.N.K. strategy on page 197.
- Have students connect this strategy with the NVA^2 strategy on page 66.
- Add an S to the acronym for Support, Summarize, or Say More as another extension.

Digital Direction

- Instead of having them write down their suggestions on the template, put students in Zoom breakout rooms and have them focus on a specific aspect of the strategy.
- Use Flipgrid to discuss digitally how to make the adjustments on the template.
- Use Padlet to post suggestions for each letter of the template.

Lesson Lead-Ins

- Use this as a lead-in into research-based writing or other extended pieces.
- Have students complete this as a warmup before completing peer conferences.
- Use this strategy as an opener for lessons on citing evidence and using research to support claims.
- Work this strategy in as a bell ringer when drafting and crafting arguments as they find support for their claims.

SLINKY PARAGRAPHS

As a young child, I remember seeing commercials for Slinkies on the television where children proclaimed their fascination and awe over watching this metal toy "walk" down the stairs. At that time, I lived in a single-story house, so when I received one for Christmas, I was beyond disappointed that my Slinky would not "walk" and instead, became a tangled mess of metal wire.

Years later, when teaching a middle school writing class, for whatever reason, I remembered that Slinky and while I was not impressed with its entertainment factor, it seemed like a great visual aid for writing class. You see, good writing that flows contains a mixture of long and short sentences. If you include too many simple sentences, your writing sounds choppy and staccato. Include too many overly verbose sentences, and your reader can get bogged down in the words. Instead, crafting a careful mix of simple, compound, and complex sentences can ensure that your writing is fluid and effective. Believe it or not, a Slinky can actually *show* students this characteristic in another form.

> **Quick Tip!**
>
> Dollar stores, online retailers, and retail stores like Target still carry Slinky toys for under $5; when you see them, stock up! You'll need one for yourself for modeling and a few for kids to use in group work.

Putting It to Work

1. Show students a writing sample as a whole class.
2. Remind students that good writing should contain a mix of long and short sentences to create an effective flow.
3. Show students the Slinky. Model stretching the Slinky in and out to mimic how the sentences in a composition should flow. For example, stretch the Slinky out to represent a long sentence. Hold it closer together to mimic a short sentence.

4. Model with the Slinky how a fluid composition would look. Think about an accordion; your hands should stretch and shrink the Slinky.

5. Have the class read aloud the sample together. While the students are reading, use the Slinky to mimic the long and short sentences.

6. Ask students to comment on what they noticed about the Slinky as they read. Did it stay about one length? Were there times when it was stretched farther than the teacher could reach? Did it vary in length from long to short?

7. Based on these observations, have students determine what revision actions they might take. For example, if the Slinky stayed about the same short length, they may recommend adding more details to the sentences to stretch them.

8. Put students in a group or with a partner.

CHAPTER 1 Writing Fitness
CHAPTER 2 Writing Warmups
CHAPTER 3 Targeted Training
CHAPTER 4 High Intensity Training
CHAPTER 5 Cold Starts and Cooldowns
CHAPTER 6 Rest, Recover, Revise
CHAPTER 7 Stretch Day

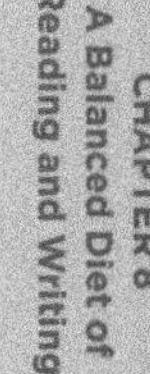

CHAPTER 1 Writing Fitness
CHAPTER 2 Writing Warmups
CHAPTER 3 Targeted Training
CHAPTER 4 High Intensity Training
CHAPTER 5 Cold Starts and Cooldowns
CHAPTER 6 Rest, Recover, Revise
CHAPTER 7 Stretch Day
CHAPTER 8 A Balanced Diet of Reading and Writing

9. Provide them with one Slinky per group.
10. Have students take turns reading their paper while their partner acts out the paper with the Slinky.
11. Switch roles.
12. Discuss revision actions.

When to Use It

- When you want students to have a visual and tactile example of what effective writing is.
- If you are working on sentence composition and structure and want to address it using another method.
- As a literacy station task.
- When you want to focus on collaborative and/or peer revision and conferencing.

Quick Tip!

Want to see this strategy in action? Head over to www.drrebeccagharper.com and watch the Slinky Sentence video with a live demonstration.

Why It Works

- Incorporating a tangible visual with an object, along with movement, can aid students in understanding the task.
- It utilizes both oral and listening skills along with physical movement.
- Having an object to hold often helps students who might otherwise not feel comfortable working in a group setting or reading their papers aloud.

Modifications

- Complete the Slinky Paragraphs as a whole class activity. Provide each student with a Slinky and have them perform the paragraph collectively.
- Use the strategy in a literacy station for a small group activity. Include Slinkies and sample writing compositions at a station for small groups to work with.
- Invite ELL students to read aloud their papers in their native language and have their partners perform the paragraph.
- Use this as an individual strategy for students to add to their revision toolbox. For example, if after reading a student's paper, you notice that this strategy would be beneficial, have them use a Slinky to evaluate their own papers.

Extensions

- Extend this strategy to include the NVA^2 strategy on page 66.
- Have students use this strategy to evaluate speeches and other literary works.
- Extend this lesson into a fully involved fragment, run-on, and sentence types unit.

Digital Direction

- Allow students to record their performances for feedback from their classmates.
- Play the video recordings of the performance on mute and have students make inferences about the writing simply based on what they observe in the video.

Lesson Lead-Ins

- Use this as a springboard into targeted and individual revision days. This can be used as an additional tool for students to evaluate their own writings.
- Connect this to the Level Up strategy on page 212 since that strategy focuses on specific words in sentences.
- Offer this as a lead-in when teaching dialogue as a visual reminder of how actual speech sounds *and* looks.

WRITING SURGERY

For years, I had a wonderful best friend who worked with me in the College of Education on several writing lessons and workshops. Dr. Jeannie Hill and I were well known for our classroom antics, which included dressing up in exercise clothes for writing workouts, prison uniforms for writing crimes, and scrubs for Writing Surgery. Let me tell you, there's nothing more exhilarating that flying down a hall on top of a media center cart giving chest compressions to a dying paragraph. Who does that?? Yours truly!

Writing Surgery is a strategy that is effective for revision due to several factors. It capitalizes on some of the most common writing problems, such as run-ons, off-topic sentences, lack of organization, and so on, and pairs them with an engaging method in which to address them. While some might say that this feels a little primary, we often perform surgery on our academic writing during our collegiate careers. Cutting? Pasting? Extracting sentences? Transplanting details? These all sound surgical to me!

With this strategy, you can really get dramatic, with scrubs and first aid kits, or you can keep it a little more low key. Regardless, the strategy is motivational, hands-on, and engaging no matter how fancy you make it.

Putting It to Work

1. Prepare for the lesson by drafting a sample paragraph on a large piece of chart paper. This paragraph needs to be one that has a number of writing issues such as run-ons, fragments, missing punctuation, and so on.

> My sister and I ate popcorn at the circus. My mom took us to a birthday party. We saw elephants, horses, and monkeys at the circus. Going to the circus is a lot of fun. One time, we got tickets to go to the circus from a contest we won at school. We had the best time on our trip to the circus. It was late when we got home. We ate cake at the birthday party and we had fun. After we watched the animals perform we ate cotton candy we ate popcorn we rode the rides at the circus and we talked to our friends.

2. Display the paragraph for the students to see and read it aloud for the class.

3. Solicit volunteers to be the surgeons.

4. As a class, determine what parts of the paragraph need to be revised. This might include physically cutting out off-topic sentences, adding sticky note punctuation to appropriate parts, or transplanting words.

5. Once the paragraph has been surgically modified, read it aloud again and compare the two samples.

6. Have students discuss how the revisions affect the overall readability and flow of the composition.

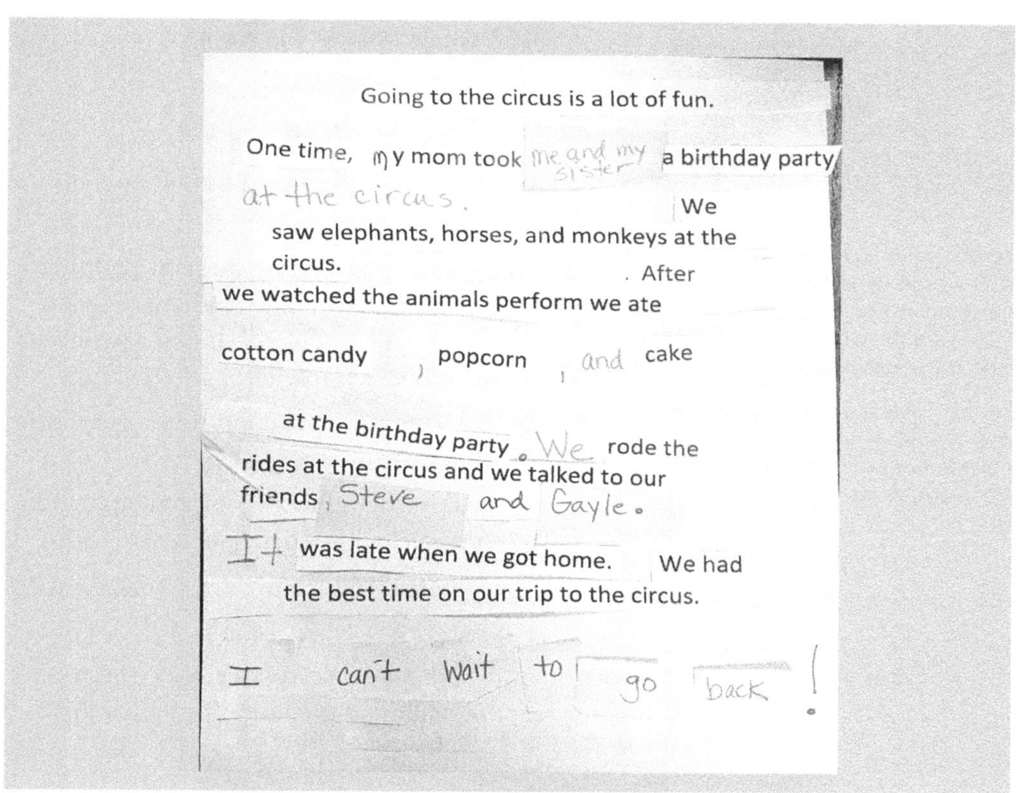

7. Provide students with individual sample paragraphs in need of surgery. Have the students revise their samples. Individually or with a partner, closely model what was observed during the whole class session.

When to Use It

- As a revision strategy that focuses on organizational and writing structure.
- If you want students to work collaboratively when revising.
- To make revision more fun and engaging.

- When you want students to have a visible and physical example of reorganizing a composition.

Quick Tip!

Here are some tips for taking Writing Surgery to the next level:

- Use pencil boxes for "writing first aid kits" that include highlighters, scissors, tape, sticky notes, and markers.

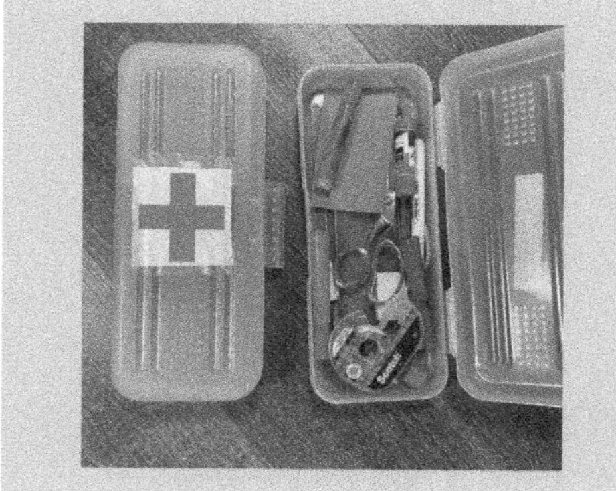

- Wear scrubs when you teach this lesson. You can buy secondhand scrubs at thrift stores for super cheap. In fact, I have a full class set that I use when I go into classrooms.
- Make up fun illnesses to diagnose (a bad case of the run-ons, fragmentitis) or silly treatment options (in need of a plot transplant, word augmentation).

Why It Works

- It incorporates a physical, hands-on component into learning.
- Collaboration is natural with this strategy so it offers opportunities for peer feedback and interaction.
- It can be modified for multiple content areas, genres, and grade levels.

Modifications

- Use Writing Surgery in small groups or as a station activity.
- Instead of having the students perform surgery initially, have students diagnose a paragraph and recommend a treatment plan. For example:
    - Diagnosis: Paragraph A has a bad case of the run-ons.
    - Treatment Plan: Incorporate punctuation at appropriate places.
    - Follow-Up: Return for a reread on XX date.
- Offer a specific focus for surgery instead of a holistic approach. For example, focus specifically on word choice, punctuation, or organization individually.

Quick Tip!

This modification could be further modified by using the same writing sample with the whole class but a different revision focus for each group. With this in mind, teachers would have a "word choice" group, a "punctuation" group, and an "organization" group.

Extensions

- Extend this engagement to incorporate a specific surgical procedure on word choice using the Level Up strategy on page 212.
- Use this strategy as a way to segue into research by having students look at research articles for specific information. Have them cut out the thesis, methodology, background literature, and so on.

- Connect this strategy to summarization strategies where students have to cut extraneous information and rely on succinct statements and specific word choice.
- Once students have practiced surgery on sample paragraphs, have them apply the revision strategy to their own compositions.

Digital Direction

- Instead of completing the surgery physically, perform all the operations digitally using word processing tools such as cut and paste.
- Complete the whole class paragraph surgery digitally on an interactive board. Use the erase, cut, paste, and insert tools to perform the surgery.

Lesson Lead-Ins

- Use this as a lead-in to writing lessons that are focused on organization and structure of compositions.
- Have students apply this strategy and concept to extended research writing engagements.
- Revisit and reorganize prior compositions and literary texts with this strategy.

LEVEL UP

Stop & Think:

I had a huge anchor chart of a tombstone with dead words listed on it in my middle school classroom. At the beginning of each semester, my students and I crafted a list of overused words that we collectively agreed would be off-limits in our writing compositions. The next day we held a funeral for these words in each class. I borrowed a shovel from the maintenance supervisor, wore a black suit to work, and chose a student to perform the eulogy as we walked around campus burying dead, overused words. I can't even begin to tell you how many words are buried in random places on that middle school campus! The first time our classes did this, the school principal, Dr. Randy Stowe, found every single hole I dug and came out to my mobile unit to ask what was going on. My response to him was, "You are the only person on the planet who would locate five random holes on a four-acre school campus before seventh period!" His response to me? "You are the only teacher on this campus who would dig five random holes on this campus. Just don't dig near the trees," as he shook his head and walked off.

One comment I hear from teachers on a regular basis is regarding students' overreliance and overuse of the same words: *nice*, *good*, *bad*, and *sad*, just to name a few. Using the same words repeatedly is something that all writers are guilty of. In some instances, using the same words has to do with the accessible written vocabulary a student possesses. In some instances, it comes down to spelling. (I'd love to write the word *melancholy*, but I can't spell it, so I'll use *sad* instead.) Lots of times students know what words mean, but they don't necessarily use them, which is often based on multiple factors. Determining how to exchange these overused words for new words can often be challenging.

One way to achieve this goal is to focus specifically on overused or generic words with the strategy Level Up. With this strategy, students focus on certain words for a specific and targeted purpose. Depending on the writing composition, students might focus on vivid vocabulary, whereas other academic content areas might hone in on academic or technical vocabulary.

Putting It to Work

1. Utilize a whole class example with words that are simply overused or too generic. For example, you might include a passage that incorporates the same types of character trait words, a passage with informal word choice, or one that includes overused adjectives. (Use oversized chart paper or project an oversized image on the interactive board so everyone in the class can see.)
2. Have students read the selection together and collectively share their noticings about the word choice.
3. Determine, as a class, which words need to be Leveled Up.
4. Mark the targeted/highlighted words on the class sample.
5. Once the targeted/highlighted words have been identified, provide students with sticky notes
6. Instruct them to come up with an alternative word for each of the targeted words. Students should write each alternative on a sticky note. For example, if the class chose three targeted words, students should produce a total of three sticky note alternatives—one for each highlighted word.

7. Have students come and place their alternative words on the sample so that they create a vertical string of options for word replacements.

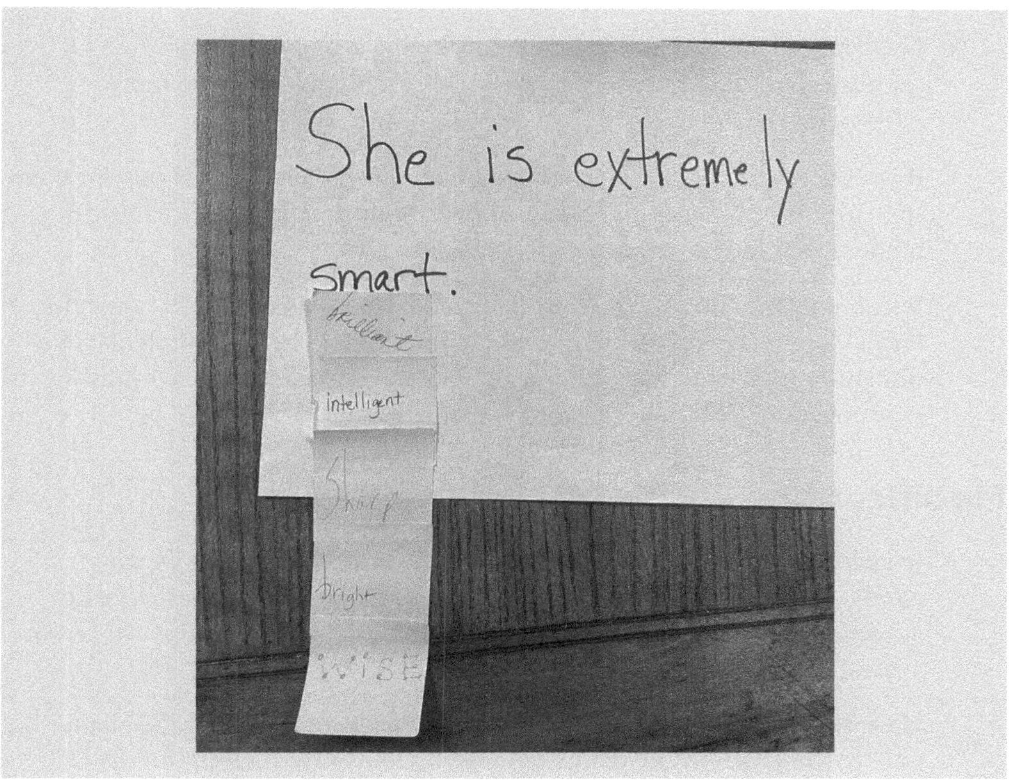

8. As a class, determine which of the options best fits the flow of the sentence.
9. Repeat for each targeted/highlighted word.
10. Have students utilize their personal writings and follow the same procedure for completing a Level Up.

This strategy operates with the understanding that students have a solid baseline of Level 1, 2, and 3 words. For example, Level 1 words are typically informal, whereas Level 2 words straddle the fence between informal and formal. Your most formal and academic vocabulary words are typically Level 3. Not understanding this will greatly impact the success of the lesson. Want more information on levels of words? Check out *Write Now and Write On: 37 Strategies for Authentic Daily Writing in Every Content Area* (Harper, 2022).

When to Use It

- As a way to focus on word choice, academic vocabulary, and specificity of detail in writing.
- When you notice that students rely on the same words in multiple compositions.
- If students have a solid draft that could benefit from a revision strategy that is focused on a specific quality rather than a revision approach that is holistic in nature.

Why It Works

- It addresses a specific component of the text.
- Focusing on individual words and developing synonyms or more sophisticated substitutes for them can help students complete more purposeful revision.
- It is student specific. Because students can utilize their own writings for this strategy, they can base their chosen words on the needs of their writing in tandem with their own academic strengths.
- Vocabulary building is indirectly addressed using this strategy. Though no formal definitions are written when completing this activity, students must display an understanding of the word's meaning to effectively substitute a new one.

Modifications

- Instead of having students Level Up words, have them Level Down words. Provide students with writing samples that include more formal academic terms. Have the students level the words down so the text is more accessible.
- Have students partner up and read each other's compositions. Students choose the words in the compositions that they want their partner to Level Up.

Extensions

- Save the extra words that you didn't use and keep them displayed on a chart in your classroom. Use the chart to collect words throughout the year that students can use in their own writing. I like to call this chart "Barely Read Words" or "Gently Read Words." Students can go to the chart and select any of these leftovers for use in their own writings.
- Extend this strategy to include leveling up dialogue. Have students identify parts in their writings that could benefit with the inclusion of dialogue.
- When writing arguments or research pieces, use Level Up to indicate areas where students might add research or support to strengthen their writings.

Digital Direction

- Use Jamboard to collaboratively suggest multiple options for the words.
- Create a Wordle (https://www.edwordle.net/) to collect all the suggested synonyms.
- Have students notate their word choices using an annotation application such as Diigo.

Lesson Lead-Ins

- Use this as a lead-in for lessons on vivid, descriptive vocabulary or academic vocabulary.
- Start with this activity when building classroom charts of Levels 1, 2, and 3 words (Harper, 2022).

LIVING PARAGRAPHS

One way to get students more involved with revision is with strategies that employ hands-on activity and movement. Getting students up and moving can help them stay focused and may circumvent potential classroom management issues that might prevent learning. Plus, because there is no one right way to revise, offering students opportunities to see this in action can have powerful effects in the classroom. For some, seeing paragraphs broken down into sentences and then rearranged like a puzzle can offer another tangible example of what the concept of revision is. Living paragraphs capitalize on all these factors and allow for maximum classroom participation from all students.

Putting It to Work

1. Using a well-developed paragraph as a model, transfer each sentence of the paragraph onto a sentence strip so that the paragraph is broken down sentence by sentence. It does not matter about the content or genre of the paragraph, but it does need to be on a topic that the students have background knowledge about.

2. Pass out the individual sentences to students. I suggest using paragraphs no longer than about eight sentences to begin.

3. Start the lesson by explaining that some students have sentences that are related to topic X.

4. Ask the students who have sentence strips to read their sentences and determine if they think their sentence is the opening sentence. Invite that student to come to the front of the room. They should hold the sentence strip in front of them so the class can read it.

5. Now, ask the other students who are at their desks holding sentence strips, "Who thinks you have a sentence that goes with this one?" Invite that student to come to the front of the room.

6. Repeat these steps until all sentences have been used.

7. Once all the students who have sentences are in front of the room, ask the students to each read their sentence.

8. Ask the students in the audience to comment on the placement of each sentence and make suggestions if needed. You might ask questions like, Does any sentence need to be moved? Does any sentence not belong? What would happen if we moved this sentence to here?
9. If you see that there is an off-topic sentence that needs to be removed, simply have that student take their sentence and move to another area in the classroom. You might also notice that some sentences need to be switched or regrouped. Have those students physically move around and then have the whole group reread the paragraph. Obtain feedback from the classroom observers.
10. Pass out blank sentence strips to the students who are in the classroom audience.
11. Instruct the audience to write one sentence that they think would go with the other sentences displayed in the front of the room.
12. Have students come to the front of the room and place themselves where they should be in the paragraph.
13. Repeat Steps 7 through 9 if needed.

When to Use It

- When you want students to physically experience revision by moving around.
- As a concrete example of how sentences and paragraphs are constructed.
- If you want students to break down a composition and reorganize it for clarity.

Why It Works

- It gets students up and moving.
- This strategy works well with all grade levels and content areas due to its versatility.

- It is buildable; you can start with a few sentences and then branch off into living multiparagraph samples.

Modifications

- Instead of having ready-made sentences constructed, provide students with a topic and have them generate their own sentences. Color code the blank sentence strips if you want specific types of sentences (topic sentences, interrogative sentences, conclusions, declarative sentences, supporting details, etc.).
- To ease into this strategy, instead of starting with sentences, start with words on notecards and build sentences word by word. This is a great modification for younger students, ELL students, or international language classrooms.
- Have ready-made sentences completed, and also include one blank sentence strip so students have to determine the missing detail.

Extensions

- Have students use the sentences from the Living Paragraph to write their own composition about the same topic.
- Use different colored blank sentence strips to indicate a specific type of sentence. For example, if you have a blank blue sentence, you have to add a question. If you have a green blank sentence strip, you have to cite a source in your sentence.
- In international language classes, create subtitles for the paragraph using different colored sentence strips. For example, beige-colored paint strips are for sentences in English and blue-colored sentence strips are for the French translation.

Digital Direction

- Use an application like PowToon and have students create characters for each of their sentences. Play and record.
- Have students send in digital images of themselves holding their sentences and use PicCollage or a Google Document to arrange the pictures in the best order.

Lesson Lead-Ins

- Use this as a lead-in for Slinky Paragraphs on page 204.
- If working on the inclusion of transitional phrases, use this as a springboard for adding "living" transitional sentences.
- e this as a lead-in for building multiparagraph compositions.

CANDY REVISION

When students are revising, sometimes it is hard to know just what to focus on first. Should I upgrade my vocabulary? Add additional evidence? Try some figurative language? These are decisions that might be difficult for some students based on the genre of writing. One super cool way to revise is by using candy to guide your revision. Yes, I said candy! In this revision activity, students are given a small fun size package of multicolored candy to use when making their revision decisions. (Skittles, Spree, and M&Ms work well for this activity.) The different colors of candy that are included in each individual package dictate the revision activity the student will complete. Once the students complete the revision, they can eat the candy. Who knew revision could be fun and delicious, too!

Putting It to Work

1. Display a well-developed composition for the entire class to see. It is helpful to give each student a copy of this sample as well so they can follow along at their desks.
2. Give each student a few pieces of colored candy. For this part of the lesson, everyone should receive the same colors of candy.
3. Refer students to a class chart or one of the templates on the companion website that indicate what each color means. For example, if you have a red candy, you might add figurative language somewhere in your writing. If you have a green candy, you might look for a place to add dialogue. *Note:* There are multiple templates for different genres of writing on the companion website. Because different genre of writing warrant different types of revision, make sure you choose appropriately.
4. Have students start with a specific color and discuss how they would make that revision in the class paper.
5. Repeat for all colors of candy.

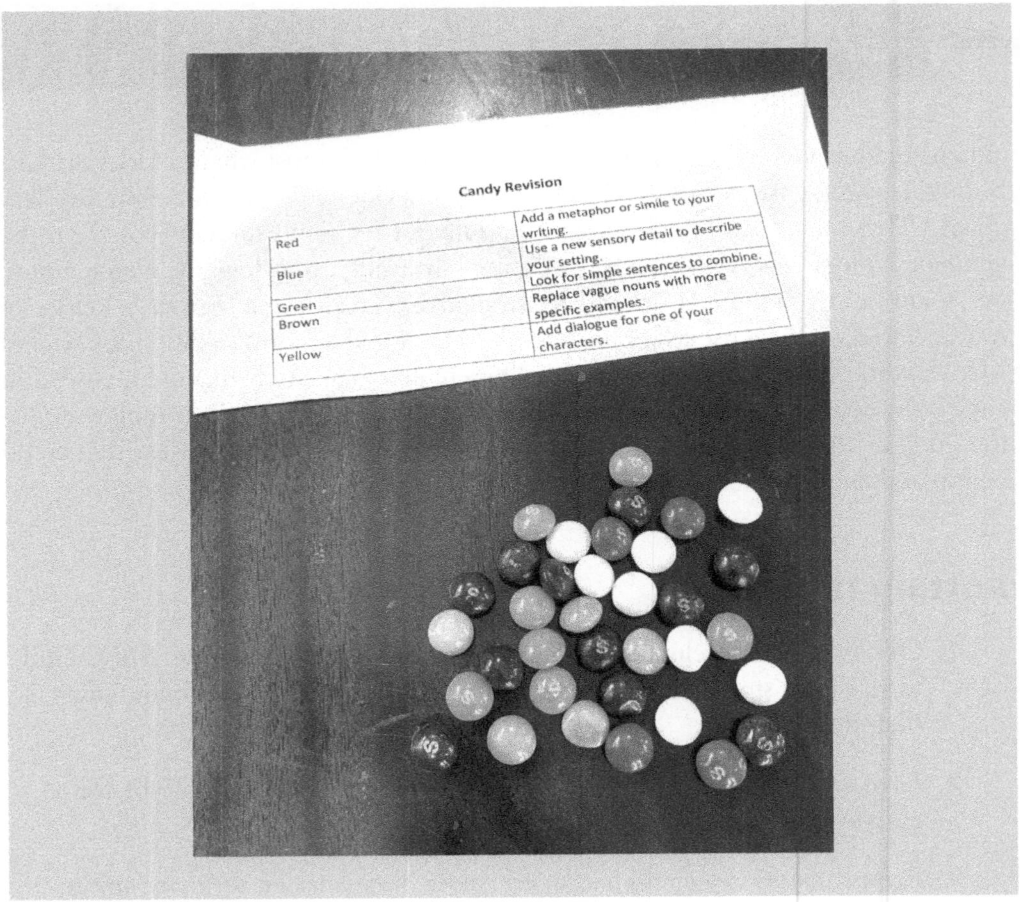

Candy Revision

Red	Add a metaphor or simile to your writing.
Blue	Use a new sensory detail to describe your setting.
Green	Look for simple sentences to combine.
Brown	Replace vague nouns with more specific examples.
Yellow	Add dialogue for one of your characters.

Quick Tip!

Don't be tempted to skip this whole group modeling and working through the first Candy Revision together. It is necessary for successful independent work.

6. Determine what writing composition of the students will be the focus for revision. For this revision activity, it is important to use a composition that is well along its way to completion. You really don't want to use short compositions that aren't well through the drafting phase since those won't offer you the same revision opportunities.
7. Pass out individual fun size bags of colored candy. If needed, provide students with a new Candy Revision template on the companion website based on the genre of focus.
8. Have students use their individual bags to complete their revisions of their own papers.
9. Discuss as a class or in peer groups if needed.

When to Use It

- When you want students to all work on revising an extended composition at the same time, but you want there to be an individualized component as well.
- As a way to get students to reread and reexamine their papers for specific and varied purposes.
- As a fun way to incorporate revision into classroom instruction.

Why It Works

- While each student is receiving individualized revision ideas based on their candy in the bag, since each color has a specific task associated with it, students may find revision much more manageable.
- Since each small fun size bag only includes a few pieces of candy, students are able to complete the revision tasks in a shorter amount of time.

Modifications

- Start with one color of candy at a time and have students master revising for that purpose before they move on to the next color.
- Divide the colors into stations and have students rotate through stations for revision.
- Put students in groups and give them all the same sample paragraph. Have each group revise their sample for one specific color. Regroup them again by placing one color representative in each new group so that all revision activities are represented. Discuss how the revisions affect the sample overall.

Extensions

- Have students add a new color revision to the requirements that can further extend their writings.
- Use this strategy for peer revision as well. Modify the actions on the template to reflect peer revision. (Check out this template on the companion website.)
- Show students a before-and-after paper and have students determine what type of revision was made.

Digital Direction

- Have students annotate their revisions by color coding them digitally or using track changes on a word processing program.
- Use a digital prize wheel app and have revision colors randomly chosen instead.
- Collaboratively revise for different purposes using a live editable document.

Lesson Lead-Ins

- Use this as a lead-in for Slinky Paragraphs on page 204.
- Connect this to other revision strategies such as I.N.K. on page 197 and P.E.N. on page 201.
- Tee up this lesson for peer conferencing days.

Chapter 7

STRETCH DAY

When thinking about the overall writing fitness benefits of stretch days, think about how several workout plans and programs are structured. Many workout programs, especially ones that are high intensity, often include a stretch or recovery day. I have to confess that those are often the days that I want to skip, not because I don't enjoy the stretching or flexibility exercises, but because I am not certain how they pay off. Yet during this past year, after reading about the benefits of recovery days, I am sold. When physically working out, recovery and stretch days are important for a number of reasons.

- Rest days allow the tiny tears in muscles to heal after strenuous workouts.
- They reduce the chance of injury.
- Improve performance.
- Increase flexibility.
- Give the body time to recover for the next day's workout.
- Allow individuals to not only physically recover but also mentally prepare for upcoming training.

With this in mind, it is easy to see how stretch or rest days can have a number of physical benefits that can pay off for overall physical fitness.

Now, let's shift back to the classroom. Because there is a vast amount of instructional content that must be addressed in a short time, the chance of any teacher giving students an off day is not likely. Who has the time to take a full-day break, right? But you can offer students the luxury of a low-key stretch day that still addresses instructional tasks, standards, and skills, but at a lower intensity than a typical day.

The ideas in this section, though they certainly hit a variety of standards and competencies in the ELA classroom, focus more on stretching writing muscles and playing around with words. In many instances, students don't have enough opportunities just to write.

Write for pleasure.

Write for fun.

Write without being tethered to a rubric or checklist.

Write without a time limit.

Write without a script or prompt.

Think about this for just a moment. How often do students get to read or write simply for pleasure?

Sadly, most students, unless they write for fun at home, don't get many opportunities to just write due to the nature and structure of classrooms. Because classrooms are standards- and assessment-driven, these are the main forces behind the development and creation of lessons and delivery in the ELA classroom. Plus, scripted curriculum programs, pacing guides, and district lesson frameworks can limit the amount of what might be considered *downtime* in literacy classrooms. But is playing around with words and writing for fun and practice really downtime? Not at all. Instead, time to practice writing in a flexible environment can prove beneficial because it offers students the chance to stretch their writing muscles in a low-stakes environment.

Let's talk about grading for a minute. Often I hear teachers saying that if an assignment isn't graded, students don't want to complete it, and I hear you. Grades have become the driving factor behind a student's participation and motivation. However, I believe it's important to offer time for students to write with no penalty, no rubric, and no formal assessment. Many students have not had that luxury for quite some time. And others? They haven't had that luxury EVER. Students might not have had the space and place to simply read because they wanted to or write about something because it was interesting. Carving out time and space for this, even if it's only a small space and for a short amount of time, can have lasting impacts on students.

When thinking about cultivating a space for Stretch Day writing, it is important to know WHO you are teaching before you begin to plan HOW and WHAT you are going to teach. When developing stretch lessons and opportunities, consider the following:

- What are the outside interests of the students?
- What types of texts do they enjoy? Graphic novels? Comic books? Poems?
- What types of writing are students doing outside of class? Texts? Snapchat? Poems? Song lyrics? Notes to friends?
- Who are the students in your class? Are they reading on grade level? Do they like sports? Are they interested in music?

Thinking through who the students are as individuals before you plan the types of stretch lessons, which often are ungraded, can help you determine what types of engagements, materials, and resources to use that will be motivational without necessarily having a grade attached.

When planning instruction think about this. In many instances, students are tasked with reading a complex text AND are required to complete a complex task that is often written. When this happens, there's simply no play, no flexibility, and not much recovery time. Think about a boxing match. Have you ever seen a boxer getting pressed up against the ropes as their opponent is wailing on them? What happens? In most instances, the boxer being attacked has little recovery time, struggles to hit back, and often opts to simply attempt to block the shots instead of gaining solid footing. Their saving grace comes in the sound of a bell signifying the end of the round.

Now think about students. When students are given a complex text (think *Letters from a Birmingham Jail* or *The Hobbit*) paired with a complex task (crafting an argument, using multiple sources as evidence, or synthesizing material, etc.), for many, they feel like the boxer against the ropes. As soon as they get hit with the difficult text, before they can recover, they are hit with a complex task. Instead of pushing through, it's simply easier to shut down, cover up, and wait for the bell.

One way to make instruction more accessible for students is by carefully considering the text and the task that students will be completing. If the *text* is complex, then the *task* should be more accessible. It might be one that is more simplistic or one that students have had a lot of experience with. If the *task* is complex, then the *text* should be more accessible. For example, it might be a genre that students are familiar with, might be on a lower grade level, or could be a visual or digital text. It is important to consider both task complexity and text complexity as instruction is planned. Doing so can improve the success of a lesson.

The strategies and engagements in this chapter, though still related to ELA standards and skills, offer students the opportunity to practice these competencies in more relaxed and fun settings. Many of these might be implemented and not graded, while others might be used as warmups or used on high intensity assessment days (the days when EOCs are administered or state testing dates). Implementing stretch lessons on those days can still not only achieve the goal of purposeful instruction but also take into account the needs and overall well-being of the students.

SOAP OPERA STORIES

While it has truly been a hot minute since I consistently watched a daytime soap opera, I spent many days at my grandmother's house watching the entire NBC lineup, which began around noon and ended around four o'clock. What is interesting, and to be commended for that matter, about soap operas is that the writers have mastered the art of ending an episode right at the peak of the action. If you diagrammed a week's worth of soap opera episodes, I bet it would look something like this:

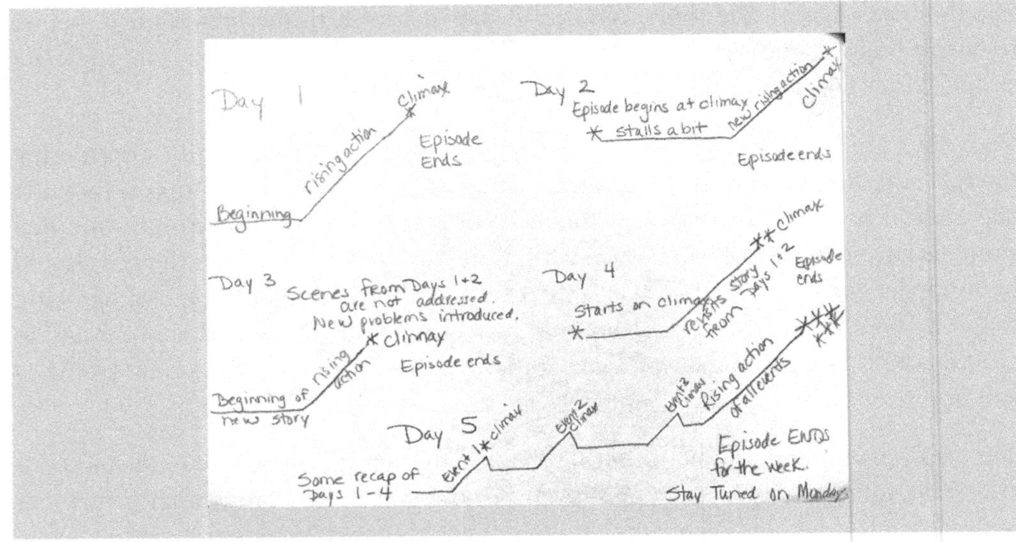

While soap operas are great examples of dramatic dialogue and cliffhanger plots, utilizing soap operas that are in different languages offers infinite possibilities for writing. They are easy to drop into instruction, offer multiple opportunities for students to express their creativity, and are a fun way to practice dialogue and the construction of a story.

Putting It to Work

1. Locate a clip of a soap opera in another language and/or produced in a different country. This clip should be about 3 to 4 minutes long. Make sure that in the clip you choose, the entire scene is played out so that students get a full idea of the entire event. (I typically look for soap operas in languages that I know no one in my class speaks. For example, I often use Portuguese soap opera samples because of their close connection to the Spanish language. You could also use other foreign television shows and sitcoms. I have found that dramas work best.)

2. Give students a notecard or sticky note.

3. Explain to the students that they will watch the video clip twice: once to initially examine the clip and the second time to write about it. Don't skip this part. It is important that students see this clip twice. The first time, they are simply going to pay attention to what is occurring in the video. After they have seen it for the first time, it will make writing about it much easier.

4. Show the video the first time. (Don't be surprised if students are shocked that it is in another language; that's the point.)

5. Discuss briefly what happened in the clip.

Why soap operas? Because they are overly dramatic and offer multiple opportunities for students to let their creativity show. Finding clips is as easy as a YouTube search. Just make certain that you preview the clip BEFORE you use it to make certain that are no inappropriate scenes. Good scenes to use are:

- Restaurant scenes
- Arguments
- Conversations between two or more people
- Scenes where someone is on the telephone
- Hospital or doctor scenes

6. Next, instruct students to use their notecard while watching the clip the second time. This time, while watching the clip, they are to construct a story of what they think is happening in the clip.

7. Repeat the clip, then ask students to share what they wrote.

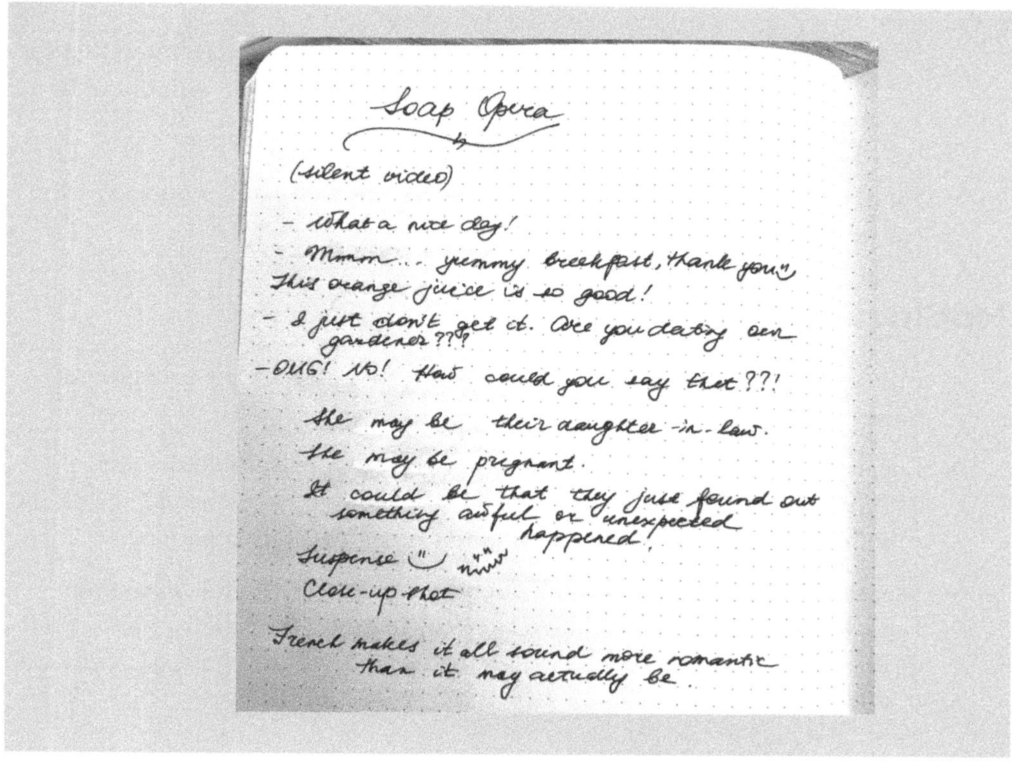

8. Draw attention to the fact that since there was a language barrier with the video, students had to rely on other information such as body language, volume in voice, tone, facial expressions, and so on to help them understand the clip. Have them share what cues informed their interpretation of the story.

9. Discuss how what they experienced can be used in their own writing. (For example, describing gestures and body language of characters, using dialogue, adding information about the volume of the speaker, etc.) All these things enhance how readers make meaning from a piece of writing.

Quick Tip!

Don't want to use a soap opera? Try these options as well:

Sports games with foreign commentary

Popular television sitcoms dubbed in another language

Scenes from foreign movies

Nature shows with animals

Clips from silent films

When to Use It

- As a fun, low-stakes way to get creative ideas flowing.
- When you want students to use visual media to construct a story.
- As a means to bring relevant media into the classroom for instruction.

Why It Works

- It is a quick writing engagement that can be completed in a short amount of time.
- It employs the use of video clips, which can aid striving readers.
- Popular culture is the center of this strategy, so it serves as a reminder of the real-world writing opportunities.

Modifications

- Instead of using foreign clips, use any film clip, but mute the background noise.
- Locate a clip that also includes subtitles. Have students watch the clip without the subtitles and discuss their thoughts. Then play the video with the subtitles and have them discuss how their version/account changed.
- Break the class into groups labeled setting, problem, dialogue, narration. Have each group watch the video and only focus on the task they have been given. Come back together as a class and use the material from each group to build a story about the clip.

Extensions

- Have students write and perform a follow-up scene to the one shown in class.
- Pay specific attention to the characters in the clip. Have students generate character traits and features for each one and predict the character's next actions.
- Challenge students to write the scene that led up to the clip. What events occurred before the scene in the video? What might come next?
- Develop backstories for each of the characters.
- Extend the dialogue lessons to include proper punctuation and the inclusion of tags.

Digital Direction

- Have students assume the roles of the characters from the clip and perform their scene. Record their performance and share with the class.
- Use the same video clip but mute the dialogue and background. Have students complete a voice-over where they create their own dialogue that accompanies the scene.

Lesson Lead-Ins

- Use this as an opener for teaching dialogue.
- Connect this to units focused on drama, performance, or theater.
- Include this as a fun writing engagement during exam weeks or other assessment-heavy time periods.

WALK-OUT SONGS

As I have mentioned, all my children are competitive swimmers, so I log countless hours in the stands at swim meets during the year. At championship meets where there are preliminaries and finals, the top seed in finals gets to choose a walk-out song that is played when the swimmers walk to the blocks. At one meet in particular, I noticed that some of the walk-out songs that were chosen seemed a little odd. For example, one swimmer chose the *Little Einsteins* theme song, and yet another chose an audio recording of the Pacer Fit Test. You heard me correctly: The. Pacer. Fit. Test. Little. Einsteins. Does no one know how to pick a walk-out song anymore?

Sitting in the stands, I began to think of ways to use this idea in my classroom. My first thoughts went to boxing matches, where boxers enter the ring with their entourage while a specific song, typically one that is upbeat, high intensity, and energetic is played. Boxers enter the ring to songs like Survivor's "Eye of the Tiger," Kanye West's "Stronger," and AC/DC's "Thunderstruck." When have you ever heard a boxer walk out to Air Supply's "I'm All Out of Love" or Olivia Rodrigo's "Drivers License"? Probably never. Those songs belong in another setting for another mood.

Walk-out songs should have a certain level of intensity and should, in some way, connect to the character or individual doing the walking. Knowing that songs can elicit certain moods and that lyrics can be used as evidence of said mood and character connections, Walk-Out Songs address several academic elements in the classroom, all while offering yet another opportunity for students to play around with writing.

Putting It to Work

1. To prime students for this activity, provide them a list of the sports figures or celebrities you'll show clips of in the next step. Ask students to generate a list of character traits about each of the figures who will be shown before you show the clip. This can activate prior knowledge and get them thinking about who the person is BEFORE they watch the walk-out. Make sure they are familiar with the individuals to complete this part.
2. Show students clips of different sports figures or celebrities entering an arena with a walk-out song.
3. Have students jot down noticings about each character and their chosen song.
4. Go back to the discussion about the characters/figures. Talk about these traits and how they are reinforced or highlighted in the choice of music. (This can be done in pairs or in small groups as well.)
5. Distribute the lyrics to the songs used in the walk-outs. Have students highlight the lyrics that best match the character traits they identified in the class discussion.
6. Share with the class.

7. Using this lesson as a frame, have students choose their own walk-out song. Have them make a list of their character traits and then find a song that they'd like to use as their walk-out song.

8. Use the template on the companion website for students to match their qualities and character traits to the chosen lyrics.

Walk-Out Song

Song I chose: Nobody's Fool by Kenny Loggins

Character Traits/Adjectives That Describe Me (one trait per box)	Song Lyrics That Support
Determined	"I'm going all the way" "Don't care how long it takes"
Pressure does not bother me	"You can turn up the heat" "Don't care how long it takes"
Successful	"I'm going all the way"
Intelligent	"I may not look so smart, but I'm nobody's fool"
Quick on my feet	"Got to learn to be on the ball"

9. Share with the class their choice of walk-out song and why they chose it.

When to Use It

- As a getting-to-know-you activity at the beginning of the year.
- When you want students to practice the skill of textual evidence in a low-key setting.
- Use this strategy as a way to capitalize on student interest by allowing them to bring in their personal song choices.

Why It Works

- It combines academic skills (textual evidence, character traits, mood, and justification) with popular culture and music.
- It is a personal writing that is individualized.
- It utilizes writing in tandem with music and can be completed in a short amount of time.

Modifications

- Assign students a partner and have them choose and justify a walk-out song for their classmate.
- Have a song bank already available for students to choose their walk-out song. (Use this modification if you are concerned about inappropriate lyrics, want to save time with searching, or if filters and security at your school prevent students from downloading music on campus.)
- Include a piece of artwork or a symbol that could also be used to represent them. You might encourage students to create their own logo, choose a pen name, or design a symbol that represents them. Hey, if Prince could do it, so can we!

Extensions

- Revisit this idea throughout the year and have students complete a "Me Playlist" with songs that best illustrate who they are as a person.
- Have students write an extended piece utilizing the lyrics as justification for their choice of song.
- Use collaborative groups for students to brainstorm other possible walk-out songs that follow the same theme and mood.
- Show students a character that they are familiar with. Play a sampling of songs and have students choose the most appropriate choice based on the character's traits. Justify and explain their choices.
- Play a song and have them determine which character from a provided list goes with the song.
- Extend this to the Music Infographics strategy on page 15.

Digital Direction

- Record a new walk-out song using a program like Guitar Band, Soundtrap, or Music Maker.
- Have students create a digital presentation using specific clips from their chosen song that best illustrate their individuality.
- Have students create a Wordle using the lyrics from their chosen song that best illustrate who they are as a person.

Lesson Lead-Ins

- Use this as a lead-in to the Music Infographics on page 15.
- Offer this stretch strategy as a reinforcement for textual evidence since lyrics are used to justify their choices.
- Connect this to the Greeting Cards lesson on page 77 or the Songs for Voice lesson on page 86.

SOCIAL SQUARE CHALLENGE

A couple of years ago, I read about a social media phenomenon known as the Dolly Parton Challenge where my idol, Dolly Parton, posted a tiled version of four separate images that would be used on four very different social media platforms. While this certainly was meant as a fun, jovial way to joke at the ways in which we represent ourselves online, this challenge is fantastic for addressing the notion of audience and purpose. Because it includes platforms that many students use in their personal lives, plus has a visual component, it can be a home run in the ELA classroom.

One reason this strategy is beneficial is because in many instances, students write for one audience: themselves. This often means that the language frequently used is rather informal and loose and may even include text message abbreviations, which really bothers some educators. However, part of why this occurs is because many students don't have a solid, comprehensive grasp of how much audience impacts their writing. In fact, whom you are writing something for directly impacts how it will be written and in what format. An easy way to bring this concept to life with images is through a classroom Social Square Challenge.

Putting It to Work

1. Provide students with the Social Square Challenge template on our companion website. You can use a variety of social media platforms for this activity. Some popular ones you might choose are Snapchat, Facebook, LinkedIn, Instagram, or TikTok. Ask your students which platforms they use regularly and want to use for this engagement.
2. Discuss each part of the square by addressing the purpose, audience, and content. This is an important step for this strategy to be effective. If students are not sure of the purpose and audience of each social media platform, it will be difficult for them to complete the engagement. Even though an overview is included on the instructions template, make sure you discuss this as a class, too, so you can clear up any misconceptions or incomplete information.
3. Show students an example of a complete Social Square Challenge. You can use one that you created as a sample or use any of the celebrity examples that are easily found online.
4. Have students choose a character from a literary work or an author that has been a focus in the ELA class.
5. Once they have chosen the character or author, have them draw a picture or find an image of that character that would fit with each social media platform.

6. Add a post for each social media platform that would accompany the image. Make sure to show students examples of different types of posts that would be appropriate for different platforms.
7. Have students justify their choices for each image and post on page 2 of the template.
8. Have students share with the class.

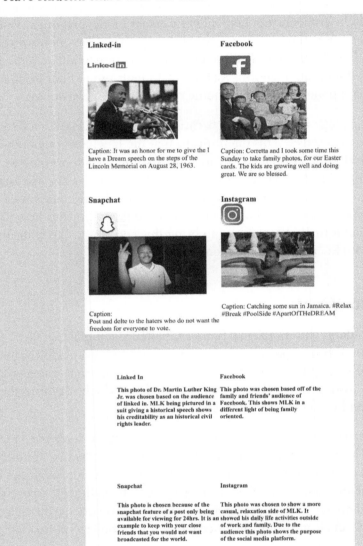

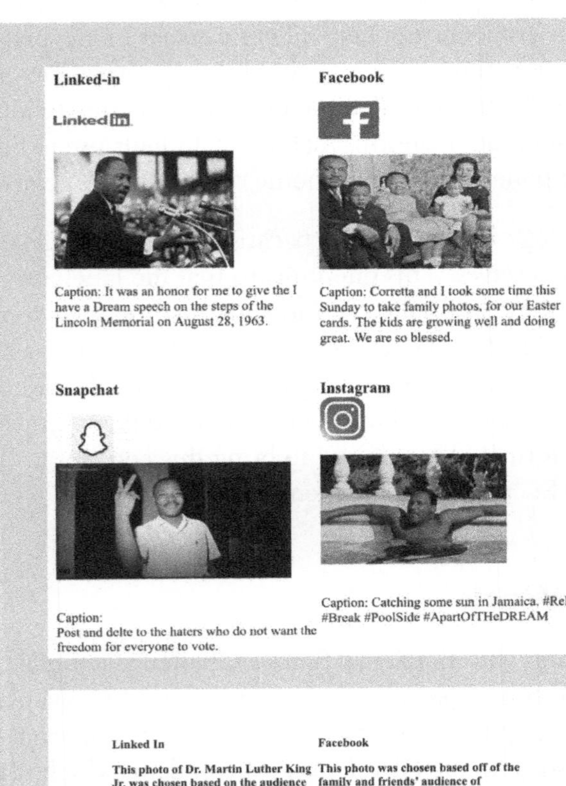

Linked-in

Caption: It was an honor for me to give the I have a Dream speech on the steps of the Lincoln Memorial on August 28, 1963.

Facebook

Caption: Corretta and I took some time this Sunday to take family photos, for our Easter cards. The kids are growing well and doing great. We are so blessed.

Snapchat

Caption:
Post and delte to the haters who do not want the freedom for everyone to vote.

Instagram

Caption: Catching some sun in Jamaica. #Relax #Break #PoolSide #ApartOfTHeDREAM

Linked In

This photo of Dr. Martin Luther King Jr. was chosen based on the audience of linked in. MLK being pictured in a suit giving a historical speech shows his creditability as an historical civil rights leader.

Facebook

This photo was chosen based off of the family and friends' audience of Facebook. This shows MLK in a different light of being family oriented.

Snapchat

This photo is chosen because of the snapchat feature of a post only being available for viewing for 24hrs. It is an example to keep with your close friends that you would not want broadcasted for the world.

Instagram

This photo was chosen to show a more casual, relaxation side of MLK. It showed his daily life activities outside of work and family. Due to the audience this photo shows the purpose of the social media platform.

When to Use It

- As a way to connect social media platforms from the real world to the academic setting.
- When you want students to evaluate a character from different perspectives.
- As a way to engage students in character discussions and analysis.
- As another way to address audience and purpose.

Why It Works

- It incorporates a visual element along with a written component. Students have to include a pictorial representation of their characters along with a justification for their choices.
- It capitalizes on relevant personal knowledge by utilizing platforms that students are familiar with, including social media.
- There are numerous authentic examples of this task online so students can easily see how real people attempted the challenge.

Modifications

- Assign a character or author to a group and have each group member assume responsibility for one of the social media platforms.
- Start with two social media platforms, one that has a career focus and one that has a personal focus. Use those two differing platforms to start the conversation on audience and purpose.
- Prior to beginning the activity, have students research each of the social media sites chosen and gather background information on each of the platforms.

Extensions

- Have students extend this activity by requiring them to draft additional posts that would be appropriate for each of the platforms.
- For certain social media platforms, have students develop supplemental documents that might be used in tandem with the application. For example, students would craft a résumé or work history that could be added to the LinkedIn profile. Students might include a bio for the Instagram profile as a supplement.
- Have students determine, based on a character's traits and personality, which social media site would best meet the needs of their character.
- Ask students to include a song that could accompany each of the posts.

Digital Direction

- Create a digital version of the Social Square Challenge using a collage-making program like PicCollage or Canva.
- Have students include audio recording explanations of their choices on their Social Square.

Lesson Lead-Ins

- Use this as a lead-in to the Social Media Profile Slide strategy on page 111.
- Connect this stretch activity to other character description/analysis strategies.
- Use this as a way to review multiple characters from an extended work of literature.
- Review different authors from multiple works of literature using this strategy.

POST PROMISE OR STORY WORTHY?

Having arrived to the social media world late, I often have questions about just how each platform works. Take Instagram for example. This platform offers the option for users to post information or add items to their stories, which are only viewable for a specific amount of time. I couldn't understand what types of details would warrant which. What should I post? What should I add to my story? How could I determine what went where? Like I do in most situations like this, I started asking teenagers. In this case, it happened to be at a swim meet where I was serving as a timer stationed at one of the starting blocks. As swimmers would come to the blocks, I would start a conversation with them that went something like this:

> "Hey, do you use Instagram?"
>
> If they said yes, I would proceed.
>
> "How do you decide what goes on your story and what goes on as a post?"
>
> Here are some of the responses I got:
>
> "I post stuff that is important."
>
> "I put stuff on my story that is happening now."
>
> "My story is stuff that isn't really important but is just funny or cool."
>
> "I post pictures that I want to keep and stay."
>
> When I asked my own daughter, Macy Belle, what the difference was, she gave me this example.
>
> "So 'I got a dog' would go on my posts and 'My dog's birthday is today' would go on my story."

Here's what this means: Important details go on posts and extraneous, supporting information goes on the story. Sound academic to you? Actually it is. What these young people described to me at the swim meet and what my daughter explained later is an understanding of the *difference* between important and supporting details, something that most ELA standard sets address. In almost every grade level and multiple subject areas, students must distinguish between the difference in important and extraneous details; that is the starting point for the skill of summarization.

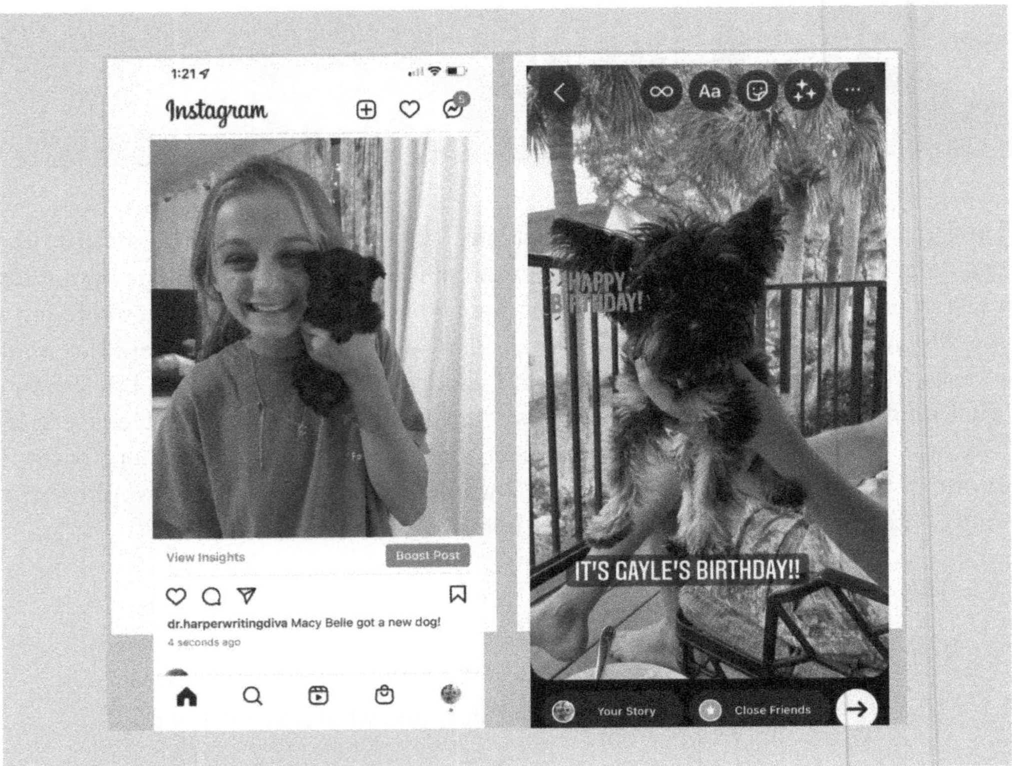

If students are actively making these distinctions in their daily lives, why not capitalize on this in the classroom? It is highly likely that many young people have not made the connection between this personal activity and its academic implications. Yet this can be turned into spendable classroom capital with the Post Promise or Story Worthy strategy.

Putting It to Work

1. After completing a unit, novel, or literary work, put a statement about the work on display for the students to see.
2. Activate prior knowledge by asking students about the social media platform Instagram.
3. Discuss what items they would post versus which ones would go in their stories.
4. Have them return their attention to the posted statement.
5. Choose whether they would post this item or put it in the character's story.
6. Discuss their choices.
7. Have them craft one statement that shows Post Promise and one detail that is Story Worthy to include on their character's Instagram.

It was a regular day, the single mother of 2 kids had woken up and got her children ready for school. She waited with them for the bus to come and went back inside. A few hours later the mailman had arrive and was curious to see if her door was locked and it wasn't. He noticed that she was all alone and saw in on his desire to kill and left immediately. No one had known she died until 3 in the afternoon when her oldest child got home. He instantly called the police and told them everything he knew, she wasn't involved in any conflict, he didn't know anyone who would want to kill her. When the police arrived they did some basic observations, they saw bruises around her neck and assumed she was strangled, her body was still kinda warm (97.4), and she was extremely stiff. The police figure she has been for about 8 hours.

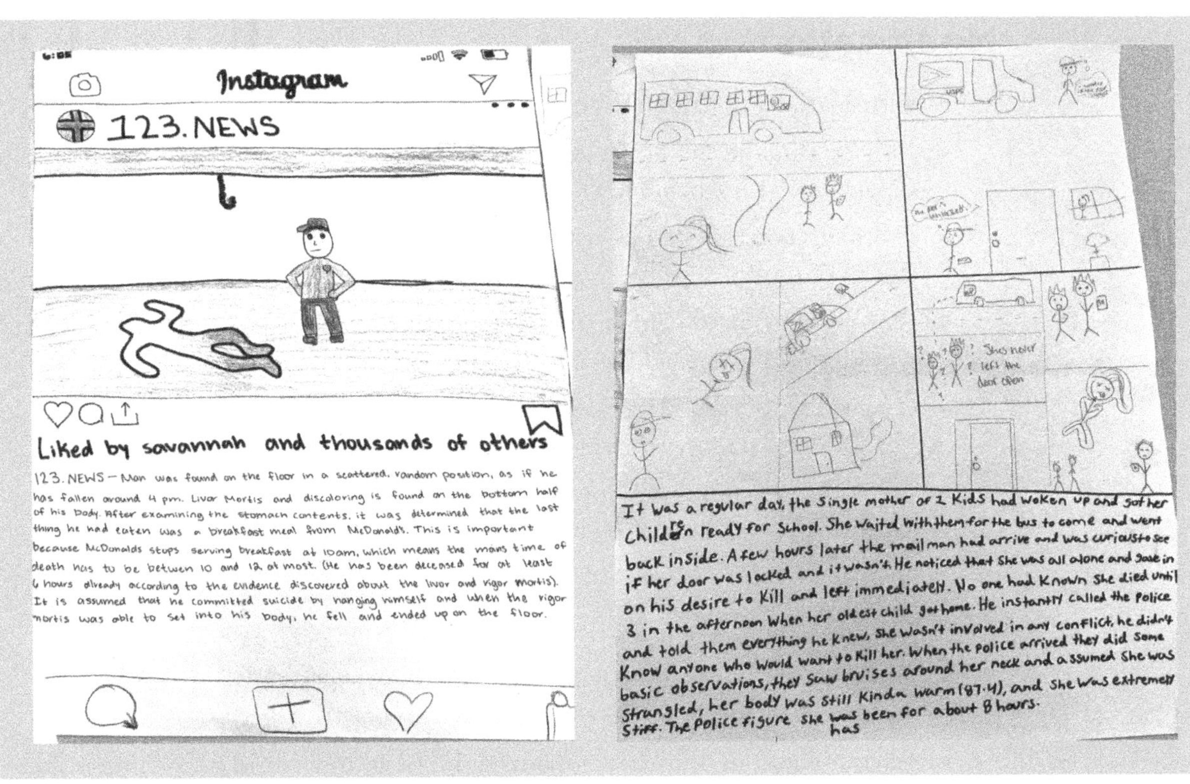

8. Record these on sticky notes.

9. Discuss with the class.

When to Use It

- Use this when finishing up a novel, extended literary work, or unit.

- As a quick way to summarize a concept or idea.

- When you want to connect an academic task to a contemporary platform.

- Connect this to writing by having students determine which details in a writing are most important depending on the purpose and/or audience.

Why It Works

- It capitalizes on personal interests and contemporary platforms.

- Because students are focusing on one statement at a time, it makes it easier for them to determine whether it shows Post Promise or is Story Worthy. Looking at smaller amounts of text can help students determine which details are important.

- It utilizes short bursts of time for completion and can be used as a bell ringer, parachute writing, or closing exercise.

CHAPTER 1 Writing Fitness

CHAPTER 2 Writing Warmups

CHAPTER 3 Targeted Training

CHAPTER 4 High Intensity Training

CHAPTER 5 Cold Starts and Cooldowns

CHAPTER 6 Rest, Recover, Revise

CHAPTER 7 Stretch Day

CHAPTER 8 A Balanced Diet of Reading and Writing

Modifications

- Instead of using written statements, use images as choices.
- Provide students with a set of images with accompanying texts. Ask students to determine which character's story or post the samples are from.
- Have students collaborate with a partner to determine which samples are stories or posts.
- Start by focusing on either stories or posts. Have students create examples that would go with stories, then progress on to posts.
- Give students a ready-made list of statements. Have them classify them into Post Promise statements and Story Worthy statements.
- Break the class into two groups and have one half focus on developing Story Worthy items while the other half develops texts that show Post Promise.

Extensions

- Once students determine where their detail or statement would go, have them draw or locate an image that could accompany the text.
- Have students develop accompanying hashtags that could go with their stories or posts.
- Extend this strategy by having students construct a written justification about why they chose to classify the sample a certain way.
- Have students create an image reel for their character.

Digital Direction

- Use Canva or PicCollage to create a mock Instagram post or story.
- Have students include a video clip or audio recording to include with their social media post or story.
- Use a quiz application to quickly tally class results for the examples.

Lesson Lead-Ins

- Use this as a lead-in for Instagram Summaries (Harper, 2022).
- Complete this activity as a review or culminating comprehension engagement when completing a unit, novel, or extended literary work.
- Connect this to any of the Character Props on page 49 and Walk-Out Songs on page 230.

DO I NEED TO REPEAT MYSELF?

When studying author's craft, one specific and easy-to-implement craft lesson is that of the repeated line. Whether they realize it or not, students have a lot of experience with repeated lines. Think about where we see repetitive texts.

- Easy-to-read, predictable books (*Brown Bear, Brown Bear, What Do You See?*)
- Choruses in songs
- Poems with repeated stanzas
- Speeches ("I Have a Dream")

Repeated lines help early readers as they begin to read due to the predictability of the text. Yet as readers become more sophisticated and skilled, repeated lines shift from those whose purpose is for readers to anticipate the words, to that of emphasis and importance. Think about the chorus of a song. Often those words communicate the overall theme and message of the song; they are the ones that are most important and carry the most weight.

Repeated lines or repeated phrases can be used in a variety of ways. In some instances, a short burst of the same three or four words might be used multiple times in a paragraph, and in other writings, an entire line might be repeated at multiple points in the passage for emphasis. Yet in other examples, sentences might start out the same way as a means to draw home a specific point or idea. Regardless, repeated lines are a fun aspect of an author's craft that can easily be integrated into many writing lessons. Do I Need to Repeat Myself? is a strategy that focuses specifically on this aspect of craft.

Putting It to Work

1. Begin by utilizing a variety of literature that utilizes the repeated line. Children's books make great examples, as do poetry and song lyrics.
2. Discuss how a repeated line or refrain can create predictability but also can be used for creating emphasis.
3. Use a sample of text from a student paper or use excerpts from other literary works for students to amend and plan around with. Poetry is also a great resource for this strategy.

When I teach the craft of a repeated line, I also incorporate the Nelly and Tim McGraw song "Over and Over" because it is an auditory example of a repeated line. Not only does it include a chorus that repeats, but it includes a repeated refrain of "over and over" that emphasizes the point as well.

4. Have students read the sample and then have them craft a line that could be repeated throughout the passage for emphasis.
5. Ask the students to determine where the new line should go and how often it should be repeated.
6. Make these revisions to the sample and then have the class read it and discuss how the addition of the repeated line affected or altered the original passage.

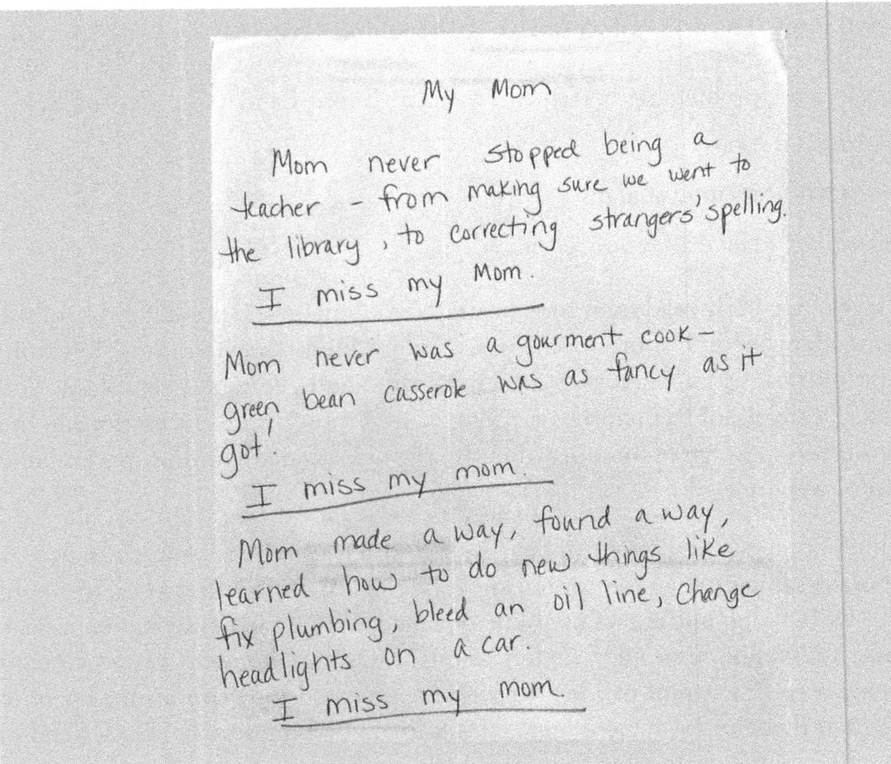

My Mom

Mom never stopped being a teacher - from making sure we went to the library, to correcting strangers' spelling.

I miss my Mom.

Mom never was a gourment cook— green bean casserole was as fancy as it got!

I miss my mom.

Mom made a way, found a way, learned how to do new things like fix plumbing, bleed an oil line, change headlights on a car.

I miss my mom.

7. Have students try the repeated line on their own writing.
8. Share with a partner or a small group.

Quick Tip!

Some of my favorite picture books that include repeated lines include

- *When I Was Young in the Mountains* by Cynthia Rylant
- *Momma, Where Are You From?* by Marie Bradby
- *When the Relatives Came* by Cynthia Rylant
- *Tough Boris* by Mem Fox
- *My Mama Had a Dancing Heart* by Libba Moore Gray
- *I Want My Hat Back* by Jon Klassen
- *One Plastic Bag* by Miranda Paul

When to Use It

- Use this as an addition to personal narrative writing units.
- As a low-key way to revise and play around with narratives or other excerpts from literature.
- As a way to use picture books as mentor texts with narratives.

Why It Works

- Because it focuses on a specific way to revise and add detail, and completing the task is easier for students.
- It combines a variety of mentor texts (songs, books, poems, speeches, etc.) as models for a specific writing task.
- Personal narratives can get ramped up by focusing on this specific writer's craft.

Modifications

- Instead of having students implement this into their own personal writing, have students take a partner's writing and use it as the sample for adding a repeated line.
- Use song lyrics as springboards by having students highlight the repeated lines and then transfer those highlighted lines into other writing samples.
- Instead of using repeated lines, have students start working with repeated words in sentences to practice alliteration.

Extensions

- Have students stretch their repeated lines using the Slinky Paragraphs strategy on page 204.
- Complete a repeated lines scavenger hunt in existing works by having students collect repeated lines from multiple novels or other literary works.

Digital Direction

- Have students record their new compositions on video and record them on Vimeo.
- Collaborate on possible repeated lines using Mural or Jamboard.
- Map out your story with repeated lines using a digital application like Dabble.

Lesson Lead-Ins

- Use this as a lead-in when analyzing song lyrics or poetry with repeated lines and stanzas.
- Connect this to other writers' craft lessons including ones on alliteration.
- Use this as an opener for Walk Out Songs on page 230.

BLACKOUT POEMS

One of my favorite ways to play around with words is through the creation of a Blackout Poem. By taking an existing text, students use a black marker to "black out" certain words to create a new, found writing. Perhaps one of the best parts of this strategy is the fact that the same excerpt of literature can turn into infinite new writings simply based on which words students choose to black out. Plus, it is a low-stakes, fun way to start dabbling in poetry and play around with words.

Putting It to Work

1. Show students a finished sample of a Blackout Poem. Explain to students that this is a poem created by blacking out words on a piece of prewritten text. (It's also a good idea to show students what the original excerpt of literature looked like before the poem was created so they can compare the two.)
2. Provide students with a sample page of text and a black marker.
3. Using the same sample, model a Blackout Poem with the class.
4. Start by reading the entire piece/excerpt aloud.
5. Focus on a small section of text to start with to create your modeled Blackout Poem. Starting with a small section of text first can help students from becoming overwhelmed. Because Blackout Poems are so unique, creative, and nebulous, it is important for students to see in small chunks how a section of text is transformed into a Blackout Poem.
6. Begin blacking out the words or phrases you don't need, don't like, or are near the phrases you do like.
7. Once you have blacked out the words you want to eliminate in that small section, read aloud the words that remain.

Quick Tip!

Though the connection to Blackout Poems is loose, you might enjoy these blackout-themed books:

- *Blackout* by John Rocco
- *Black: The History of a Color* by Michel Pastoureau
- *The Black Book of Colors* by Menena Cottin
- *What Color Is Night?* by Grant Snider

my name means hope. sadness,
waiting. number nine. muddy Mexican records
on Sunday mornings songs like sobbing.

it is mine.
born like me in the Chinese year of the horse--
born female-
women strong.

My great-grandmother. a wild, horse of a woman
as if she were a fancy chandelier.

She looked out the window her whole life
she sorry she couldn't be all the things she wanted to be.
Esperanza. her name, her place by the window.

my name funny as if the syllables were made out of tin and hurt the
roof of your mouth. name is made out of a softer something, like
silver, not quite as ugli
baptize myself under a new name, a name more like the real me,

8. Discuss how the text shifted and changed.
9. Proceed to the next section and repeat Steps 5 through 8 until the entire excerpt is completed.
10. Discuss the completed poem with the class.
11. Using the same sample of text, have the students create their own Blackout Poems.
12. Share with the class.

I like to sometimes use actual pages from old books. You can purchase some old books at thrift stores and use real book pages for this activity. You can also use newspapers or magazines as another alternative. If you don't want to go that route, photocopies work just as well. You can use excerpts of novels the class has already read as the printed samples for this activity. This way, the students are seeing the text once again.

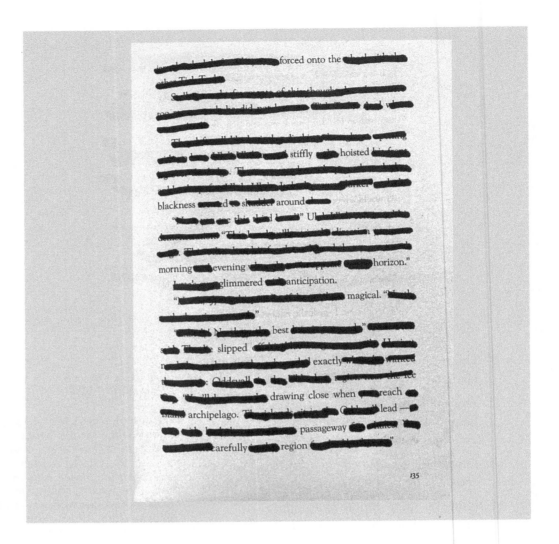

When to Use It

- As a fun way to introduce poetry to the class.
- When you want to revisit a text that's been read prior, but in a new way.
- If you want students to use another author's words to make a brand-new piece of writing.
- As a way to encourage and motivate striving writers.

Why It Works

- Because this strategy starts with a precreated sample of writing, students are basically beginning with a word/sentence bank from which to write.
- Blacking out certain words helps students think through how words, phrases, and sentences function because they have to be strategic about which items to remove and which ones to keep.

- There's no wrong way to do a Blackout Poem, and each one can be as unique as the student who crafted it.

Modifications

- Since poems might be a little intimidating for some, have students practice blacking out words to make sentences.
- Have students work with a partner to create a collaborative Blackout Poem.
- Instead of creating a poem, have students black out all the words that aren't figurative language, prepositional phrases, transitional phrases, or other snippets of language.

Extensions

- Have students compile their Blackout Poems into a poetry anthology.
- Instead of creating poems, have students create a story that is continued by utilizing multiple excerpts from different literary works to create the extended story.
- Have students take a personal narrative that they have written and whittle it down into a Blackout Poem.
- Once students have blacked out the words they don't want to use, have them use magazines to locate the words they are planning to keep and create a version of a Ransom Note poem (Harper, 2022).

Digital Direction

- Snip the chosen words using a digital application or the snipping tool on Microsoft Word. Paste them into a document like a collage.
- Have students load the excerpt of text into a drawing application online and then use the marker tool to digitally black out the words.

Lesson Lead-Ins

- Use this as a lead-in for units on poetry.
- Integrate this activity into lessons on found phrases, figurative language, or personal narratives.

BLOCK POEMS

Ransom note poems (Harper, 2022) are great ways for students to play around with words and build their own poetry examples that bear a close resemblance to ransom notes. Another way to play around with words and build poems is by building Block Poems. With this activity, students physically build poems using words pasted on construction blocks to make their own writing construction. What a great hands-on way to write!

Putting It to Work

1. Paste a variety of words to construction blocks, one word per block. You can use Jenga blocks, traditional building blocks, or LEGOS.

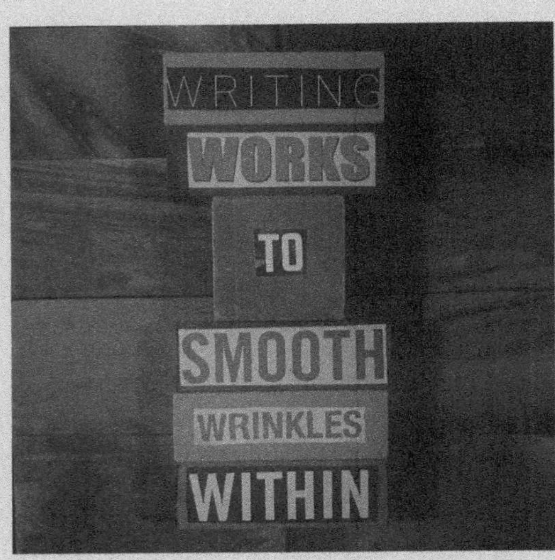

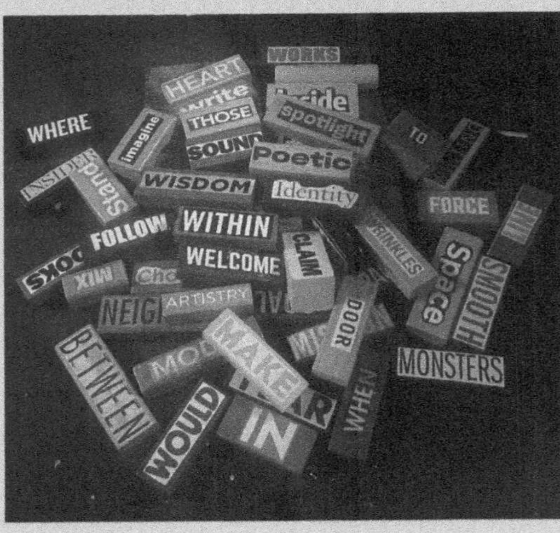

2. Show students a poem that you have built using word blocks. Talk about the word choices you made and why.
3. Provide students with word blocks.
4. Have them work individually or with a partner to build their own poem using the words they were given.
5. Share with the class.

When to Use It

- When you want students to physically construct a writing composition using tangible physical materials.
- As a way for students to see how writings are physically created and revised.
- As a low-stakes way to integrate poetry with students.

Why It Works

- Students can create their own unique poems by building words into written compositions.
- Revision is easy to model because students can construct new poems simply by adding and removing blocks.
- Many students like hands-on activities using manipulatives, and this can make the learning more concrete.

Modifications

- Instead of using blocks, use cut-out words like in the Ransom Note poem strategy (Harper, 2022).
- Give students a specific topic to write about when they construct their poems.
- Instead of creating poems, have students collect word blocks that focus on a specific concept or idea.
- Color code the words on the blocks to represent certain parts of speech so students know which ones to include when they write their own poems.

Extensions

- Have students collaborate with a partner to write a poem in two voices using the blocks.
- Give students blank blocks and have them add new words that could be used to create poems.
- Build a poem collaboratively by having one person start with one word and then solicit volunteers to add to the words, thus creating a whole class poem.
- Create poems specifically for certain characters, events, or concepts.

Digital Direction

- Use a program like Canva to build a digital example of the poem.
- Host a virtual poetry slam online showcasing the Block Poems created.
- Display the poetry using a virtual exhibition program such as Art.Spaces or Artopia.

Lesson Lead-Ins

- Use this as a lead-in to Prepositional Phrase Poems on page 251.
- Connect this to summary lessons, other poetry lessons, or vocabulary strategies.

PREPOSITIONAL PHRASE POEMS

Teaching grammar and sentence structure can get a little boring, especially when taught in the old-school, traditional format. In traditional grammar instruction, student experience with concepts such as prepositional phrases, transitional sentences, direct and indirect objects, and so on often occurs via worksheets with students identifying and labeling parts of sentences and speech in a rudimentary way. As a literacy educator, I am much more interested in utilizing lesson engagements that help students understand how language and writing function instead of labeling and diagramming. One way to play around with language and grammatical elements is using Prepositional Phrase Poems. With this activity, students focus on drafting poems that are composed entirely of prepositional phrases.

Putting It to Work

1. Provide students with a prepositional phrase word bank. These can be from the template on the companion website, or you can have students collect a list of prepositional phrases by locating samples from other literature.
2. Show students a sample of a Prepositional Phrase Poem.

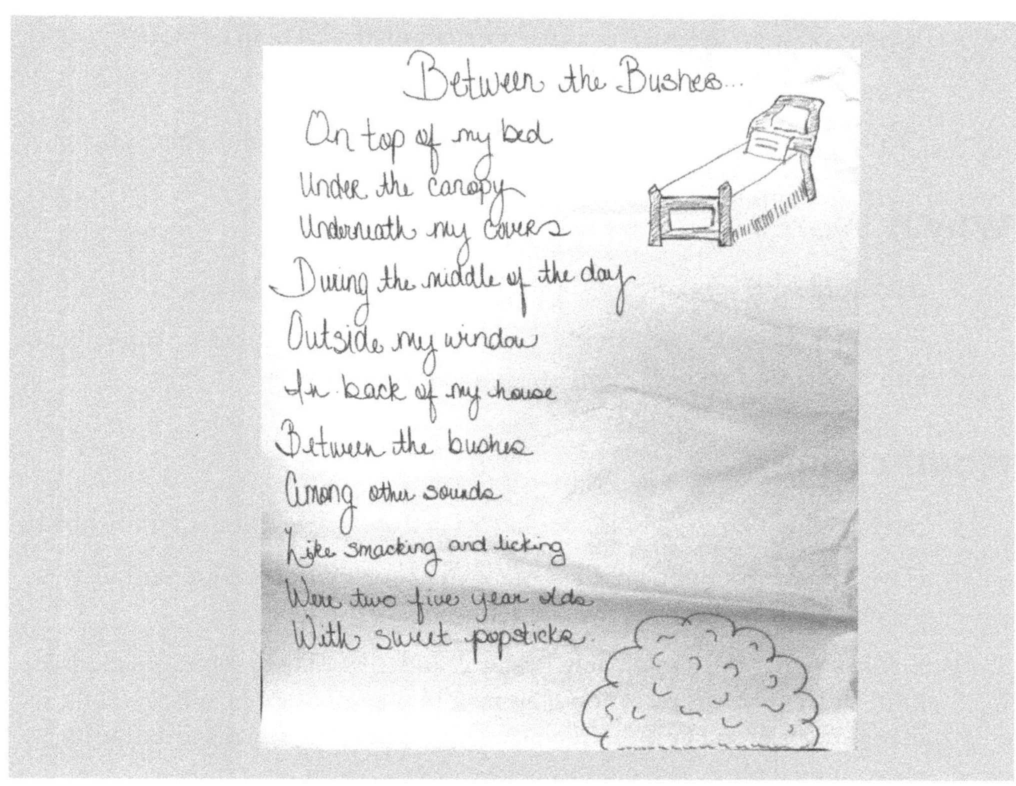

CHAPTER 1 Writing Fitness

CHAPTER 2 Writing Warmups

CHAPTER 3 Targeted Training

CHAPTER 4 High Intensity Training

CHAPTER 5 Cold Starts and Cooldowns

CHAPTER 6 Rest, Recover, Revise

CHAPTER 7 Stretch Day

CHAPTER 8 A Balanced Diet of Reading and Writing

Quick Tip!

You may want to give students a minimum number of phrases to include so you don't get the question, "How long does this have to be?"

3. Remind students that poems take on a variety of forms and do not necessarily have to rhyme.
4. Explain to students that for this writing task, they will only write in prepositional phrases.
5. Using the phrase bank, create a class poem together.
6. Have students brainstorm a list of possible topics or overall themes that may be used when writing their poems. (You don't have to create a list of possible topics, but it may be helpful for some students to have a topic idea instead of having to develop one on their own.)
7. Allow students to work with a partner to create their poems.
8. Make sure they know to use the phrases from the phrase bank to draft their poems.
9. Share with the class.

When to Use It

- When you want to focus on a specific grammatical skill in context.
- As a way to integrate poetry into grammar lessons.
- To develop a deeper understanding of the function of a grammar concept.

Why It Works

- It addresses a grammar concept in context and not in isolation.
- Because poems are often shorter than other compositions, some students may find them more accessible when writing.

Modifications

- Instead of writing Prepositional Phrase Poems, try Transitional Phrase poems.
- Have students focus on another grammar or sentence structure skill like dependent clauses, appositives, or interrogative sentences.
- Before starting this stretch activity, have students collect prepositional phrases from a variety of samples including picture books, songs, poems, and other literature excerpts. This can help students as they begin writing and using prepositional phrases in context.

- Record these poems on paint strips. Based on the number of blocks on the strips, that's the number of phrases that are needed.

Extensions

- Have students find images that best illustrate the prepositional phrases they have chosen in their poems to use with their poems.
- Try using repeated prepositional phrases to emphasize a specific point. Use the Do I Need to Repeat Myself? strategy instructions on page 241 for assistance.
- Have students create partner Prepositional Phrase Poems where students practice a "call and response" type of poem.

Digital Direction

- Start the lesson off by having students collaboratively post prepositional phrase ideas on Jamboard or Padlet.
- Animate the poems using Canva, Adobe Spark, or Haiku Deck.
- Create a digital poetry book using Storybird or Little Bird Tales.

Lesson Lead-Ins

- Use this strategy to introduce and reinforce prepositional phrases. Have students practice incorporating them into their other writings.
- Lead into specific revision suggestions with a lesson like this one.
- Use this as a starter for a unit on poetry.

PARTNER POEMS

Partner Poems have a lot of the same characteristics as the Bio Poem (Harper, 2017). Students I taught loved Bio Poems because there was a specific formula and length requirement included. This type of template made it easier for many students because they were able to see exactly what material was needed for completion.

Partner Poems are similar in the sense that they follow a template, BUT they are performed in two voices, with two students performing their poems together, which creates a lovely, unique, collaborative writing engagement. Plus, Partner Poems are excellent getting-to-know-you activities.

Putting It to Work

1. Provide students with the Partner Poems template on the companion website.
2. Show students an example of a completed poem, or draft your own poem live while going over the template.
3. Have students complete their own templates.

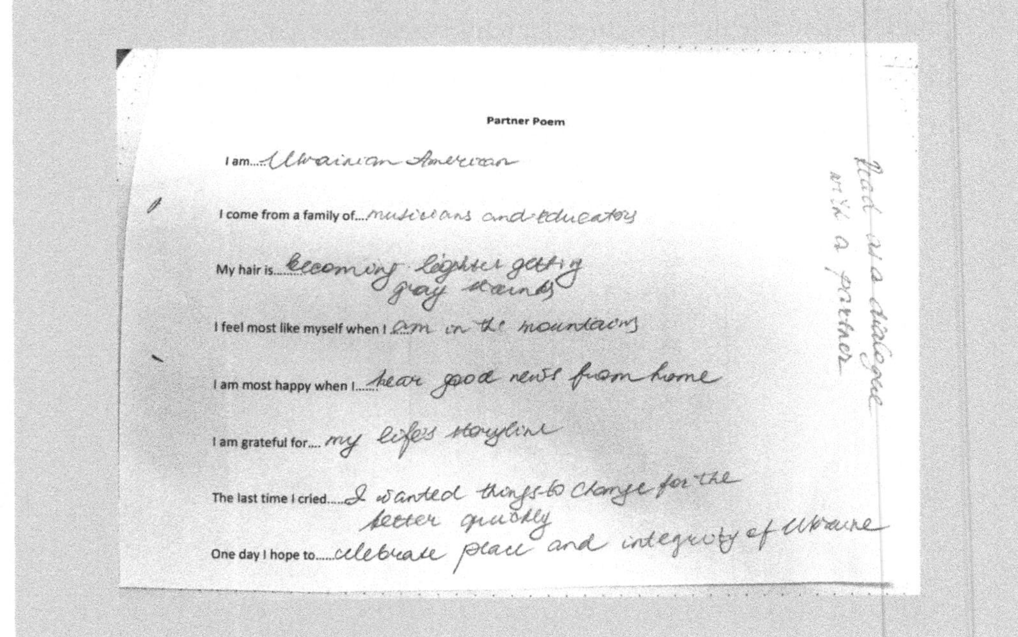

Partner Poem

I am.....Ukrainian American

I come from a family of....musicians and educators

My hair is..........becoming lighter getting gray strands

I feel most like myself when I am in the mountains

I am most happy when I.......hear good news from home

I am grateful for.... my life's storyline

The last time I cried.....I wanted things to change for the better quickly

One day I hope to......celebrate peace and integrity of Ukraine

Read as a dialogue with a partner

4. When it is time to share, pick two students to read their poems aloud.
5. Alternate voices. For example, student 1 will read the first line and then student 2 will read the first line. This continues until the whole poem is performed.

Want to see this in action? Check out www.drrebeccagharper.com for a video demonstration.

6. Switch up the students and perform another poem.
7. Discuss how the poems shifted and changed based on who was paired.
8. Have students circulate the room and find a few classmates to perform their poems with.
9. Give students 5 to 7 minutes to collaboratively perform in small groups.
10. Share their noticings with the class.

When to Use It

- As an icebreaker or getting-to-know-you activity.
- When you want students to practice writing poems.
- As a way for students to develop a collaborative culminating product.

Why It Works

- It involves a collaborative final product, yet it depends solely on individual construction until the performance component.
- Because it utilizes a template, students can determine exactly the material needed for inclusion.
- It can be completed in a short amount of time.

Modifications

- Instead of having students complete all the parts, have them choose a few sentence starters on the poem to complete and then share with a partner.
- Have students create partner poems for characters in a novel.
- Change the sentence starters from "I . . ." to "You . . ." or "They . . ." and have students write about one of their classmates.

Extensions

- Have students add another sentence starter to the poem template.

- Create a class collaborative poem by combining information from multiple student examples to draft a class poem.

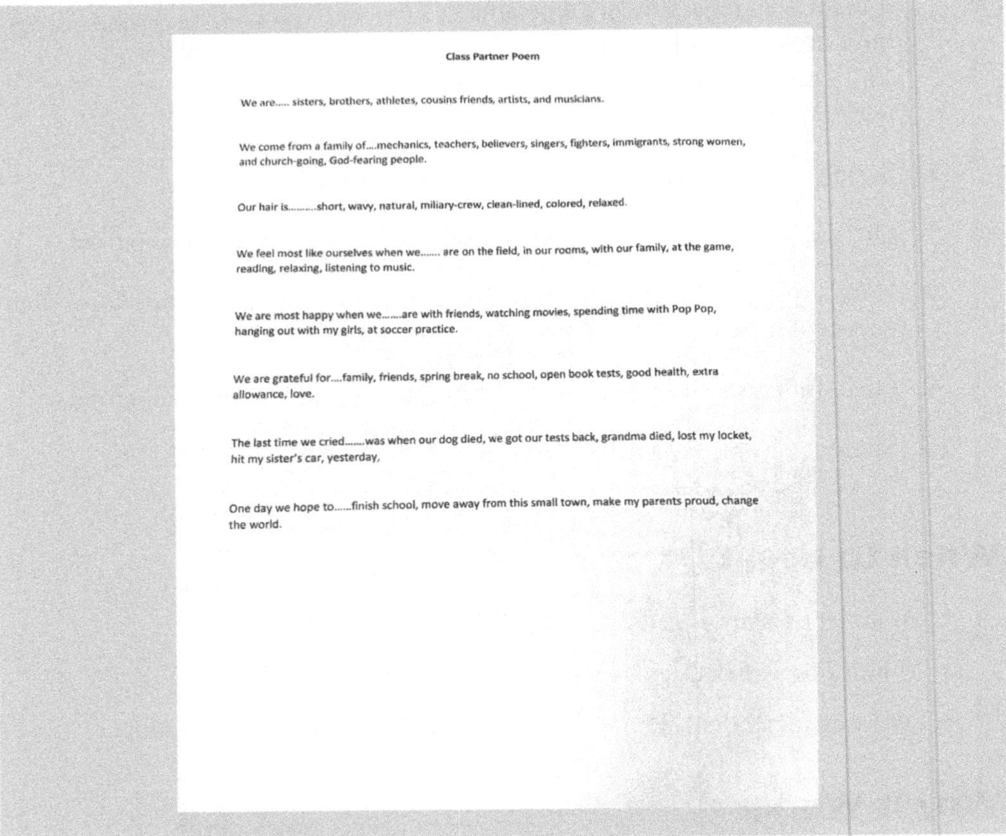

Class Partner Poem

We are..... sisters, brothers, athletes, cousins friends, artists, and musicians.

We come from a family of....mechanics, teachers, believers, singers, fighters, immigrants, strong women, and church-going, God-fearing people.

Our hair is..........short, wavy, natural, miliary-crew, clean-lined, colored, relaxed.

We feel most like ourselves when we....... are on the field, in our rooms, with our family, at the game, reading, relaxing, listening to music.

We are most happy when we.......are with friends, watching movies, spending time with Pop Pop, hanging out with my girls, at soccer practice.

We are grateful for....family, friends, spring break, no school, open book tests, good health, extra allowance, love.

The last time we cried.......was when our dog died, we got our tests back, grandma died, lost my locket, hit my sister's car, yesterday,

One day we hope to......finish school, move away from this small town, make my parents proud, change the world.

- Have students form small groups and have them combine their poems into one that they perform in unison.

Digital Direction

- Use Zoom breakout rooms for students to perform their poems with a digital partner.
- Connect to classrooms across the country and perform Coast to Coast Partner Poems online.

Lesson Lead-Ins

- Use this as a lead-in for personal narratives.
- When starting units on poetry, try Partner Poems as icebreakers.
- Use these as lead-ins for performance poetry or studying poems in multiple voices.

A BALANCED DIET OF READING AND WRITING

The Literature and Writing Students Need to Thrive

Simply working out isn't the only part of developing a healthy lifestyle and obtaining good overall health. Instead, to achieve optimal health, physical fitness, healthy eating, good lifestyle habits, and attention to mental and emotional health aspects are addressed. You won't see results if you only go to the gym and don't follow it up with healthy eating and lifestyle habits. Good health won't come simply by running three miles on the treadmill and then eating burgers and fries all the time; it simply doesn't work that way. Similarly, eating celery and carrots all the time while neglecting your physical fitness won't really lead to overall health. Overall health is a combination of multiple aspects that, together, improve overall health and wellness.

Writing fitness is no different. For students to be in good writing shape overall, they can't just write one way or write a few times a week. They need to do more than only train for personal narrative experiences or expository writing tasks. And they certainly can't cram 9 weeks' worth of writing instruction into the week before the big assessment. (We've all been there, right?) Instead, writing must be a regular activity, of varying intensity, across several genres and purposes. Plus, writing must be combined alongside quality literature in several formats, including print and digital. Making certain that students have a well-balanced diet of quality literature, along with plenty of time to train as readers and writers, can set students up for success.

In the pages that follow, I provide an overview of the other components of a balanced diet of reading and writing—all pieces that can enhance these writing workouts and build students with healthy literacy lives.

Literacy Passports

When I think about writing and how students gain proficiency at a variety of writing tasks, it really is less about the genre and structure and more about *experiencing* writing. For some students, their experience with certain types of writing are a one and done, and in fact, many standard sets and pacing guides are set up so that is exactly what happens. Persuasive writing? Check. Narrative writing? Check. The problem with this is that teaching writing genre by genre, and then moving on to the next one, only allows students limited experiences. How many of you have standards sets or pacing guides that focus on a particular genre for each nine weeks? Now, that certainly is not a bad approach because it *does* ensure that students at least get exposed to a variety of genres, but it limits their depth and understanding of the subtle nuances of each genre. Consider a schedule like this:

- First 9 weeks (personal narrative)
- Second 9 weeks (expository)
- Third 9 weeks (persuasive)
- Fourth 9 weeks (personal narrative)

With a model like this, students focus on one particular genre for each quarter and then move on to an entirely different genre for the next 9 weeks. As a result, these genres become compartmentalized and exist in silos, thus giving students limited experiences with each. Once the first 9 weeks is over, many students won't experience a specific genre again until later in the year, if they *do* experience it again. This can be problematic for a few reasons. For one, it creates the belief that different genres of writing always exist in their own vacuums. Yet it is not at all uncommon to see components of the persuasive genre show up in personal narratives. Similarly, components of arguments can also be informational as well. When teaching genres in silos, it can nurture the belief that all genres are bounded sets that do not merge, and exist as black and white, not grey. However, genres and stylistic components can merge and bleed over, and in fact, acknowledging these qualities can help students develop a deeper and more thorough understanding of writing. (Remember the tandem training genres/writings in Chapter 6?)

Here's where a literacy passport can come in handy: Let's say that I have never traveled to Paris, France, before. On my first trip there, I will probably see the real touristy places that everyone sees when they go to Paris for the first time. You would probably go to the Eiffel Tower, the Louvre, and Moulin Rouge. After visiting on this first trip, you get your first stamp in your passport for a visit to Paris, France. You can check France off on your Places to Visit list since you now have evidence that you have visited. Once. Now imagine that you return to Paris on several occasions and as a result have multiple stamps in your passport.

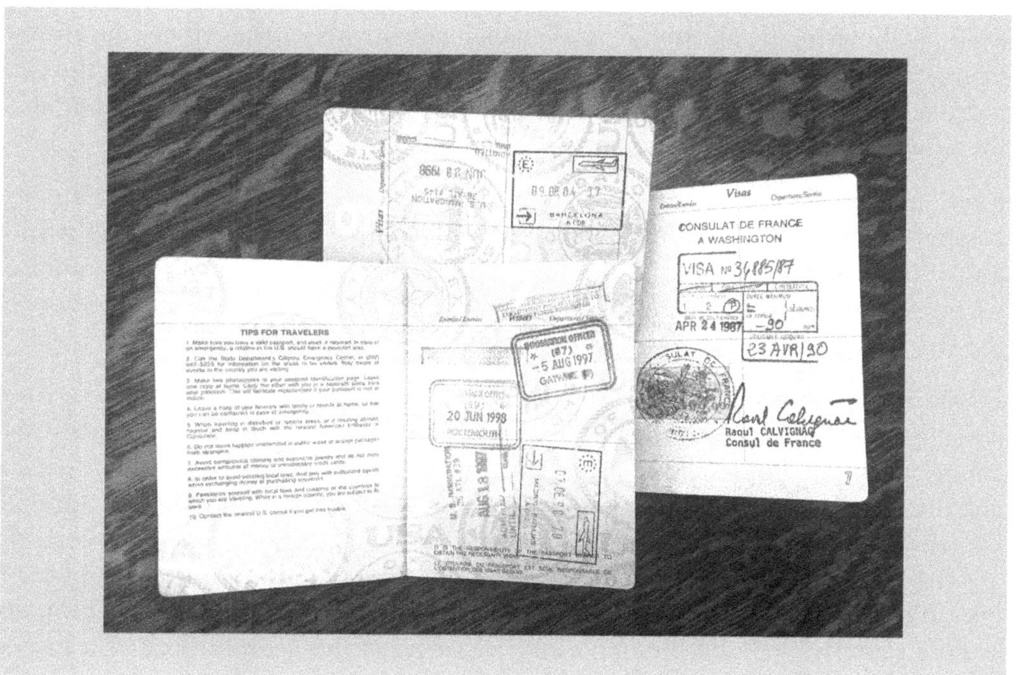

While you might return to those first three landmarks, since you have checked off the must-see places, you might now venture off onto side streets and try out local bakeries for pastries. Stop in a quaint gift shop and buy a trinket or head into a local bistro for a cup of coffee. You see, returning to a place that you have visited before and often allows a visitor to explore new areas, shops, and dining. While you may return to the Eiffel Tower each time you head back to Paris, it is likely that you will venture out into places that only those who live in Paris or are frequent visitors know about. In other words, you have developed a deeper understanding of this place. You know it because you have visited it on multiple occasions, during different seasons, and with different traveling partners. Thus, your experience with Paris is different than someone who has only visited once. Plus, when you spend an extended time in a location, that prolonged engagement offers its own benefits because your longer visit allows you the luxury of lingering. Ask yourself, how often do we allow students to linger along the pages of a book or with the words they write?

How does that relate to writing? First off, many students only have a few stamps on their literacy passports. For example, they might have one persuasive stamp, one personal narrative stamp, and one expository stamp on their literacy passports. In other words, it would be the same as going to Paris, France, one time and only seeing those three landmarks that everyone sees. Then going to Australia and only visiting the Sydney Opera House and the Outback and then heading off to Egypt and only seeing the pyramids. In each of these examples, the travelers are barely brushing the surface of the wonders of each country. The same holds true for only visiting the persuasive genre once for 9 weeks. Sure, you learn that to persuade someone you have to state your position and provide evidence that gets your reader to side with you, but that is it. Only visiting that genre once doesn't allow students the opportunity to get to know the subtle nuances of persuasive writing, like for example, how the use of carefully crafted dialogue might help convince your reader, or how opening with a vignette or quote can serve as an effective hook. You see, those qualities are only experienced when you return often and on a regular basis, for a variety of purposes and topics.

Even more concerning though are those students who have blank literacy passports because they haven't had the opportunities to see the writing world. Sadly, many students haven't had the occasion to truly engage with the craft of writing in their academic settings. And they are missing out on the wonders of the writing world.

For students to truly understand how a particular genre of writing *functions*, they must visit and revisit it often over an extended time for a variety of purposes, audiences, and about a number of topics. It is not enough for students to write an argumentative essay and then move on. They really need to experience the genre of argument in multiple content areas, utilize it for short and extended writing pieces, and craft arguments on a variety of topics. When this happens, students are essentially visiting an argument over and over again, thus gaining multiple literacy passport stamps and developing a more sophisticated and thorough understanding of the genre instead of a simple surface-level, drive-by approach.

When planning writing engagements and experiences to help students fill their literacy passports, consider the following:

- Is this the student's first experience with this genre? If so, you need to hit the high points or the main attractions first.
- Who is the intended audience?
- How much time are you able to devote to this writing task?
- When will students see this again?
- What other writing genres or components of authors' craft are closely related to this genre?
- What types of supports will students need to successfully complete this type of writing? For example, if students are writing a research composition, what types of mini lessons might also be included? Ones that focus on credible sources, academic tone and jargon, along with citation components would be lessons that should be taught in tandem.
- Do I really need to grade this? Can you get the information needed through a more informal method of assessment?

Considering these bullet points can help plan writing engagements that are purposeful and effective in today's busy classroom because they help focus the lessons on the endgame, ask yourself, "What is my endgame?"

Time to Write

One of the most important items to consider in the ELA classroom is time. For students to get better at writing, they have to be given the time to practice this craft. Carving out space within the class period is integral for success. But how much time is enough? The real answer to that question is that there never can be too much time to write, but in today's classroom, time is a precious commodity. In fact, many teachers find that the instructional time they are allocated each week is often cut into by administrative or school-based initiatives. These can range from interruptions like fire drills and lockdowns, discipline issues, to special programs like pep rallies and club meetings, to assessment days. Recently I was in a middle school where the sixth- through eighth-grade teachers indicated that for the 3 weeks prior, they had been administering a variety of assessments ranging from benchmarks to county assessments all leading up to the state assessment, and they had only had about 7 days for solid instruction. That's right: 7 days over 3 weeks.

Unfortunately, this loss in instructional time is not unique or unusual and happens on a regular basis in classrooms across the country. Plus, with the nation still reeling from COVID-19, many teachers find themselves with their backs against the wall as they try to catch students up on almost 2 years of instability in the school system and world. It's not just academics; many teachers are spending time helping students reacclimate to the structure and format of in-person schooling. In fact, the most recent data from the Census indicates that even though many students are back in school, parents of over 50% of students say their children are spending less time on learning activities than before the pandemic (US Census Household Pulse Survey, 2022). Plus, other data indicates that over 80% of teachers and parents are concerned with their students meeting academic standards (Institute of Education Sciences, 2022). Yet, even if we had all the time in the world, increased instructional time does not automatically equate into effective instruction. Quality instructional time is the main focus here, keeping a laser focus on what your end result or goal is.

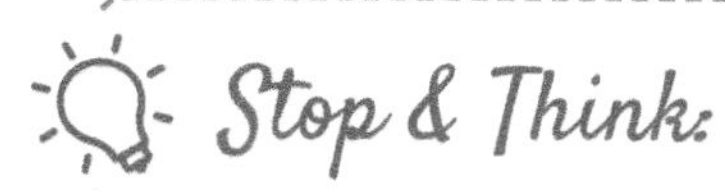

Remember the table from Chapter 1 on page 4 where instructional goals are laid out? Go back to that. Determine the instructional goal and what activities and strategies are going to be more effective in getting you there.

Really, that idea isn't simply for the classroom; it works in life as well. One of the best professional lessons I have learned in the past year came from reading Angela Duckworth's *Grit* (2016). Her chapter about goals and focus have been extremely insightful as my new mantra for work-related activities and instruction is always: "Does this help me get to my endgame?" If the answer is no, I don't do it. If it helps me get to my endgame, then I say yes.

Here's how I have laid out some of my professional goals:

Goal	Increase my national presence in the literacy field	Develop literacy strategies for classroom implementation	Develop professional relationships on campus with colleagues	Increase the Augusta University Writing Project's footprint in the local community
Tasks that help me accomplish this goal	Presenting at conferences; submitting articles in literacy journals; volunteering to speak at literacy organizational meetings; serving on boards for professional organizations	Professional learning; classroom visits; partnering with classroom teachers	Serve as university ombudsman; serve as chair on important committees like Promotion and Tenure	Author book clubs; Scholar Series; family literacy nights; obtaining grant funding with community organizations; partnering with local news media outlets

Having a chart of what activities help me get to my goals has greatly helped me determine which activities have the best payoffs. Classroom instruction is no different. One of the easiest ways to determine this is to ask yourself a few questions as you plan your teaching.

- Will what I am doing today help or hinder my instruction?
- What crossover engagements can be planned that hit multiple skills at once?
- What is the desired product or goal of my instruction? Working backward from that goal, what steps need to be taken to achieve these results?
- Are there instructional strategies that I am using that aren't yielding the most profitable results?
- Are there lessons/novels/texts that you dread teaching? Maybe now is the time to change it up with something new that could work better.

Pass the Poetry, Please

When I collected data for my dissertation, one of the participants in my study indicated that because she hated poetry, she waited till the absolute last minute to cover it. As a result, for most years, she didn't include it as she often found herself out of time. How convenient. Yet I would argue alongside the iconic Jason Reynolds (2015), whose interview on PBS encourages teachers to embrace poetry because it can hook striving readers. Fewer words on the page and more white space on the page can prove beneficial for many, because it certainly takes less time to read a poem than an epistle. I love Jason's analogy that compares a reluctant reader to that of someone deathly afraid of dogs. Would you take someone afraid of dogs to a pit-bull breeder and then to the movie theater to see *Cujo*? I think not. Yet every single day we send scared and reluctant readers to those *Cujo*-like theaters in the form of word after word on the page. Like Jason suggests, why not ease them into reading much like you would ease a dog-fearing person into acceptance by taking them to a puppy daycare with inobtrusive and slobbering pups, yelping in their infancy?

Try the same tactic in your classroom in the form of poems. Instead of hitting students with extended texts, try poems first. For readers who lack stamina and might be performing below grade level, poems offer access to those who might view reading as intimidating and vicious. Plus, poems can be used to teach almost every possible ELA standard known to man. Figurative language? Try Walter Dean Myers's "Summer" or one of Kwame Alexander's poems in *The Crossover*. (My personal favorite is "Filthy McNasty.") Character development? Try an excerpt from Jason Reynolds's *Long Way Down* or one of the poems included in Nikki Grimes' s novel in verse *Bronx Masquerade*. The theme of love, loss, acceptance, and heroics? Try Stevie Smith's "Not Waving but Drowning," or Ralph Fletcher's "Owl Pellets."

You see my point? You don't need the New Testament or Whitman's "Leaves of Grass" to effectively teach literary components. Instead, you just need words with a message, however brief and conserved. Each of these examples offers students the chance to interact with smaller excerpts of text, but still address the main focus of the lesson. Plus, reading poems on a regular basis can help students build their reading stamina, much like quick writes and warmups help them build their writing stamina.

> **Quick Tip!**
>
> Using novels in verse can make read alouds a cinch. In fact, one year, we completed a whole school read-aloud using Jason Reynolds' *Long Way Down* in one day. How you ask? We purchased a copy for every teacher in the building and gave them a specific page amount to read each period. By seventh period, every single kid in that school had heard the entire *Long Way Down* novel. Talk about powerful!

And just a quick reminder that you don't have to simply use poems that stand alone. There is a plethora of novels written entirely in verse that offer the same benefit. Kwame Alexander's *The Crossover*, Jason Reynolds's *Long Way Down*, Rajani LaRocca's *Red, White, and Whole*, and Nikki Grimes's *Bronx Masquerade* listed above offer entire novel-length stories told entirely in verse. Use one example from the book as your starting point or read the entire novel; it is completely up to you and your class. Plus, novels in verse are awesome choices for read alouds because you can sail through multiple pages in record time due to the limited number of words on the page. In fact, I once stopped by a fifth-grade class to read *The Crossover* and found myself almost 100 pages into the novel only 20 minutes into the class period. Talk about an effective use of time! Plus, novels in verse can help students see tangible success in the form of multiple pages read much faster than with a traditionally constructed novel. In fact, I would be willing to bet that I could read half of the entire book *The Crossover* in the same amount of time as it would take me to read Chapter 1 of *The Hobbit*!

Don't Settle Down Yet; Play the Field!

When I taught middle school, I found that many of my students who did enjoy reading were hooked on one particular genre or author. Venturing outside of that comfort zone was difficult for many, but it is necessary. Otherwise, students get boxed into one genre or author, and when that author quits writing, they don't know where to go next. (Think about Robert Jordan and the *Wheel of Time* series. Imagine how disappointed his fan base was when he passed away and they realized that the series they had hitched their wagon to was done!)

One of the best ways you can address this issue is by reading aloud different types of texts from multiple genres. Maybe your students have not experienced sci-fi yet. Now is the perfect opportunity to read them a few pages from *The House of the Scorpion* by Nancy Farmer. If they love that, then they might want to also read *The Ear, the Eye, and the Arm* or the *Lords of Opium* by the same author.

Read alouds, when done well and often, become like commercials or promos for genres and authors. I often utilize books that have highly engaging opening chapters in an effort to hook readers. Some of my favorites are *Out of My Mind* by Sharon Draper, *Luna* by Julianne Peterson, and *The Absolutely True Diary of a Part-Time Indian* by Sherman Alexie. When using these as read alouds, I incorporate cliffhanger or especially poignant chapters to share in hopes that students will want to read more.

Don't stop at books though. Use songs, movie clips, comic strips, photos, and more to hook students on different genres. Wordless picture books are another fantastic resource due to the fact that students rely only on images to create the story. (Check out the Wordless Picture Books strategy on page 107 that specifically uses wordless picture books.) As a result, reading levels, command of the native language, and other traditional instructional impacting factors are removed from the equation.

And while read alouds and teacher-led engagements can certainly expose students to multiple genres and authors, times for students to make genre choices independently are important as well. Here is a super easy way for students to take ownership of their own reading choices: use the book pass. Here is how it works:

- Provide students with the Book Pass template on the companion website.
- Give students a stack of books to sift through.
- As students look at a specific book, they record the information on their template and then make any comments regarding their opinions/reactions to the book.
- Pass books around about half a dozen times.
- Once students have completed their template, they now have a list of books from a variety of genres that they may choose to check out in the library.

In short, using a book pass helps students see a variety of books from multiple authors and a variety of genres they may choose to check out at a later date. In fact, it offers them one more chance to interact with multiple books across several genres and authors. In this situation, exposure is the key. No more getting to the library and wandering around without any direction. Now, students have a list of books that they might choose to check out when they head to the library.

Another way to increase exposure to multiple authors and genres is through the integration of First Chapter Fridays. In this strategy, teachers share only the first chapters of books so students can get an idea about the overall book. Other ideas include Book Tastings where a student who has read a book offers a brief overview of the story and shares this with students. Book Tastings are set up so that students can rotate through stations and hear the highlights of a book before moving on to the next. Think about it like a wine flight. You get a sample of each book and then based on your reaction to the sample, you decide if you want to try out the entire text. Book Speed Dates work well, too. Students spend 2 to 4 minutes telling the high points of their books before they move on to a new partner or date to share their talking points. Regardless of how you choose to do this, each of the strategies listed here addresses the important component of getting students exposed to multiple genres and authors.

Switch It Up!

While routines are super important, spontaneity certainly has its place in the classroom, too. When I work out, I don't only train my shoulders every day for 45 minutes. Instead, on some days I focus on shoulders, other days legs, and yet another day I might target my back. Similarly, I don't always do an hour-long lift routine. Sometimes I lift for an hour, other times I do HIIT training for 30 minutes, and sometimes I only work my abs for 10 minutes. The point of this is variety. I don't always train at a lower intensity level for a longer amount of time, nor do I always train at a high pace for short bursts of time. I also don't always stick to the same workout program. Sometimes I work out with Shaun T, other times it's me and Tony Horton, and on other days Amolia Cesar is my best friend. My point is that I don't stick to one specific workout routine. Instead, I mix and match based on what I need. Notice the scale tipping up a bit? I'll key up a cardio video. Almost swimsuit season? Let me start working on that six pack. Stressed out at work? Namaste, ya'll! What I need physically and mentally has a significant impact on what workout routine I complete.

Much like my workout routines, when planning and implementing writing lessons in my classroom, I have to consider similar factors. I can't only train my students to complete super quick and short writing bursts when at some point they will have to write complete extended pieces. Likewise, I can't only focus on extended fully executed and involved pieces when they need time to simply draft and process information. Instead, I must carefully mix up the types of writings I want my students to do. Daily writing and extended pieces are going to look different because they have different academic demands, yet both are equally important. Plus, nothing burns out a student faster than training them too hard on back-to-back days or not giving them time to rest and recover. Building a writing routine doesn't mean sticking to the same routine necessarily. Instead, it means that students expect that they will write every day, routinely, but the task, purpose, genre, and topic are anything but routine.

Connecting writing tasks/engagements to my instructional goals can help me plan the most effective writing lessons based on my needs. It might be helpful for you to create a go-to chart that can easily be dropped into your lesson plan templates. Here is one I started; you can use the Standards Matrix on the companion website to create a template that fits your curriculum needs.

Writing to process information	Quick writes, reflections, written conversations, Drop Drafts; writing breaks
Research writing	Stop/Go Sources; Text Mapping; Mix and Match Writing
Character analysis/development	Cast the Character; Character Evolution paint strips

Grammar-Schrammar

One of my least favorite items to focus on is grammar. As someone who has a PhD in language and literacy, I am not sure I could correctly diagram a sentence, but I do know how language functions, which, in my opinion, supersedes any ability to appropriately label a dangling participle or underline a complete predicate. I am most interested in how language *functions*, not how to identify specific components.

Allowing students the ability to practice writing, playing around with phrases, and combining and revising sentences can achieve all the grammar standards listed in your standard set, but within context. No more teaching grammar in isolation, because we know this doesn't work. Give me a kid who has a sophisticated understanding about how to articulate an idea, organize a paper, and craft sentences that are lyrical and purposeful over any student who can diagram a sentence accurately. Knowing how to write and how to leverage words so that the message is clearly articulated will pay off substantially more than a 100 on a grammar worksheet. Plus, students need time to play around with language and grammar. Strategies that channel this type of playing with language are ones like the Prepositional Phrase Poems on page 251, Soap Opera Stories on page 226, or the NVA[2] strategy on page 66. Ask yourself, "Do my students know how language *functions*?"

Celebrate Even Small Victories

For many of our students, simply getting a coherent sentence recorded on a paper is a monumental feat. Celebrate it! One of my favorite students, Byron, was a habitual fragment writer. I mean the kid was proficient in writing sentences that started with the words *and but*. A self-proclaimed "fragment addict," Byron needed validation when he got a sentence constructed correctly and completely, even if he only had one correct sentence in his whole paper. Praise your students' success. Now I certainly don't mean that you coddle them or refrain from holding them to high standards. What I mean is that you celebrate small victories, especially for those writers who lack self-confidence and who are striving. Doing so can buy spendable capital in the classroom, which you never can have enough of.

On a related note, call or send notes home to caregivers when students do something well in class. Many of the students who were in my classes had discipline problems, so I made a point to call parents and give positive news. I made sure that I called at least two parents/caregivers per week with good news. I can't tell you how many parents or caregivers told me that no one had ever called to tell them anything good about their kid. Wow! Think how the dynamics might shift in your classroom if you committed to making one positive phone call a week!

We're Well Into the Twenty-First Century

While there will always be a place for the classics in literature and the classic genres in writing, don't be afraid to branch out. Now I certainly don't mean throwing the baby out with the bath water. Instead, integrate contemporary literature along with the canon. Merge pop culture writing along with the sophisticated academic genres. For example, when teaching Shakespeare's *Romeo and Juliet,* don't only rely on the primary text for meaning making. Instead, combine a contemporary title like *YOLO Juliet,* part of the OMG Shakespeare series, along with a video clip and Andy Griffith's rendition of *Romeo and Juliet.* Use an excerpt from Sharon Draper's *Romiette and Julio* and include a theatrical or dance version of the play. By utilizing multiple mediums, it is much more likely the students will develop an overall understanding of a complex text.

Similarly, when teaching writing, think about the types of formats that writing lives in when in today's world. Students might not be writing research papers for fun, but they are posting Snaps, recording TikToks, and responding to classmates in less than traditional manners. Every single one of those venues offers possibility in the classroom, *IF* leveraged appropriately. One of my first students, Michael, came into my writing class daily and professed that he was not a writer and did not want to be in my class. Yet this self-proclaimed nonwriter shared with me that he was a rapper who wrote lyrics at home. He later brought in stacks of composition notebooks filled with raps he had written: not for a grade; not for school; not for any assignment. He wrote them for himself. How can this student, who produced more tangible evidence of written expression than I had written in an entire semester, not believe he was a writer? Probably because he didn't see himself as a writer based on the bounds and qualifications that the school setting used to define what a *writer* was.

Ask yourself this: "How many students are in my class who don't see themselves as writers? How can I see them for who they are and give them opportunities to see themselves as writers?"

The First Step Is . . .

Just like the first step when getting in physical shape starts with getting in the car and going to the gym or walking into your basement and picking up the weights, getting started with writing fitness involves the first step of picking up the pencil and writing. As an ELA teacher, giving students the place and space to pick up the pencil is just as important. Building a nurturing classroom environment where students feel safe to share their words and ideas can help young writers grow and flourish.

Victoria Jamieson, author of *Roller Girl* and *When Stars Are Scattered*, once told a group of teachers, "Everyone has a story; the only difference is that writers write them down." That one sentence has stayed with me because it posits that we all can be writers *if* we get the words on the page and write our stories down.

Let today be the day that the students in your class write theirs down. The world is waiting.

REFERENCES

Ballard, J. (2020). Exercising and sticking to a healthy diet are the most common 2021 New Year's resolutions. *YouGovAmerica*. https://today.yougov.com/topics/society/articles-reports/2020/12/23/2021-new-years-resolutions-poll

Bliss, B. (2020). *Thoughts and prayers*. HarperCollins.

Buckholz, W. (2010). *Understand rap: Explanations of confusing rap lyrics you and your grandma can understand*. Abrams.

Duckworth, A. (2016). *Grit: The power of passion and perseverance*. Scribner.

Graham, S., McKeown, D., Kiuhara, S., & Harris, K. R. (2012). A meta-analysis of writing instruction for students in the elementary grades. *Journal of Educational Psychology, 104*, 879–896. https://doi.org/10.1037/a0029185

Harper, R. G. (2017). *Content writing that rocks (and works!)*. Shell Education.

Harper, R. G. (2022). *Write now & write on: Grades 6–12*. Corwin.

Institute of Education Sciences. (n.d.). *2022 school pulse panel*. Author. https://ies.ed.gov/schoolsurvey/spp/

Lenhart, A. (2008). *Writing, technology and teens*. Pew Internet and American Life Project.

Lisle, J. T. (2006). *Black duck*. Puffin.

Lloyd, N. (2014). *A snicker of magic*. Scholastic Press.

Luciani, J. (2015). *Why 80 percent of New Year's resolutions fail*. https://health.usnews.com/health-news/blogs/eat-run/articles/2015-12-29/why-80-percent-of-new-years-resolutions-fail

Murphy, M. (2020). *This is the month when New Year's resolutions fail—Here's how to save them*. https://www.forbes.com/sites/markmurphy/2020/02/11/this-is-the-month-when-new-years-resolutions-fail-heres-how-to-save-them/?sh=aa9ed16272f0

National Council of Teachers of English. (2018). *Standards for the English language arts*. Author. https://cdn.ncte.org/nctefiles/resources/books/sample/standardsdoc.pdf

Paulsen, G. (2003). *How Angel Peterson got his name*. Yearling.

Reynolds, J. (2017, December 15). *How poetry can help kids turn a fear of literature into love*. https://www.pbs.org/newshour/show/how-poetry-can-help-kids-turn-a-fear-of-literature-into-loveencourages

US Census Household Pulse Survey. (2022, September, 9). *Household Pulse Survey: Measuring social and economic impacts during the coronavirus pandemic*. https://www.census.gov/programs-surveys/household-pulse-survey.html

INDEX

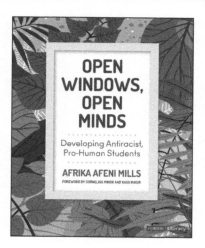

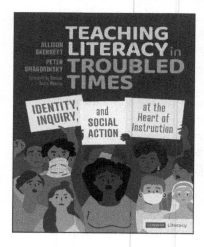

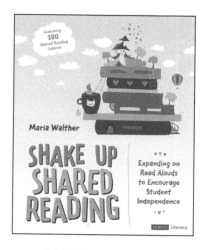

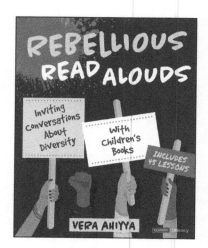

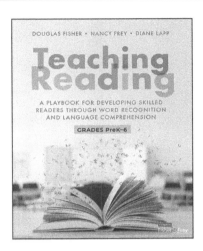

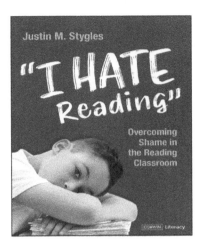

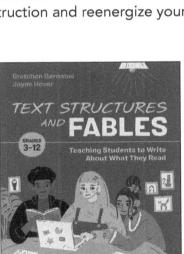

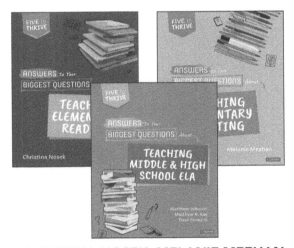